Audubon Plantation Country
COOKBOOK

Audubon Plantation Country
COOKBOOK

BY ANNE BUTLER

PELICAN PUBLISHING COMPANY

Gretna 2004

Originally published as *More than a Cookbook: An Eclectic Collection,* 1988, 1989, 1992
Published by arrangement with the author by Pelican Publishing Company, Inc., 2004

First edition, 1988
Second printing, 1989
Third printing, 1992
First Pelican edition, 2004

Library of Congress Cataloging-in-Publication Data

Hamilton, Anne Butler.
    Audubon plantation country cookbook / Anne Butler.— 1st Pelican ed.
        p. cm.
Rev. ed. of: More than a cookbook. 1992.
Includes index.
    ISBN 1-58980-131-8 (hardcover : alk. paper)
  1. Cookery, American—Louisiana style. I. Hamilton, Anne Butler. More than a
cookbook. II. Title.

    TX715.2.L68H33 2003
    641.59763—dc22

                                                            2003022450

Printed in Singapore
Published by Pelican Publishing Company, Inc.
1000 Burmaster Street, Gretna, Louisiana 70053

CONTENTS

St. Francisville and the West Feliciana Parish Area of Louisiana

Indexes

INTRODUCTION

There are people in this picturesque plantation country who'll swear that there are other people here whose feet never touch the floor each morning until that entire day's menus are planned to perfection.

While I can't personally swear to that myself, I must admit that food does carry a lot of weight around here, and that it is the center of a lot of our activities, our gatherings, our rituals and rites of passage, our recreations and our religions . . . well, all right, our every waking breath. This is true for all of us, whether we excuse ourselves daintily after one tiny helping by saying we've had "a gracious plenty" or "an elegant sufficiency," or whether we belly up to the table and gobble down four servings before calling ourselves "tight as a tick!"

What makes food so important? It's not just the planning and preparing; it's the *sharing*. If it's debatable whether there's any sound when a tree falls in a forest when there's no one there to hear, then it's equally questionable . . . just for the sake of argument, say . . . whether a delectable bite of bourbon pie or a heavenly slice of rum cake tastes as good when eaten alone with no one to *mmm* and *ahhh* with.

Does ever a watermelon taste so good as the one chilled in running creek waters and shared by naked, knock-kneed, sunburnt boys at the old swimmin' hole? Was ever a cucumber sandwich so divine as that devoured daintily by three-year-olds at tea, swathed in Grandma's lace gown and long white gloves, dripping with jewels and shaded by Mama's garden-party rose-covered hat?

The sharing of food is not something we voluntarily do with enemies; we eat only with friends and

family, given our druthers. It's almost a religious fellowship, as explained to me by our affable former Episcopal minister here in St. Francisville, who describes himself as "in the Friar Tuck mode" in between trips 'round the block on his bicycle in vain attempts to work off some of the sinfully rich culinary creations parishioners insist on stuffing him with. How could he possibly turn down such offerings of love, prepared as such acts of faith, maybe even atonement?

Of course he couldn't, no more than could the prodigal child who, having finally escaped his mother's clutches, returns on visits to hear how "poorly" he looks, how desperately in need of his mama's fare to put a little meat on his bones.

Food is an offering of love. It was also used for discipline in our growing-up years. With constant reminders of all the starving children in Africa or China or Algeria, we were admonished to clean our plates, punished for mischief by banishment to bed without supper, and rewarded for good behavior with favorite food treats and sweets, so that you can almost tell how good we were as children by counting the number of our adult fat rolls.

And so for each celebration, we share food, and we mourn together over food as well. But besides marking the milestones of today, our food embodies our heritage, reflecting the diverse cultural influences and flavorings cleverly blended by some divine recipe into our own unique history and development.

We are, after all, what we eat, and how diverse that is! Food is part of our history, part of our heritage to be passed down from generation to generation, a continuing legacy from our forebears, some of whom might more appropriately be shown

in those foreboding oil portraits wearing chef's hat or apron, for while we may have been lucky enough to have inherited a little land or a favorite brooch, what we treasure most are our great-grandmother's receipts, our grandmother's cookbooks, our mother's helpful kitchen hints.

Particularly on special holidays, though we may use a few modern-day shortcuts, we often try to recreate old family favorites of our ancestors year after year after year. This is English Plantation Country, distinguished from our Creole and Cajun neighbors to the south, and our Christmas dinners to this day feature roast goose or turkey, cornbread dressing, flaming plum pudding with hard sauce flavored with plenty of good whiskey, and other dishes brought straight from the British Isles by our first settlers.

As growing children in other climes learned to recite poetry and equally erudite stuff, we chanted silly rhymes like

I eats when I'm hungry,
I drinks when I'm dry.
And if the devil don't get me,
I'll live 'til I die.

I suppose that's along the same lines as that wonderful quote author Ellen Gilchrist put into the mouth of her overweight professor: "When you're hungry, eat; when you're sleepy, sleep; pass the cornbread," repeated just before he's mashed by the careening car of a crazed dieter while waiting in line at the donut shop. There are priorities in life, and the satisfactions of good food are high on the list. Witness the abbreviated grace:

Good bread,
Good meat—
Good God,
Let's eat!

I guess that's what gave me the idea of doing a book centered around food, but not *just* a cookbook . . . a book that would include history and humor, people and places . . . a book that would cover *life.* What could make a recipe more interesting or inspiring, after all, than knowing its origin, hearing stories of its servings, seeing in word pictures or actual vintage photographs the very persons who invented it or used it to best advantage?

Did people think that was a crazy idea?

Not around here, they didn't!

It reminds me of an elderly friend who went to purchase a hat, knowing exactly what he wanted. As he dubiously regarded the model that the solic-itous salesman had perched on his head, he asked, "But is it a *Stetson?*" The salesman's reply: "Of *course* it's a Stetson! It's *better* than a Stetson!"

Which might seem to be mutually exclusive. But perhaps it's not.

So this book, filled as it is with recipes for some of the South's most mouthwatering dishes, is a cookbook, all right, but it's *better* than a cookbook, too! It's full of personalized recipes stamped with the identifying mark of actual history, measured and molded by real people in real places during real periods of time.

Now which would you rather cook? An impersonal, strange, and unknown recipe from some faraway kitchen? Or a recipe whose lineage is known, an old friend, so to speak, maybe even a member of the family?

I *thought* so!

Audubon Plantation Country
COOKBOOK

ABBREVIATIONS

Standard

tsp.	=	teaspoon
tbsp.	=	tablespoon
oz.	=	ounce
qt.	=	quart
lb.	=	pound

Metric

ml.	=	milliliter
l.	=	liter
g.	=	gram
kg.	=	kilogram
mg.	=	milligram

STANDARD-METRIC APPROXIMATIONS

⅛ teaspoon	=	.6 milliliter		
¼ teaspoon	=	1.2 milliliters		
½ teaspoon	=	2.5 milliliters		
1 teaspoon	=	5 milliliters		
1 tablespoon	=	15 milliliters		
4 tablespoons	=	¼ cup	=	60 milliliters
8 tablespoons	=	½ cup	=	118 milliliters
16 tablespoons	=	1 cup	=	236 milliliters
2 cups	=	473 milliliters		
2½ cups	=	563 milliliters		
4 cups	=	946 milliliters		
1 quart	=	4 cups	=	.94 liter

SOLID MEASUREMENTS

½ ounce	=	15 grams		
1 ounce	=	25 grams		
4 ounces	=	110 grams		
16 ounces	=	1 pound	=	454 grams

NATCHEZ AND THE ADAMS COUNTY AREA OF MISSISSIPPI

Grand Village of the Natchez Indians

World famous for its antebellum culture, grand mansions, and well-established pilgrimages, Natchez is less well known as the site of the Grand Village of the Natchez Indians, a mighty tribe of sunworshippers whose culture reached its peak several centuries before the coming of the first white explorers.

From the writings of French explorers and priests, as well as from archaeological excavations of the site, a fairly accurate picture of life in Grand Village has been reproduced, complete with historical artifacts and authentic reproductions, and the village has been designated a National Historic Landmark, administered by the Department of Archives and History.

The Indians' first significant contact with European explorers came in March 1682, when LaSalle, representing France in the New World, declared the Natchez bluffs the most desirable site for settlement on the river and spent at least one night in a Natchez Indian village, smoking a calumet with the chief.

Iberville established relationships with the Natchez in 1700, a peaceful contact that deteriorated into the First Natchez War against the French. By 1716 Bienville and a group of French settlers had established Fort Rosalie and a settlement they called Natchez, reestablishing friendly relationships until French expansion and infringement on native property rights led in 1729 to the

Indian massacre of the French garrison at the fort; over 200 were killed. French retaliation wiped out the entire Natchez nation within the next few years.

The five villages occupied in this area by the Natchez Indians were much like that recreated at Grand Village, with its typical thatched-roof house of clay. Their community, ruled by the Great Sun, consisted of rigidly defined classes of tribesmen, the nobility claiming descent from the sun and the commoners being called Stinkards; this class system was hereditary through the maternal line.

Upon the death of the Sun, his wives and other loyal retainers were ceremoniously strangled to accompany him into the afterworld and his house was burned, the mound upon which it sat raised to a new height to support the home of his successor. A perpetual sacred flame, symbol of the sun from which the royal family descended, was maintained in the inner sanctum of the temple where the bones of the Suns were interred; negligent attendants paid for letting the fire go out with their lives.

Agriculture formed the basis of this culture, and, like hunting, was a community activity, the entire village gathering for planting and harvesting the major crops of corn, beans, pumpkins, and melons.

Besides farming, hunting was the major occupation of the men of the Natchez tribe. They used bows made of long-lasting black locust wood, strung with twisted bark or animal sinew. Arrows with fire-hardened tips and feathers were common. For hunting big game, a bone head was attached to the arrow, with feather midriffs soaked in fish glue.

Major hunts were group affairs, with deer driven within a circle of hunters for the kill. All able-bodied villagers took part in bison hunts. The game was brought home by the women, with some meat preserved by smoke drying.

The Natchez ate bison, deer, bear, and dog meat, as well as fish, wild turkey, and other fowl. All possible parts of game animals were preserved for use in the tribal life. Deer skins were tanned for cloaks, the sinews beaten and spun for thread, and the rib bones bent and polished as bracelets. Bison skins were dressed with the wool intact for use as quilts and robes; bison wool was also spun for belts, ribbons, and garters. Bear skins were made into carrying straps, and oil was extracted from the fat. Even the fur of the opossum was spun into belts, dyed red. Porcupine quills were split and used to decorate cloaks of animal skins or mulberry bark, and bird feathers were also used for decoration, the type of feather marking the class of the wearer.

While the buffalo no longer roam the banks of the Homochitto, the consumption of canines is discouraged, and bear are getting scarcer even in the swamps, the wild turkey has made a comeback and white-tailed deer remain plentiful in Mississippi and Louisiana, nimbly challenging the hunter much as they did in the days of the Natchez Indians. Their sinews may not be spun into thread nor their rib bones polished as gentlemen's bracelets, but the venison is consumed with gusto just as considerable.

Venison Marinade

½ cup soy sauce
3 tbsp. vegetable oil
2 cloves garlic, minced
1 tbsp. grated or ¾ tsp. ground ginger
3 tbsp. honey

Combine all ingredients. Place venison in glass, enamel, or stainless-steel dish and cover with marinade. Marinate several hours at least, turning occasionally. Broil or grill venison. This marinade works well with round steak and would probably work nearly as well with shoe leather, tenderizing and imparting a wonderful flavor.

Harvard Bardwell's Smoked Venison in Bacon

1 leg venison
1 cup balsamic vinegar
1 cup olive oil
2 oz. Worcestershire sauce
½ oz. Tabasco sauce
1 6-oz. bottle Bayou Bengal Cajunpeppa
    Sauce
3 oz. soy sauce
1 lb. bacon
1 6-oz. bottle Bayou Bengal Cajunpeppa
    Sauce
¼ cup Worcestershire sauce
4 dashes Tabasco sauce
Seasoned salt and coarse-ground black pepper
    to taste

Place venison in a large container or hefty bag and marinate for 4 days in marinade made of vinegar, olive oil, 2 oz. Worcestershire, ½ oz. Tabasco, 1 bottle Cajunpeppa Sauce, and soy sauce. Turn daily. Marinate bacon overnight in marinade made of 1 bottle Cajunpeppa Sauce, ¼ cup Worcestershire, and 4 dashes Tabasco. Remove roast from refrigerator at least 1 hour before cooking. Season generously with seasoned salt and black pepper. Wrap bacon over the top of roast, and smoke in a smoker about 6 to 8 hours, until tender. Don't overcook.

Lucie Butler's Venison Shish-Kabobs

½ cup lemon juice
1 tbsp. Worcestershire sauce
1 clove garlic, pressed
3 lb. tender venison, cubed
12 slices bacon, cut in thirds
1 lb. small onions, parboiled
3 bell peppers, cut in large pieces
16 large mushrooms
1 pt. cherry tomatoes
Salt and pepper to taste

Make marinade of the lemon juice, Worcestershire, and garlic. Toss with the cubed venison and allow to stand several hours, stirring once or twice. Alternate venison, bacon, and vegetables on skewers and season with salt and pepper. Baste with your favorite barbecue sauce or lemon-butter sauce. Cook until medium-rare; don't overcook.

Ormond Butler's Wild Turkey

1 tbsp. flour
Turkey-sized brown-in-bag
1 wild turkey
Salt and cayenne pepper
Worcestershire sauce
Bacon grease
1 apple, quartered
1 stalk celery, chopped
½ medium onion, chopped
½ orange or lemon, sliced
4 slices uncooked bacon

Place flour in cooking bag, following directions on package. If the turkey is large, cut off drumsticks at the second joint and reserve for making gumbo later. Sprinkle turkey inside and out with salt, pepper, and Worcestershire. Oil outside of bird with bacon grease. Stuff cavity with the fruit, vegetables, and bacon. Bake according to directions on cooking bag. Remove turkey from bag and cool. Degrease the juices completely. Slice turkey and reheat in degreased pan gravy. Leftover turkey slices will stay moist if frozen covered with pan juices.

Natchez Trace

The old Natchez Trace was a wilderness road that grew from wild animal and Indian trails and was stamped by thousands of feet into an important link between the Mississippi Territory and the rest of the early United States. Now preserved by the National Park System, the trace parkway is a 450-mile route through history from Natchez to Nashville.

When early French explorers arrived on the Gulf Coast just before 1700, the Old Southwest was occupied by Indian tribes; archaeological evidence indicates habitation of the area some 8,000 years ago. A 1733 French map shows an Indian trail from Natchez to Choctaw villages near Jackson, Mississippi, and then on to Chickasaw villages in northeastern Mississippi.

The old Indian trade route was increasingly traveled by French traders, soldiers, and missionaries. It was called the "Path to the Choctaw Nation" on British maps after 1763, when France ceded the region to England and a large number of English settlers moved into the Natchez area.

After the American Revolution, Spain claimed the area, and by 1785 a thriving trade had been set up with New Orleans and Natchez markets. Flatboaters from Ohio, Kentucky, and the western frontier floated down the Mississippi River with products like flour, pork, tobacco, hemp, and iron; their only way home was to walk or ride horseback up the old Indian route to Nashville, which they did with such increasing volume that the trace was trampled into a crude road.

When Spain surrendered claim to lands north of the 31st parallel, the United States created the Mississippi Territory, with Natchez as capital. Communication between the territory and Washington became increasingly important, especially when Congress in 1800 extended mail service to Natchez. Complaining that the road was only a

wilderness trail, the postmaster general described it as "no other than an Indian footpath very devious and narrow." Pres. Thomas Jefferson in 1801 ordered the army to clear the road, and in 1808 Congress appropriated funds for the postmaster to contract for improvements, thus turning the trace into a significant frontier road.

Inns, called "stands," were erected along the trace from 1804 on, with more than 20 operating by 1820. During this period the trace was the most heavily traveled road in the Old Southwest, with boatmen, soldiers, postmen, missionaries, Indians, pioneer settlers, circuit riders, outlaws, and adventurers sharing the dangers of its passage: steaming swamps, floods, insects, natural disasters, as well as robbers and unfriendly Indians.

When the United States declared war on England in 1812, Gen. Andrew Jackson marched down the Natchez Trace to protect New Orleans from Britain's ally Spain. In 1815 Jackson stopped the British at the Battle of New Orleans, then shared a victory march back up the trace with his men.

The coming of the steamboat, as well as new roads and towns, replaced the Natchez Trace as a vital roadway and allowed it to return to a quiet forest lane for a century or more. Now the Park System has preserved this significant part of American history with a modern parkway roughly following the route of the original trace.

Along the parkway near Natchez are scenic stopping places with loess bluffs, sections of the old trace roadbed, an immense Indian mound covering nearly 8 acres erected around 1300 by ancestors of the Creek, Choctaw, and Natchez Indians, and Mount Locust, one of the first of the inns along the old trace, with frontier furniture and living-history demonstrations spring through fall.

Probably built around 1780, Mount Locust by 1784 had been purchased by a Virginia merchant, farmer, innkeeper, magistrate, and sheriff of the region, who enlarged the house and operated it as an inn, with meals cooked in the brick-floored outside kitchen and served in the big house to travelers, who spent the night in a separate building called Sleepy Hollow.

The main house has been preserved and authentically furnished to give visitors a look at an early inn and working plantation along the old trace.

Guides in period clothing portray life in the early 1800s and demonstrate carding and spinning cotton, making soap, splitting rails, and making shakes for roofing with original or reproduction tools.

Just in the first 15 or so miles above Natchez, the trace parkway offers stops sufficient to provide an understanding of life along the old trace, called "a bond that held the Southwest to the rest of the nation, a channel for the flow of people and ideas, a memorial to the thousands whose footsteps stamped into the American land." Traveling farther along the trace reveals such spots of interest as a handicraft center with demonstrations, sorghum mill, burial spot of Meriwether Lewis, fall county fair with fiddlin' contest, self-guiding trails, and Civil War demonstrations. Speeding, hunting, and disturbing the natural state of the parkway are prohibited, and rangers patrol to enforce park regulations and offer help.

There are pleasant picnicking spots located at regular intervals along the parkway, often along sandy creeks, so pack a picnic hamper and enjoy an unforgettable history lesson at the same time along the Natchez Trace. Never mind what Mama always told you; there are so many nice insulated bags and containers these days that you can even enjoy such old-fashioned favorites as cold salads made with mayonnaise without fear of ptomaine poisoning.

Spinach Salad

1 cup oil (not olive oil)
2 tbsp. sugar
5 tbsp. red-wine vinegar
4 tbsp. sour cream
Coarse-ground black pepper
2 tsp. chopped parsley
1½ tsp. salt
2 cloves garlic, crushed
½ tsp. dry mustard
2 10-oz. pkg. fresh spinach, washed and
   dried
4 hard-boiled eggs, chopped
8 strips bacon, crisply fried and crumbled

Mix dressing at least 6 hours before using by combining oil, sugar, vinegar, sour cream, and seasonings. Toss spinach with desired amount of dressing, then top with eggs and bacon.

Paella Salad

1 7-oz. pkg. yellow rice, cooked
2 tbsp. tarragon vinegar
⅓ cup oil
⅛ tsp. salt
Black pepper to taste
Worcestershire sauce to taste
⅛ tsp. dry mustard
¼ tsp. Accent
2 cups diced cooked chicken
1 cup boiled, shelled shrimp
1 small can green peas
1 large tomato, chopped
1 bell pepper, chopped
½ cup minced onion
⅓ cup thinly sliced celery
1 tbsp. chopped pimiento

Mix hot rice, vinegar, oil, and seasonings. Cool to room temperature. Add remaining ingredients. Toss lightly and chill. May prepare night before. Serves 6 to 8.

Curried Chicken Salad

4 large chicken breasts
1 can sliced water chestnuts
2 lb. green grapes, cut in half
2 cups chopped celery
2 cups slivered almonds
1 cup mayonnaise
1 tsp. soy sauce
1 tsp. lemon juice
1 tsp. curry powder

Cook chicken breasts, cool, and dice. Put in mixing bowl and add water chestnuts, grapes, celery, and almonds. Mix dressing by combining mayonnaise, soy sauce, lemon juice, and curry powder. Toss dressing with chicken mixture, then chill before serving. Serves 8.

Long Island Soft Ginger Cake

1 cup butter
1 cup sugar
1 tsp. baking soda
½ cup sour milk
3 cups sifted flour
2 tbsp. ground ginger
2 cups molasses
4 eggs

Cream butter and sugar until light. Dissolve soda in milk and add to mixture. Add flour, then ginger and molasses. Beat eggs until light and fold into batter. Pour into 9x13x1½" pan, and bake in 350-degree oven for about 30 minutes. This is an old recipe belonging to Mrs. William J. Minor; her father-in-law, Stephen Minor of Concord Plantation, was a powerful leader in Natchez under the Spanish regime in the late 1700s.

Rosalie

On the loess bluffs towering 250 feet above the waters of the Mississippi River, declared by LaSalle the most desirable site on the river in 1682, Bienville and a band of French settlers would establish a fort in 1716.

They called this first fort on the Mississippi Rosalie in honor of the beautiful Duchess de Pontchartrain, and they called their settlement Natchez for the Indian tribes who had dwelled here for some 500 years. By 1729 those same Indians had massacred the French settlers and priests; retaliatory attacks three years later all but wiped out the Indians.

The area fell under the control of the British in 1763, then under the Spanish, both crowns granting large land grants for the establishment of plantations growing corn, indigo, and tobacco. The Spanish governor commissioned a surveyor to lay out the town atop the bluffs, and Natchez as we know it began taking shape, by 1798 becoming part of the United States.

It was in 1806, 11 years before Mississippi would become a state, that 13-year-old Eliza Lowe became a bride. Her parents, succumbing to yellow fever in one of the tragically regular epidemics that spread like wildfire to decimate entire families, begged Peter Little to take care of their young daughter; he did, marrying her and the same day sending her away to boarding school in Baltimore.

When she returned, grown to womanhood, he built for her the lovely home called Rosalie, situated on the site of that early fort, overlooking the Mississippi River and Natchez Under-the-Hill. It has been said that Peter dreamed of grand parties and entertainments in his new home, but the pious Eliza leaned toward austere chicken dinners and lengthy visitations from Methodist circuit riders, whereupon her long-suffering husband built a parsonage across the street for use by visiting preachers.

Eliza would die of yellow fever herself during the epidemic of 1853, her husband following her several years later. The home was sold to Andrew Wilson, who formalized the parlor with the addition of fine carpets, gilded mirrors, and a complete set of intricately carved rosewood furniture made by the master craftsman Belter.

During the Civil War, Rosalie served as headquarters for Union general Walter Gresham and his staff, who left the imprints of their spurs on the cypress floors. The parlor mirrors had been buried in the hillside before the city of Natchez was occupied; the carpets were rolled up and stored in the attic along with the fine furnishings during the occupation of 1863, when Gen. U. S. Grant slept here while on his way from Vicksburg to New Orleans.

Since 1938 Rosalie has been the property of the Mississippi Society, Daughters of the American Revolution, who open the house for tours and sell in their gift shop *The DAR Recipe Book* of Rosalie recipes, a collection to which "Daughters" from across the state contributed cherished family recipes handed down through the generations, some originating during the same period as Rosalie, a few reprinted here. Proceeds from book sales further the work of the Mississippi Society, DAR.

General Grant's Pudding

⅓ lb. butter
⅓ lb. sugar
4 tbsp. milk
⅓ lb. flour
⅓ lb. orange marmalade
2 tbsp. baking powder
3 egg yolks, beaten
3 egg whites, beaten
½ cup butter
1 cup sugar
½ cup tepid water
Whipped cream

Cream ⅓ lb. butter and ⅓ lb. sugar and add milk, flour, marmalade, baking powder, and then the eggs, folding whites in last. Pour into buttered mold and steam for 3 hours. Make Foamy Sauce by creaming ½ cup butter until soft, adding by teaspoonfuls 1 cup sugar, and then adding by teaspoonfuls the water. Put sauce in pitcher, set in boiling water, and cook for 30 minutes until all foam. Pour sauce over pudding and top with whipped cream. Serve at once. This recipe is said to have been brought home from China by Gen. U. S. Grant.

Syllabub

½ cup sugar
1 tbsp. lemon juice
1 cup light cream
6 ladyfingers
½ cup sherry
Pinch cinnamon
Pinch nutmeg

Mix sugar, lemon juice, and light cream. Do not beat; stir with spoon. Soak ladyfingers in sherry. Place in 6 wine or sherbet glasses. Pour cream mixture over ladyfingers and sprinkle with cinnamon and nutmeg. This is said to have been served in sugar-plantation homes along the Mississippi River in antebellum days.

Lady Baltimore Cake

2 cups seeded raisins
12 figs
Sherry or brandy (optional)
1 cup butter
2 cups sugar
4 eggs
3½ cups cake flour
4 tsp. baking powder
½ tsp. salt
1 cup milk
1 cup sugar
½ cup water
2 tsp. vanilla extract
2 tsp. almond extract
2 cups sugar
⅔ cup water
2 tsp. corn syrup
2 egg whites, beaten stiff
2 cups pecans or walnuts, minced
Almond extract
Vanilla extract

If desired, soak raisins and figs overnight in small amount of sherry or brandy. Mince. Cream butter until light and fluffy. Add 2 cups sugar gradually and continue beating to the consistency of whipped cream. Add eggs one at a time and beat thoroughly. Sift flour, baking powder, and salt together three times. Add to butter mixture alternately with 1 cup milk. Bake in two 9 or 10" cake pans in 350-degree oven about 30 minutes. Make a thick syrup of 1 cup sugar and ½ cup water. Add vanilla and almond extract. Spread this over the layers as soon as they are removed from pans. For frosting, mix 2 cups sugar with ⅔ cup water and the corn syrup; cook until it forms a firm ball in cold water. Pour gradually into the egg whites, beating constantly. Add raisins, figs, and nuts. Add almond and vanilla extract to taste. Spread between layers and on top and sides of cake. This is said to be the glamorous Lady Baltimore Cake recipe from Charleston's Lady Baltimore Tea Room.

The Misses Rumble's Christmas Charlotte Russe

1 tbsp. gelatin
¼ cup cold water
4 eggs, separated
4 heaping tbsp. sugar
1 pt. whipped cream
Vanilla extract
2 lemons (optional)
Ladyfingers
Cherry

Soak gelatin in cold water, then dissolve over hot water. Beat yolks of eggs and sugar. Add gelatin. Fold in whipped cream and stiffly beaten whites of eggs. Flavor with vanilla. Add the juice and rind of 2 lemons, if desired. Line mold with ladyfingers and pour in custard. Top with cherry and put in icebox until firm. From *Feliciana Recipes* published years ago by Grace Episcopal Church, this recipe is attributed to "the Misses Rumble of Rosalie, Natchez, Mississippi," who served it for Christmas dessert.

Concord

Built in 1794 and burned in 1901, Concord Plantation was closely associated with the earliest leaders of the Natchez area: Gayoso de Lemos, who commanded the military post at Natchez for the Spanish, and Stephen Minor, who would be his successor and help bridge the gap between Spanish and American rule.

Born in Mapletown, Pennsylvania, which was then a part of Virginia, in 1760, Stephen Minor descended the Mississippi River in 1779 bound for New Orleans with a load of merchandise. He was not quite 20 but was already involved with politics and power, for the trip apparently was a screen for obtaining war materials being secretly supplied by Spain to the American revolutionaries in the West.

His party and the war materials were ambushed on the return trip north, with Minor escaping death only because illness had delayed him some miles behind.

Returning to New Orleans, he helped the Spanish under the governor of Louisiana, Bernardo de Galvez, in attacks against the British at Manchac, Baton Rouge, Mobile, and Pensacola. Once West Florida was Spanish, Minor was awarded military rank and granted the land upon which the city of Natchez was built. He was held in high esteem by the governor of the Natchez District, Don Manuel Gayoso de Lemos, beneath whom he served as adjutant.

Adept at serving the interests of both Spain and

the earliest inhabitants of Natchez, Minor eventually replaced Gayoso de Lemos and became governor of the area until Spain was forced out and the area became American.

From 1797 Minor owned Concord, and, in addition to his military and political duties, he was a successful planter, raising indigo, tobacco, and cotton on his huge acreages (at one point, 40,000 acres) of rich bottomlands. He also raised cattle and was an avid breeder of fine Thoroughbred horses, belonged to the Fleetfield racetrack society, and became an early president of the Bank of the Mississippi.

In 1792 Stephen Minor married Katharine Lintot of Natchez, whose sister Fanny was wife of Philip Nolan, a name familiar to readers of Edward Everett Hale's fictional patriotic tome *Man Without a Country* as that attributed to the young military officer whose boredom with service at a backwater post like Fort Adams led to his ill-fated involvement with Aaron Burr. The Minors would rear his son Philip after the senior Nolan lost his life while on what was said to be an illegal horse-hunting expedition in Texas in 1797.

Many of the Concord recipes were preserved in handwritten manuscripts saved by Minor descendants at Southdown Plantation in south Louisiana, built on land acquired in 1828 by Stephen Minor's son William. William Minor's son Henry Chotard Minor kept even more meticulous notes, and the compilation of these add interest to a Southdown fundraising cookbook called *Good Earth*, featuring Minor receipts, household hints, and time-honored advice covering every problem from dressing calves' heads to cleaning ostrich plumes to removing bullets or other foreign objects from the alimentary tract.

The Concord Receipt for Gumbo

Chicken
Black pepper and salt to taste
Okra
Rice

Cut up your chicken, lay it in cold water till the blood is drawn out, and fry it to a nice brown color. Season it with black pepper and salt. Have a large soup plate full of okra and chop fine, throwing away the heads and tips of the same, as they are hard. Always use the long white, it being more tender and better flavored than the other kinds. Stir in this with the chicken, and it will partake of the taste and seasoning of the chicken. Fry it a little, and have ready some boiling water, pouring over, say, 3 quarts, and allow a sufficient quantity to boil away. Let all boil down until the chicken becomes perfectly tender, so that it may easily be torn to pieces with a fork. If fried, it requires more pepper and salt, which should be added before it is thoroughly cooked. The gumbo thus made will be very thick. If you do not like it made this way, do not boil so much, as it spoils all kinds of soups to boil down and fill up again, as many do, with cold water, and besides it is never so rich. Have rice boiled tender, but be careful that the grains are separate.

The Concord Receipt for Making Frozen Punch

6 lemons
3 qt. water
2¼ lb. sugar
4 egg whites
Brandy
Rum

Take lemons and squeeze the juice into the water. Add sugar. Beat the egg whites, stir into the lemonade, then add 3 wineglasses each of the best brandy and rum. Freeze it as ice cream.

The Concord Receipt for Pickling Pork

Cut up the hog in pieces to suit yourself; then sprinkle it with salt, on a table or board to extract the blood. Hard salt is the best. Fine salt answers very well but it requires more of it. It can remain in the salt for 2 or 3 days if the weather permits. Then pack in the barrel, sprinkling salt between every layer, skin side down; then put the pickle on it, which is made by dissolving 6 oz. of saltpetre to every 100 lb. Add ½ lb. of brown sugar and as much water as will cover the pork well.

Stephen Minor Receipt for Dressing Salads

2 egg yolks
2 tsp. salt
2 tsp. mustard
Black and cayenne pepper to taste
6 tbsp. oil
1 tbsp. vinegar

Take the egg yolks, put them in a soup plate, then add salt, mustard, and peppers. Then stir well with a fork. Stir in sweet oil very slowly, then add by degrees the vinegar. Pour on the salad just before eating.

The Concord Receipt for Making Mint Sauce to Eat with Roast Mutton

Fresh mint
Vinegar
Sugar

Take a handful of mint, wash the dust well off it, squeeze all the water out of it, then put it in a tumbler. Pour as much vinegar on it as you wish sauce. Let it remain for 2 hours. Then strain it into a sauce bowl. Add as much fine loaf sugar as will suit the taste, making it rich with the sugar. It is then fit for use.

Historic Jefferson College

Children, and some unthinking adults as well, tend to think of life in the Old South as all elegance and ease, all gaiety and jubilation.

And it's true, in privileged places there were servants with silver trays catering to every whispered whim, and plentiful occasions for joyous celebration.

But at the same time, life on the early plantations for the most part required hard work and struggle and plenty of elbow grease, not to mention blood, sweat, and tears. There were the dangers of the frontier to face, and the difficulties in wresting from the wilderness fields for planting. Men's bodies were early aged and broken by the constant succession of days filled with backbreaking toil, and women's hearts were broken as well by the tragically

high numbers of offspring going straight from cradle to grave.

To balance the times of glory there were sweeping tragedies: floods or droughts wiping out the cash and food crops upon which plantation empires depended, terrible epidemics of yellow fever or cholera spreading like wildfire to wipe out entire families, the ravages of war and the deprivation of its aftermath when homes were burned and wives and mothers lost a generation of grown men on the battlefields and plenty of boys as well.

To give today's children a real understanding of what life was like for their counterparts several centuries ago in Mississippi and its environs, Historic Jefferson College in Washington, just

above Natchez, hosts a number of activities geared toward young students throughout the year. At Christmastime, Mississippi elementary students carefully recreate Victorian decorations to hang on trees at the college; in the summer, visitors sprawl under the spreading shade trees and listen with rapturous delight to storytelling in the best old-time tradition of oral entertainment; and at other times there are classes in basketry.

A summer session called "Pioneer Week—The Way It Was" gives children aged 7 to 12 hands-on lessons in just exactly how things were done by their counterparts 150 to 200 years ago. Food preservation lessons include gathering beans and okra from the garden bright and early one morning, then stringing the beans to make "leather breeches" beans, a technique used to preserve them for later use during the winter off-season. Green apples and okra are sliced and dried to extend their use over the seasons as well, and eggs, always more plentiful in summer, are preserved in crocks of waterglass kept in cool places for making holiday cakes and pies during the winter. Yeast bread is also made and butter is churned.

One session concentrates on household chores, the children sweeping with sagebrush brooms, polishing furniture with mint leaves, washing clothes with lye soap, cooking stew, and making apple but-ter; they also bake a crumb cake on an open fire using a recipe published in *Early American Life* magazine. A scarecrow is made to protect growing vegetables in the all-important garden, and the decorative art of stenciling is introduced.

For the nature session, bird walks along the nature trail and the making of cornhusk flowers are featured. The crafts session highlights the making of rag rugs, crocheting, spinning, weaving, and smocking. A final session of plain old fun includes some good old-timey storytelling, lively early 1800s banjo music, and old-fashioned games like hopscotch and potato races, jump rope and horseshoe pitching. Like pioneer children before them, youngsters get the chance to keep diaries and learn sayings once they've completed their chores. Since books were scarce in most early settlers' homes, children were often instructed by having to memorize verses, usually ones that taught morals.

The setting for all this is an appropriate one, for Historic Jefferson College was incorporated in 1802 as the first educational institution in the Mississippi Territory and named for Pres. Thomas Jefferson. Now an official state historic site and an ongoing restoration project, Historic Jefferson College includes on its grounds the Burr Oaks, where, tradition has it, Aaron Burr was arraigned for treason in 1807.

Nix Kucha

1½ cups brown sugar
2½ cups all-purpose flour
½ cup butter, or combination of butter and lard
½ tsp. salt
1 tsp. baking soda
1 cup sour milk or buttermilk
1 egg

The name of this cake means "Nothing Crumb Cake," an indication of its simplicity . . . nothing can go wrong when you make it. Mix sugar, flour, and butter together as you would for pie crust or until crumbly. Remove half the crumbs and set aside to use on the top of the cake. Add salt and baking soda to milk and add this to the remaining crumbs. Beat in the egg. Mix well and pour into a well-buttered Dutch oven. Sprinkle reserved crumbs on top and bake 30 to 40 minutes. The cake is best served fresh.

Natchez Under-the-Hill

Back in the days when cotton was king and the Mississippi River the main highway connecting the rich plantation country with the wonders of the world, life was lived with a graceful and rational formality—gentlemen were chivalric cavaliers living by a respected and courtly code of honor, their ladies wasp-waisted belles in hoop skirts and ringlets, skilled in the social graces.

At least that was what life was like for some in the South, the cultured aristocracy of the planter class in areas like antebellum Natchez atop the bluffs.

But Natchez Under-the-Hill, the rough and rowdy port area where the first steamboat docked before 1820—ah, that was a different story.

Life under the hill in the early days, with its saloons, gambling dens, raucous dance halls, and houses of ill repute, was fast and cheap for the rough boatmen braving the perils of the river on their rude flatboats. According to some accounts, the only thing cheaper than a woman's body was a man's life. Many a productive plantation was lost in a crooked card game, and many a promising life.

Under the hill, life took its pace from Old Man River, rolling along right at its feet. As always, the river proved a fickle friend at best, beneficently bestowing unbelievable blessings and then just as easily, with whimsical cruelty, taking them away . . . its lapping waters fertilizing and nurturing and cleansing, then flooding and drowning and destroying, its gentleness turning violent and then returning with new life once again in a never-ending cycle.

Today Natchez Under-the-Hill still takes from

WINTER SCENE FROM THE BLUFFS

the river its unique character, and proves that its denizens haven't forgotten how to have a good time or appreciate the minute. The *Delta Queen* and *Mississippi Queen* paddlewheelers still dock here to disgorge tourists for visits to the historic Natchez area, so this is where the Floozy Contest is held during the annual riverboat race between New Orleans and St. Louis, with outrageously dressed "floozies" recruited from boat passengers or crews strutting their stuff to earn points to determine the winner of the race.

The Under-the-Hill Saloon on Silver Street occupies a restored building dating from the early 1830s that has been used as a bakery, grocery, pool hall, beer joint, and mostly a lively saloon with a thriving house of ill repute upstairs in the old days. It still retains much of that colorful character, the cool dark interiors full of ship models and ceiling fans, captain's chairs and hatch-cover tables, three double French doors with plenty of glass opening onto the boardwalk and allowing magnificent river views from even the smokiest of barstool perches.

Says Andre Farish, Jr., who with his father has long run the popular saloon, "There's something awfully soothing and relaxing about the mighty Mississippi being right here where you can spit in it and take a sip of your beer at the same time. It makes you feel mighty small." While he loves the river and saloon, having even been married there, he has also seen its dark side, like high-water times when river waters rise to lap right at the foot of Silver Street. Andre was also on duty as "cocktail waitress" the tragic day in 1980 when the whole hillside above the saloon came crashing down in a mudslide that killed the saloon bartender and the cook in the Bowie Knife next door.

Now the hillside has been stabilized and a through road connects this lower area with the blufftops near Rosalie, easing the access to the shops, casino, and restaurants under the hill. Since the 1970s the area has enjoyed a resurgence of popularity, and fun special events like the balloon festival bring crowds spilling down along Silver Street.

But Natchez Under-the-Hill has outlived the vices and violence of the rowdy boatmen, the rise and fall of steamboat popularity, the flooding, the mudslides, the neglect, and now the renewed appreciation. You get the impression it will continue to be around, its liveliness ebbing and flowing perhaps, but always rolling along just as steadily as that Old Man River.

Under-the-Hill Saloon Bloody Mary

1 shot vodka
Black pepper
Celery salt
Dash Worcestershire sauce
1 or 2 drops Tabasco sauce
Lime
Lemon
½ oz. beef bouillon
Tomato juice
Pickled okra

Pour vodka over the rocks in a glass, says Andre Farish, Jr., then add a couple of shakes of pepper and celery salt, Worcestershire, Tabasco, a squeeze of lime, a squeeze of lemon, beef bouillon, and tomato juice to fill glass. Shake or pour back and forth between 2 glasses to mix. Garnish with pickled okra, and you'll never find a finer Bloody Mary anywhere in the world, he says. Of course, he also says it tastes much better in one of the rocking chairs on the boardwalk in front of the Under-the-Hill Saloon watching the sunset paint a string of barges and tugs coming around a distant bend in the mighty Mississippi River, but you can try it at home anyway.

Green Leaves Audubon China

High above Rankin Street in the middle of Natchez, in the shade of huge old oaks and magnolias, Green Leaves perches in its leafy bower, filled with treasures collected by six generations of the same family.

The house with its pleasant courtyard was built in 1838; within a decade it had been acquired by George W. and Mary Roane Koontz, whose descendants continue to live in it and love it today.

Its fine furnishings have been collected over the generations, but one of the most prized treasures in Green Leaves actually predates the house itself. That's the set of bird china, which may well have been painted by the artist-naturalist John James Audubon himself.

In 1820 Audubon set out from Kentucky on his journey down the Mississippi River, bent upon starting work toward his staggering goal of painting all the birds of the entire vast North American continent. Leaving behind him a string of failed business ventures, he floated downriver aboard a flatboat, working to pay his passage and disembarking briefly at Natchez the day after Christmas, then continuing on to New Orleans, where he earned what money he could painting portraits and giving lessons in French, drawing, music, or dancing.

He spent four months of 1821 at West Feliciana Parish's Oakley Plantation, sketching more than 80 of his bird studies while tutoring young Eliza Pirrie, then returned to New Orleans, where his family joined him.

In the early spring of 1822, the poverty-ridden artist booked passage aboard a steamboat to Natchez, paying his way by executing a crayon portrait of the boat's captain and his wife. For the next year Audubon would haunt the woodlands and swamps of the Natchez area and cross the river into Louisiana, painting such birds as the white-throated sparrow, the towhee bunting, the Chuck-will's widow, the

wood thrush, the Eastern kingbird, the blue-eyed yellow warbler, and the black-throated bunting.

He supported himself by selling portraits and teaching French, music, and drawing both to private students and also at established educational institutes like Mr. Davis' Seminary and Elizabeth Female Academy. When his young sons joined him, they were enrolled at Jefferson College in nearby Washington.

Audubon was also said to have painted three complete sets of china while in Natchez, one including more than 336 pieces for the Gaillard family at Etania, featuring flowers and fruit painted on plain white Parisian china, which was then fired in a large charcoal oven built on the place for that purpose.

One of the other sets of china Audubon painted may be that at Green Leaves. Family lore has it that the French provincial china was ordered from a French factory, painted in Natchez by the great artist himself, then sent back to France to be properly fired.

There are some 200 pieces of the Green Leaves bird china remaining after all this time, each one magnificently executed with a broad blue border and brilliantly colored bird positioned in the center, each different. The china comes in a staggering array of sizes and shapes and functions, with lovely shell dishes, covered vegetable dishes that are round and oblong and square, tiny nut dishes each with its own perfectly proportioned bird, fruit baskets, stemmed compotes and cake baskets, and 7 graduating sizes of platters.

Virginia Beltzhoover Morrison, mistress of the house who shares some favorite recipes here, is careful to stress that the bird china is only *attributed* to Audubon, but there's something so fitting about birds painted by the great bird artist himself roosting high on a hill in a house called Green Leaves nestled among the Natchez treetops.

Green Leaves Turtle Soup

Terrapin
Soup meat
2 onions
Handful parsley
Thyme, minced
½ tsp. ground allspice
4 round spices
Ground mace
Salt and black pepper to taste
½ lemon
Claret or Madeira

Scald the terrapin as you would a chicken, after having taken out the gall. Scrape the outer skin off, cut the terrapin up in pieces, and wash it. Have a nice piece of soup meat and boil it with the shell of the terrapin until about 3 hours before dinnertime. Strain all the meat out of the pot, throw in the terrapin, and let it boil steadily over low heat until 30 minutes before dinner. Then season with onions, parsley, a little thyme, allspice, 4 round spices, a little mace, salt, and pepper. Just before dishing up, cut the lemon up in the soup and throw in a little wine. This is the title recipe from the grand little booklet sold for 25 cents at the first pilgrimages in Natchez in the 1930s and called *Turtle Soup & Other Choice Recipes From Natchez, Mississippi.*

Pots de Crème

2 cups milk, cream, or half & half
5-8 oz. best-quality chocolate, grated
2 tbsp. sugar
6 egg yolks
1 tsp. vanilla extract or orange rind

Cook and stir milk or cream with chocolate and sugar until blended and the milk scalded. Beat egg yolks lightly. Temper them by stirring in ½ cup of hot milk mixture in a double boiler. Add to rest of the hot milk mixture. Add vanilla or orange rind. Continue to stir until the custard begins to thicken. You may strain if needed. Pour into cups. Cool uncovered until steam is out, then cover and refrigerate.

Magnificent Melrose

Magnificent Melrose in Natchez, melding the best of the Greek Revival and Georgian architectural styles, is called by the experts "an amazing time capsule" with such impressive richness and purity as to be a "wonderful document of mid-19th-century life."

Perhaps more than any other area house, Melrose has been preserved with such sensitivity to the original design and includes so many original furnishings as to present the classic picture of life in the Old South at the zenith of the cotton culture.

The home was built between 1841 and 1845 by leading lawyer-planter John Thompson McMurran, who spared no expense in providing the perfect setting for his beautiful wife, Mary Louise, financing his efforts with proceeds from his fertile cotton plantations across the river in Louisiana.

In 1865, at the close of the Civil War, another lawyer-planter, George Malin Davis, acquired Melrose, and it would remain in his family for more than a century. The John S. Callons purchased the home in 1976 and set about the impeccable restoration.

Centering an 82-acre English park planted with flowering shrubs and trees grown to great height, the

house is still surrounded by such early dependencies as the double-galleried servants' quarters and outside kitchen, stables, and carriage house.

The interiors of Melrose were graced with the best furnishings that could be acquired in the 1840s, rare museum-quality examples of the height of skill reached by America's finest master-craftsmen. The drawing room, with its original brocatelle draperies of cooling green colored with vegetable dye and spun with real gold thread, was featured in a book detailing the hundred most beautiful rooms in the country. The delicate floral and scrolled carvings trimming its rosewood furniture were duplicated by Gorham Silver Company for the sterling pattern called Melrose.

Between the library, formal parlor, and drawing room are immense *faux bois* sliding doors trimmed in silver, and other doors throughout the home have solid silver doorknobs and trim as well. The dining room, its air stirred gently in the old days by a huge punkah of carved mahogany suspended above the table, still contains the original set of 14 Gothic Revival chairs, table, and sideboard, setting off the original 1832 silver service.

In the broad entrance foyer and Great Hall are two English woven floorcloths, handpainted and considered "extremely rare documents" by national restoration and preservation experts; the entrance foyer floorcloth is in an inlaid lozenge design, while the Great Hall's floorcloth with its 11 brilliant colors duplicates the pattern of Brussels carpeting. No other house in the country has two such floorcloths in the original setting.

Such tasteful attention to detail, such a wealth of original period pieces, such perfection of setting, and such understanding of the period displayed during the sensitive restoration of Melrose led to its designation as a National Historic Landmark by the United States Department of the Interior, citing its remarkable perfection of design and the integrity of its beautiful surroundings. More recently, the same assets have accounted for the property's becoming the centerpiece of an 82-acre national park designed to eventually link the termination of the Natchez Trace with the Mississippi River and the quintessential Southern plantation.

Today 16,600-square-foot Melrose and the Natchez National Historical Park open daily for tours, some guided by affable Fred Page, who has been the butler at Melrose since 1948 and is as much a part of the home as the dining room's crystal flycatcher or the built-in chaperone in the Victorian *tete-a-tete* parlor sofa.

Betty Callon's Seven-Layer Lemon Cake

1 cup butter
2 cups sugar
4 eggs
3 cups cake flour
3 tsp. baking powder
¼ tsp. salt
2 tsp. vanilla extract
1 cup milk
1½ cups sugar
3 eggs
3 tbsp. butter
Grated rind and juice of 3 lemons

Cream 1 cup butter with 2 cups sugar; add 4 eggs, one at a time, and beat well. Sift together flour, baking powder, and salt. Mix vanilla with milk. To the butter mixture, add flour in three parts and milk in two parts, beginning with flour. Bake at 350 degrees for about 25 minutes. This is a three-layer cake, but for lemon cake make 7 thin layers by putting just enough batter in pans to cover bottom; adjust baking time, as it will not take 25 minutes to bake the thin layers. For lemon filling, mix 1½ cups sugar with 3 eggs, 3 tbsp. butter, and lemon juice and rind. Cook in double boiler until thick; don't undercook. Spread filling between layers and on top. Betty Callon says she usually makes 1⅓ recipes of the filling so there'll be plenty to put between the layers and on top of the cake.

Betty Callon's Salmon Muffins

1 small onion
1 stalk celery
1 15½-oz. can salmon and juice
½ cup finely ground bread or cracker crumbs
1 egg
Salt and black pepper to taste
Herbs of your choice
Cayenne pepper to taste

Chop onion and celery in food processor. Mix all ingredients together. Pack lightly into greased muffin tins. Bake at 350 degrees for 20 minutes. Makes 18 small muffins, which can be served hot or cold with sauce of choice. Betty Callon makes her sauce by mixing mayonnaise with horseradish and capers, and says this makes a wonderful first course at a dinner party. She says she just created the recipe off the top of her head and her guests loved it.

BBQ Sauce for Ribs

1 cup sugar
1 pt. apple juice
1½ tbsp. salt
1 tbsp. black pepper
1 tsp. cayenne pepper
½ tsp. Tabasco sauce
3 tbsp. Worcestershire sauce
1 onion, thinly sliced
2 thick slices lemon
2 cups catsup
1½ sticks butter or oleo
3 tsp. prepared mustard

Place sugar in apple juice and heat to dissolve. Add remaining ingredients and mix all together. Bring to a boil and simmer about 30 minutes. Freezes well. Makes sauce sufficient for 6 to 8 ribs.

Betty Callon's Baked Grits Casserole

1 cup grits, not quick or instant
3 cups water
1 stick butter
1 roll garlic cheese
½ cup milk or half & half
2 eggs, beaten
2 lb. bulk sausage, browned and drained

Cook grits according to directions on box until water is absorbed. Add butter and cheese. Stir well until both are melted and blended. Add milk, eggs, and sausage. Beat well. Add spices or seasonings as desired. Pour into casserole dish and bake at 300 degrees for 45 minutes.

Squaw Corn

2 cans cream-style corn
2 eggs, beaten
¾ cup cornmeal
¾ tsp. garlic salt
¼ cup cooking oil
1 small onion, chopped
4 jalapeno peppers, chopped
8 oz. grated cheddar cheese
Cracker crumbs for topping
Butter

Mix corn, eggs, meal, salt, oil, onion, peppers, and cheese and pour into casserole dish. Top with cracker crumbs and butter. Bake covered for 1 hour at 400 degrees. Betty Callon says this is a wonderful side dish that can even be used in lieu of bread.

Steamboatin'

In the cotton-rich days of the mid-1800s, upwards of 20 huge steamboats or fast packets might be docked on any given day at the rowdy river ports of Natchez Under-the-Hill or Bayou Sara. Amid a tangle of sweating heavy-laden roustabouts and mule-drawn wagons, the muddy thoroughfares of these port settlements teemed with traffic and cattle drives, cotton bales were piled as high as the sky, and mile-long rows of warehouses overflowed.

Fanciful with gingerbread trim, the immense riverboats would be unloading the riches of the world to beautify elegant plantation homes—fine works of art, handcarved furniture of rosewood or polished mahogany, leather-bound first editions to stock libraries, lace-trimmed and embroidered linens, foodstuffs not locally available, barrels and crates packed with delicate crystal or handpainted china from Gay Paree, and the latest lush fashions from the capitals of the Continent for the ladies and the gentlemen too.

In return, the steamboats would be piled high with cotton bales for shipment to cotton factors in New Orleans, and the quicker the better . . . whole plantation empires depended on the sale of this cotton for their livelihood from year to year, for cotton was king and financed for his court an entire way of life. Thus the boats raced up and down the river, and the swiftest was granted the contract to deliver the mail and was much sought after for delivering cotton and trade goods as well. In days when a great deal of travel was by water, travelers also were anxious to book passage on the fastest boat, in spite of the threat of midriver fires and explosions, snags and sinkings, floods and other perils of river traffic.

When the steamboat *Princess,* for example, was bound for the opening of the Louisiana Supreme Court in New Orleans on February 27, 1859, it was packed with over 200 prominent passengers, including many of the most highly respected barristers in the South. Delayed by fog upriver, the boat reached Bayou Sara landing running behind schedule and hurriedly boarded such passengers as Lorenzo D. Brewer of St. Francisville. The boat's sweating crew stoked the blazing fires and tried to make up for lost time. When the *Princess* reached Conrad's Point just south of Baton Rouge, there was a fiery explosion. Dying passengers, badly burned, were hauled from the river's waters and rolled in flour on the levee, but over 70 were fatally wounded, including Brewer.

In Natchez from 1870 to 1913 there was a skilled professional photographer named Henry C. Norman recording all this action for posterity, and after his death, his son Earl maintained the family trade through the mid-1950s. Not long ago, a Natchez physician, with assistance from several other dedicated local photographers, began the monumental task of salvaging these pictorial records from the Normans' original glass or celluloid negatives. One who helped was professional photographer Ed Prince, himself descended from a long line of river pilots who owned such boats as the Royal Route Packets; he provided the photos used here to illustrate the opulence of some steamboat dining rooms.

The entire steamboatin' era has been preserved most vividly and accurately in a series of books beautifully compiled by Dr. Thomas H. Gandy and his wife, Joan W. Gandy, books concentrating separately on riverboats, on Victorian children, and on historic Natchez itself as seen through the lenses of the Normans and other early photographers. These books are available throughout the Natchez area and make for highly enjoyable and historically edifying mementos of a visit South along the Great River Road.

From the Gandys' book called *Norman's Natchez—An Early Photographer and His Town* comes a picturesquely detailed description of dining on a steamboat as recorded by this early photographer: "Norman was obviously a natural for recording river life. His artist's eye focused on gleaming gingerbread pilothouses, each with its own special style, on jauntily posed riverboat travelers, on people and pistons in the engine rooms, and on the dining rooms of special grace, where one might indulge in green turtle soup, potted fowl and tongue ornamented with jelly, *pate chaud* of pigeon, and whortleberry pie. The table settings, with their stacked silverware, were equal to the splendor of the menus. As one veteran steamboat traveler said, 'I have seen New Yorkers stand aghast at the display of every conceivable confection with which the dinner table was loaded, and the fare to Vicksburg from New Orleans . . . was only $10, a bottle of wine included.'"

Turtle Soup

10 lb. turtle meat
1 qt. vegetable oil
2-3 bunches celery, chopped
1 bunch parsley, chopped
2 bell peppers, chopped
1-2 bunches shallots, chopped
4 cups chopped onion
4-4½ cups flour
6 gal. water
2-3 tbsp. thyme
4-6 tbsp. cloves
3-4 tbsp. nutmeg
1-2 cups Worcestershire sauce
⅓ cup hot pepper sauce
1-2 tbsp. marjoram
4-5 tbsp. cinnamon
2-3 tbsp. ground ginger
1 tbsp. mace
1 tbsp. ground allspice
⅜ cup salt
12-15 bay leaves
¼ cup Accent
¼ cup sugar
2-3 cloves garlic, chopped
4 #2 cans tomato sauce

Defrost meat if frozen and save the liquid. Cut meat in small pieces and fry in oil. Then add vegetables and flour and brown. Add water, seasonings, and rest of ingredients. Cook over medium to low heat for 4 hours.

Oyster Pie

½ stick oleo
⅔ cup chopped mushrooms
1 cup fried, crumbled bacon
⅔ cup chopped green onions
½ cup chopped onion
3 cloves garlic, pressed
4 tbsp. flour
¾ tsp. salt
¼ tsp. white pepper
¼ tsp. cayenne pepper
½ cup oyster liquid
½ cup red wine
1½ doz. oysters, poached until edges curl
1½ cups sifted all-purpose flour
¾ tsp. salt
⅔ cup shortening
5-7 tbsp. cold water

In a 9" skillet, melt oleo and lightly sauté mushrooms, bacon, green onions, onion, and garlic. When onion is soft, add 4 tbsp. flour, ¾ tsp. salt, and peppers. Cook well 7-10 minutes. Blend in oyster liquid and wine, and simmer over low heat 35-45 minutes. Chop oysters and add them for the last 7-10 minutes of cooking. Allow to cool while making pie crust of sifted flour, ¾ tsp. salt, shortening, and water. Mix well and form into well-moistened ball of dough. Divide the ball in half for upper and lower crusts. Roll first ball into a crust and place in 9" skillet. Fill with oyster mixture. Roll the second ball into top crust, place atop pie, and seal edges. Cut slits in the top to release steam and place pie in preheated 450-degree oven for 10 minutes. Then reduce heat to 350 degrees and bake 40 minutes. Turn oven to low or off, and let pie sit until the crust browns slightly.

Lehmann Landing Leg of Lamb

Leg of lamb
Salt and black pepper to taste
Ground ginger
Dry mustard
1 large onion, sliced
4 tomatoes, chopped (or 1 can)
1 tbsp. tomato puree (or catsup)
1 tsp. Worcestershire sauce
Flour
2 cups cold water

Wash and dry young leg of lamb. Rub with salt, pepper, and a little ginger. Put in baking pan. Sprinkle with mustard. Add onion, tomatoes, puree, and Worcestershire and sprinkle a little flour over all. Pour in water and bake in hot oven until meat is tender, basting occasionally and adding more water as necessary.

Duck Breast Pâté

1 1-lb. duck breast
White wine
Chicken broth
3-4 bay leaves
Worcestershire sauce
Hot pepper sauce
Garlic powder
Seasoned salt
Black peppercorns
Onion, grated
Pinch dry mustard
Pinch nutmeg
Mushrooms, sliced and sautéed in butter

Cook duck breast whole in white wine and chicken broth to cover. Season while cooking with bay leaves, Worcestershire, hot pepper sauce, garlic powder, seasoned salt, and a few black peppercorns. Cook about 20 minutes or until firm but not pink. Drain and save liquid. Put breast in food processor and puree until smooth, adding a little cooking liquid, a little grated onion, mustard, and nutmeg but keeping mixture thick. Put in bowl, add mushrooms, and mix. If mixture looks too dry or crumbly, add butter from mushroom sauté. Put in mold. Can be frozen; if so, remix after thawing.

1899 Spinning-Wheel Cookbook's Fowl and Oyster Pie

1 duck or chicken
Water
Flour
Butter
Salt and pepper to taste
Pie crust
Oysters

To make this pie, duck is preferable, wild duck best of all, but chicken will answer. Cut up the fowl and stew it in plenty of water, as a great deal of gravy is wanted; thicken the gravy with a little flour and put in a generous lump of butter and salt and pepper to taste. Line a deep pan with pie crust, set it in the oven, and let it bake until light brown. Then cover the bottom with pieces of the stewed fowl. On this put a layer of oysters, then some narrow strips of pie crust that have been rolled thin and baked, then another layer of the fowl and another of oysters until the pan is filled, always letting the top layer be of oysters, on each layer of which should be put a lump of butter. Over this pour the hot gravy, of which there should be enough to fill the pan. Put a crust over the whole and bake until the top crust is brown. The *Spinning-Wheel Cookbook* was printed in 1899 by the ladies of the Spinning-Wheel Club of Woodville, Mississippi.

1899 Spinning-Wheel Cookbook's Chicken Jelly

2 chickens
Water
2 tbsp. Worcestershire sauce
1 tbsp. salt
Pinch ground cloves
Pinch ground allspice
Pinch mace
6 eggs, hardboiled
1 lemon

Place the chickens in water just to cover. Boil chickens until you can easily pull the meat from the bones. Return the bones to the broth and boil 30 minutes longer. Strain and set in a cool place, and the liquor will become jellied. The next day cut the meat into small pieces, leaving out the skin. Melt the jelly and put the pieces in it. Add Worcestershire, salt, cloves, allspice, and mace. Slice eggs and lemon, line the mold or bowl with these slices, pour in the mixture, and let it stand till the next day.

Brandy Alexander Pie

1 env. plain gelatin
½ cup cold water
⅔ cup sugar
⅛ tsp. salt
3 eggs, separated
¼ cup cognac
¼ cup crème de cacao or benedictine
2 cups whipping cream
Chocolate curls

Sprinkle gelatin over cold water in saucepan. Add ⅓ cup sugar, salt, and egg yolks. Stir to blend. Heat over low heat until gelatin dissolves and mixture thickens. Do not boil. Remove from heat and stir in liqueurs. Half a cup of crème de menthe can be substituted for the cognac and crème de cacao or benedictine, if desired. Chill until mixture mounds slightly. Beat egg whites until stiff. Gradually add remaining sugar into whites. Fold into mixture with 1 cup whipped whipping cream. Chill and decorate with swirl of remaining whipped cream and chocolate curls.

Pickled Beef Tongue

2 or 3 tongues
Salt peter
Garlic
Hot red pepper
Dash ground ginger
Dash cayenne pepper
1 tbsp. ground allspice
1 tsp. whole cloves
1 cup salt

Wash tongues and remove bones. Rub well with salt peter. Stick 3 pieces garlic in each. Stick 3 pieces red pepper in each. Put in flat-bottom crock. Add ginger, cayenne, allspice, and cloves. Cover with salt. Put cover on and put in icebox. Turn every other day for 1 week. Wash and boil until tender in large vessel of water. Skin while warm. This recipe is from the vintage *Feliciana Recipes* published years ago by Grace Episcopal Church in St. Francisville.

Dunleith

Touring one of the magnificent antebellum mansions of Natchez is an unforgettable opportunity to experience the gracious lifestyle of the Old South when cotton was king and the livin' elegant, surrounded by delicately carved furnishings of rosewood and mahogany set off by polished silver and gleaming crystal or handpainted china, walls and windows draped in silks and damasks, libraries full of leather-bound volumes of great literature, decanters overflowing with rich wines, tables groaning under the weight of innumerable courses of delectable dishes, the heady scent of fresh magnolias perfuming the air, and the joyful sound of children at play drifting through the open windows.

Touring these homes provides a glimpse of all this, but to truly experience it, try spending the night in one of the many historic Bed and Breakfasts. Savor the nightfall while rocking on the gallery, watching the swifts and swallows wheel through the darkening skies; dream the night away in a massive four-poster bed with lush hangings and perhaps even a mosquito bar; awaken to a hearty plantation breakfast fit for the master of such a fine home.

In antebellum days the visits of friends and relatives were eagerly anticipated and highly enjoyed events breaking the monotony and isolation for plantation families when transportation was slow and dangerous and home responsibilities too demanding to permit much travel. Visits, when they did occur, often lasted for weeks or months, sometimes even years, and guests were entertained royally.

So they still are today at homes like beautiful Dunleith, an immense Greek Revival townhouse set on a Natchez hilltop centering 40 landscaped acres and considered of such architectural importance as to have been named a National Historic Landmark.

Twenty-six double columns of wedge-shaped bricks surround the massive three-story home with its 16-foot ceilings and winding 41-foot staircase, its downstairs front windows opening from the floor to the ceiling so the beauteous belles of antebellum balls could waltz right through them from the broad gallery into the double parlors. Those same parlors, with immense gold-leaf mirrors to reflect and magnify the light from early candle-burning crystal chandeliers, have huge sliding

pocket doors that could be closed when the ladies wanted to retire to their own affairs, the gentlemen closeting themselves in the opposite parlor with aromatic cigars and good brandy and interminable talk of politics or crops.

The exceptionally rare wallpaper in the formal dining room was printed by Zuber and Company in France from some 3,000 woodblocks painstakingly carved by hand in 1855 to depict *Les Zones,* the climatic zones of the world, Temperate, Tropical, and Arctic. During World War I, the paper was protected from destruction by being concealed in a dank cave in Alsace-Lorraine, there acquiring small mildew spots still visible but hardly distracting from the magnificent scenes.

Dunleith was built in 1855 by Charles Dahlgren and his wife, Mary Routh Ellis Dahlgren, on the site of the home of her father, Job Routh, one of the district's largest landholders and planters; called Routhland, this earlier home burned after being struck by lightning. Dunleith's 12 spacious rooms, broad hallways, and 9,500 square feet of living space were necessary to accommodate the lifestyle of this prominent couple and their 11 children, as were the rear dependencies.

During the Civil War Dunleith was home to Alfred V. Davis, who bred fine Thoroughbreds, several of the finest of which he hid in the cellar under the dining room when rumors of impending Union requisitions reached him; the horses were luckily silent during the dinner Davis was forced to share with the Union officers who soon arrived to inspect his barns.

Today there are overnight accommodations for guests in the main house and in the courtyard wing and original dairy barn to the rear of the house, as well as in the river-view suites; the large and unusual poultry house topped with pigeonnaire serves as bakery and offices. In the original carriage house and stables is a fabulously elegant restaurant, The Castle Restaurant.

Dunleith Pumpkin Bread

1 cup oil
⅔ cup water
4 eggs
2 cups pumpkin
1 tsp. nutmeg
2 tsp. baking soda
1 tsp. cinnamon
3 cups sugar
3⅓ cups flour
½ cup chopped nuts
½ tsp. salt

Preheat oven to 350 degrees. Mix oil, water, eggs, and pumpkin in small bowl. Add remaining ingredients and pour into 3 greased and floured loaf pans. Bake until tests done, 40-50 minutes.

Miss Routh's Dewberry Vinegar

Fresh dewberries, washed and hulled
Vinegar
Sugar
Whole cloves
Whole allspice

Cover berries with vinegar. Let stand 24 hours. Then strain off and to every pint of vinegar add a pint of sugar. Strain into kettle, add cloves and allspice, and let boil hard for 20 minutes. This recipe comes from a tiny book called *Turtle Soup & Other Choice Recipes From Natchez, Mississippi,* which was sold for 25 cents at the first pilgrimages in the early 1930s.

Stanton Hall

A National Historic Landmark covering an entire city block right in the middle of Natchez, white-columned Stanton Hall crowns the crest of a hill shaded by ancient live oaks and magnolias.

The stately home was built in 1857 at the height of antebellum elegance and reflects in its design and furnishings the finest that money could buy. Sheffield silver doorknobs and hinges, bronze chandeliers depicting Natchez history, marble mantels, gold-leaf French mirrors, and richly upholstered period furnishings provide a picture of a gracious lifestyle in the South before the Civil War.

Stanton Hall was erected for wealthy cotton broker Frederick Stanton under the direction of local architect-builder Capt. Thomas Rose, using homegrown talent as artists, builders, and finishers. Its arched hallway is an impressive 72 feet long, one entire side flanked by twin parlors opening into each other, charming rooms whose end mirrors make them seem to go on endlessly.

A property of the Pilgrimage Garden Club, which purchased the home in 1938 and restored it to perfection, Stanton Hall is open for tours and is also the scene for many social functions, wedding receptions like that of Charlotte Ferguson and George Murrell (pictured here), and other gatherings. On the site of the home's original carriage house, the club operates a restaurant of the same name famed for its Southern-fried chicken, tomato aspic, tiny light biscuits and other party fare, as well as mint juleps.

Carriage House Restaurant Tomato Aspic

2 env. plain gelatin
½ cup hot water
3¼ cups tomato juice
1 tbsp. lemon juice
2 tsp. Worcestershire sauce
½ tsp. Tabasco sauce, or to taste
1 small onion, minced
2 stalk celery, minced
1 tsp. salt
½ tsp. black pepper
8 oz. cream cheese
10 lettuce leaves
Mayonnaise

Dissolve gelatin in hot water. Add tomato juice, lemon juice, Worcestershire, Tabasco, onions, celery, salt, and pepper. Stir well. Put 1 tsp. cream cheese in each of 10 4- or 5-oz. molds. Fill molds with tomato mixture. Chill until firm. To serve, unmold and place each on lettuce leaf topped with mayonnaise.

Carriage House Hot Crabmeat and Shrimp Dip

2 stalks celery, chopped
1 bunch green onions, chopped
1 stick butter
2 tbsp. flour
1 pt. half & half
1 lb. white lump crabmeat
1 lb. boiled shrimp, chopped
8 oz. Swiss cheese, grated
Salt, black pepper, and cayenne pepper to taste

Sauté celery and onions in butter until soft. Add flour and mix well. Add half & half to make a cream sauce. Add crabmeat, shrimp, and cheese. Mix lightly. Simmer on top of stove approximately 10 minutes. Add seasonings. Remove from stove and put in chafing dish to keep warm. Serve with melba rounds. If too thick, add a little more cream.

Magnolia Hall

Called one of the three most outstanding examples of Greek Revival architecture in the town of Natchez, Magnolia Hall was built in 1858, the last great mansion completed before the outbreak of the Civil War, when a cannonball from the Union gunboat *Essex* burst through its kitchen walls.

Now restored to its original brownstone appearance and operated as a museum by the Natchez Garden Club, Magnolia Hall contains extensive collections of priceless 18th- and 19th-century art, textiles, needlework, and costumes.

Some of these exhibits explain past customs relating to what was a far-too-prevalent fact of everyday life in times past . . . death. With doctors few and far between and the art of healing limited at best, with epidemics of diseases like malaria and cholera commonly sweeping away whole settlements, with life spans of only a few decades common and a man of 30 or 40 considered elderly beyond expectation, with childbirth and its perils sending many a young mother straight from the birthing bed to the grave and far too often accompanied by the poor babe, death was accepted as an everyday part of life in the 18th and 19th centuries.

So besides the gala ball gowns and lush draperies, the brightly patterned carpets and rich upholsteries setting off fine antique furnishings, Magnolia Hall, in tribute to real life as it was historically lived, also shows such relics as a stitched mourning picture, loving tribute to a lost friend or relative, among its fine collection of silk embroideries.

And just inside the spacious entrance hallway hangs an unusual portrait, a likeness captured in 1861 by the New Orleans artist Reinhart. The expression on the lovely face of the white-gowned young girl, if it looks a trifle sad, is nonetheless fitting, for Sally Polk Richards was painted after her untimely death at a young age.

Closer inspection of the large portrait reveals that the rose at her breast, setting off her white bridal costume, is wilted, and that her hand rests, ever so gracefully, upon her own flower-draped coffin. Hovering faintly visible in the darkened background may be seen the dread Angel of Death, unwanted guest at the marriage celebration.

Sally Polk Richards was the young bride of Alexander Keene Richards, who, like many wealthy planters of his day, raised fine Thoroughbreds and followed them to such races as the Kentucky Derby. When Richards married again, after the early demise of his beloved Sally, his second wife was said to have received a most unusual and probably not entirely welcomed wedding gift from Sally's aunt and uncle . . . this portrait.

Magnolia Hall today offers not only tours but refreshments as well, from romantic candlelit dinners to receptions and brunch for groups; some favorite Magnolia Hall recipes, like those here, have been reprinted in tiny recipe booklets available in area gift shops including the one at Magnolia Hall, or by mail from the Natchez Garden Club, Box 537, Natchez, MS 39120.

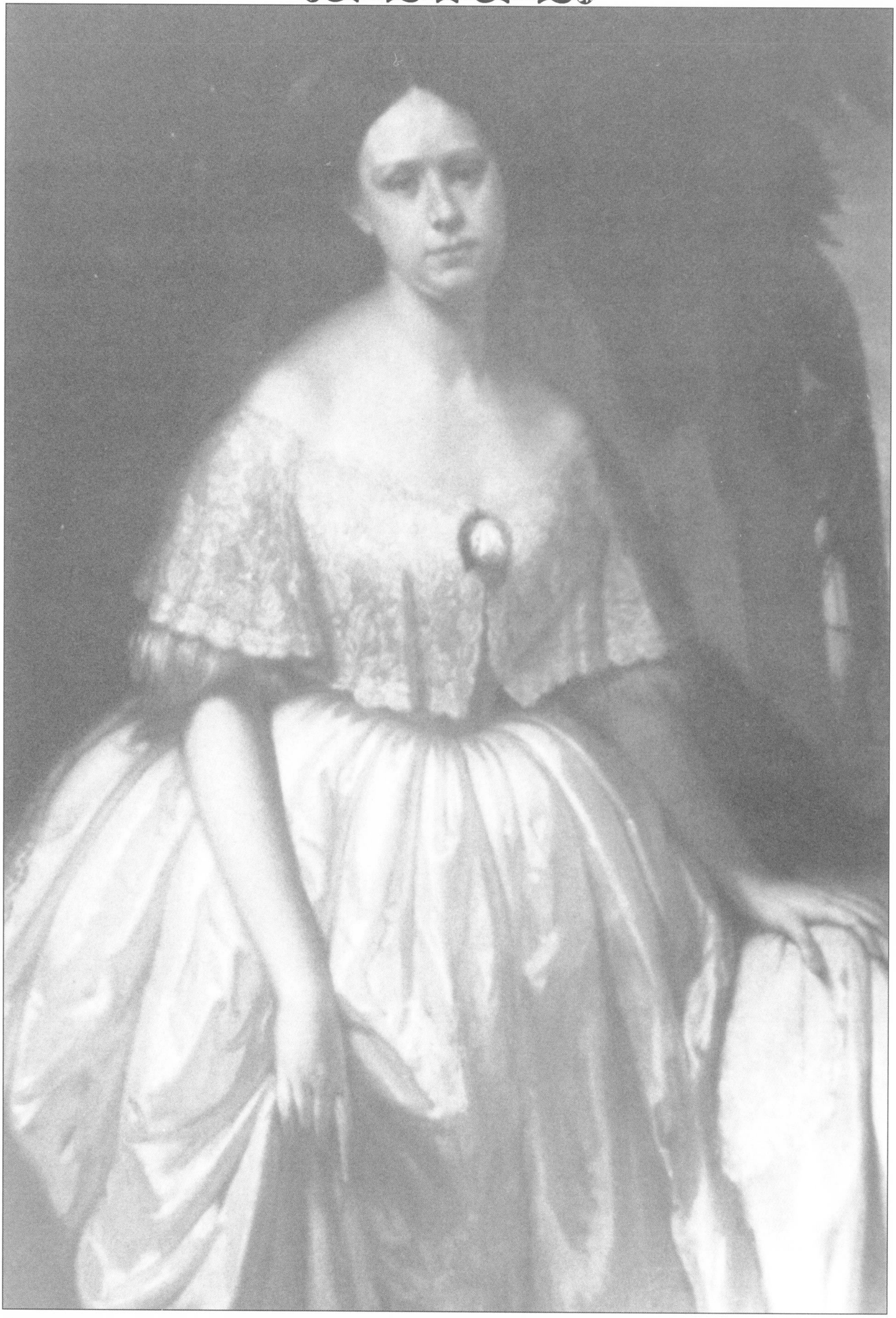

Magnolia Hall Orange Blush

1 6-oz. can frozen orange juice concentrate,
 thawed
1 cup cranberry juice
4 tbsp. sugar
1 pt. club soda
Crushed ice

Combine undiluted orange juice, cranberry juice, and sugar. Chill thoroughly. Just before serving, stir in soda and pour over crushed ice in old-fashioned glasses. Serves 6.

Cheese Grits

2 cups grits
7 cups water
Salt and black pepper to taste
1 6-oz. roll garlic cheese
½ cup milk
1 6-oz. roll sharp cheese
4 eggs
2 sticks butter

Add grits to boiling salted water. When done, add remaining ingredients. If fluffier grits are desired, separate eggs and beat egg whites. Bake for 1 hour at 350 degrees in 3-qt. casserole dish. Serves 12.

Bread Pudding

6 eggs
1½ cups sugar
2 pt. half & half
2 tsp. vanilla extract
6 dinner rolls, torn into small pieces
2 tbsp. butter, diced
2 tbsp. brown sugar

Beat eggs well; add sugar, cream, and vanilla. Blend together well. Fold torn rolls into egg mixture. Pour custard mixture into ungreased 3-qt. baking dish and bake at 350 degrees for 1 hour. Sprinkle top of hot pudding with butter pieces, then brown sugar. Pour whiskey sauce on top (see below). Top with whipped cream and sprinkle with a little nutmeg if desired. Serves 12.

Whiskey Sauce

1½ cups sugar
1 5.33-oz. can evaporated milk
4 tbsp. oleo
1 egg, beaten
3 tbsp. whiskey

Combine all ingredients except whiskey in top of double boiler. Place over boiling water and cook, stirring well, until thick. Keep warm until serving time, or make ahead and keep in refrigerator. Do not add whiskey until just before serving. Makes 1½ cups. Use to top Bread Pudding.

Jezebel Sauce

1 16-oz. jar apple jelly
1 jar pineapple preserves
1 jar horseradish
1 2-oz. can dry mustard
Salt and black pepper to taste

Combine ingredients. They will keep indefinitely in the refrigerator. Good served with meats.

Longwood

One of Natchez's most popular tourist destinations just happens, oddly enough, to be an unfinished octagonal Oriental villa called Longwood, now a National Historic Landmark maintained in impeccable order by the Pilgrimage Garden Club.

Its builder, Dr. Haller Nutt, was born near Rodney, Mississippi, and was exceptionally well educated, with degrees in both science and medicine. Owner of three working cotton plantations in Louisiana (Winter Quarters near Newellton and the now-gone Araby and Evergreen), Nutt made his money in cotton and was worth $1 million by the time he turned 20.

Like many of the antebellum homes in Natchez, Longwood was intended to be a summer house, not a working plantation; its original 90 acres have been consolidated under garden club ownership once again. Construction on the home began in 1860 from plans drawn by Philadelphia architect Samuel Sloan. Some 30,000 square feet were planned for the home, in 32 rooms on six floors, including a basement designed for recreation, a formal living and dining floor, two floors of bedrooms, and two observatory floors on top.

Constructed of brick with wood trim, the house was topped by a 16-sided cupola crowned by a Byzantine onion dome and was referred to as a "remembrancer of Eastern magnificence which looms up against the mellowed azure of a southern sky." Eight rooms on each floor were centered around a rotunda in the original plans, which provided for lower lighting through a series of mirrors and translucent marble flooring.

After some 18 months of construction, war broke out and the skilled Northern workers dropped their tools to return home. A Union sympathizer who had opened his Louisiana plantations to Federal troops, Nutt lived to see two of his

houses there burned and some $3 million in property confiscated or destroyed by Union men. When he died at age 48 in 1864, his wife said it was of a broken heart.

With the help of local labor, Nutt had managed to complete the exterior and nine rooms in the basement of the house, where his wife and subsequent descendants would live for the next century. Dr. Nutt's widow, the former Julia Williams, won a settlement of $256,000 from the government but was never able to complete the house. In 1930 her children (of 11, eight lived to maturity) received another undisclosed sum.

While many of the elaborate furnishings, mosaic floors, marble mantels, and statues that had been ordered from Europe were seized on the high seas by Federal blockades, the living quarters in Longwood's basement were splendidly furnished with fine pieces from Mrs. Nutt's dowry or from her own homeplace, Ashburn. The parlor is furnished appropriately with a rosewood Victorian set, gilded French mirrors, and fine paintings, and 85 percent of the furnishings in the rest of the basement are original to Longwood.

What were originally planned to be the billiard room, smoking room, playroom, schoolroom, office, hall, and rotunda of the basement recreational floor were turned into family living quarters, furnished as bedrooms, dining room, and

parlor instead. The rough-cut cypress flooring was to be replaced by slate and is only five inches above the ground at basement level.

The interior walls of Longwood are 18 inches thick; outer walls are 27 inches thick with a five-inch airspace. Ceilings vary from 9'3" to a soaring 15 feet. Arched windows are graced by the original shutters, which in upper floors slide into the walls.

The unfinished stories above the basement level are just as interesting as the furnished rooms below. The second story, the main living floor, may be seen on tours, while those stories above it are unsafe for visitors but may be seen through the open rotunda. In alcoves around the central room on the second story lie the original tools and buckets left from the home's construction, still where the workmen flung them as they rushed off to war.

In letters written to her son during the difficult years after the Civil War, Julia Nutt paints a poignant and moving picture of a sorrowful time of deprivation. In the face of tragedy, however, the young people proved resilient, as they have through the ages, getting together on Saturdays for dances and entertainments. Julia Nutt writes of the girls of the family making cakes for these parties, saying she would have begrudged them the use of the flour had she not been so keenly aware of the desperate need for young people to have their moments of fun even in such trying times.

Longwood Sponge Cake

1 lb. powdered sugar
½ lb. flour
10 eggs
Juice of 1 lemon
Rind of 2 lemons

Mix and bake in slow oven, increasing heat gradually until cake tests done. This recipe and the one following are from a minute treasure, only a few inches in height, called *Turtle Soup & Other Choice Recipes From Natchez, Mississippi,* sold for the princely sum of one quarter during early pilgrimages in the 1930s.

Miss Julia's Potato Nests with Green Peas

2 cups hot riced potatoes
2 tbsp. butter
1 egg yolk
Few drops onion juice
1 tsp. minced parsley
½ tsp. salt
⅛ tsp. black pepper
Green peas
Breadcrumbs
1 egg
2 tbsp. water
Hot fat for frying

Mix well the potatoes, butter, egg yolk, onion juice, parsley, salt, and pepper. Shape into little nests and fill each with 1 tsp. green peas, then cover with potato, making a small ball. Roll in breadcrumbs. Beat egg lightly with water, dip the rolled balls into this egg mixture, covering surface entirely, then roll in breadcrumbs again. Brush off all extra crumbs and fry in hot fat for 1 minute. Drain on brown paper. These are a nice accompaniment for birds, the old recipe says.

Antiques Shopping in Natchez

As the warming early-morning sun plays across the old brick and flourishing plant life of his rear courtyard, affable antiques dealer Hal Garner relaxes in a canebottomed Regency chair with painted decoration, perfectly at home in his surroundings. He could be sharing with guests a spectacular Persimmon Pudding, or perhaps a taste of Strawberries Romanoff, or some scrumptious Butter Pecan Turtle Bars or Crème de Menthe Brownies to accompany the tea he is pouring from the teapot of a 35-piece early-19th-century Miles Mason tea set of blue and white porcelain.

Garner's rambling shop overflows upstairs and downstairs and out into the brick stable across the courtyard of his beautifully restored complex on Franklin Street in downtown Natchez, an area becoming known as "Antiques Row" as more and more dealers come to roost there.

It's a highly appropriate setting. Most of the buildings were originally commercial structures dating from just after the Civil War, often with living quarters for their proprietors upstairs, and Garner feels that the antiques dealers of today find something gratifying about returning the structures to their original uses, keeping them true to their heritage, so to speak. Garner's own shop encompasses the original Liberty Saddle and Harness Shop with its stable and upstairs apartment, a meat market, and a wholesale dry goods.

The location is propitious as well, near enough to the downtown shopping district yet somewhat removed from the hurly burly, a good place for the dealers to be able to offer tourists refreshments, attentive personal service, and that "something extra" that upholds the Natchez tradition of being gracious and accommodating.

"Dealers in Natchez are able to support themselves and remain available to local customers only because of the patronage of tourists, and with us coming together in one immediate area, we can better serve them and can also communicate with one another just what visitors are interested in," explains Garner. "Many tourists come to tour, and then only incidentally find things they want to buy."

Reaching out to the visitors has turned Garner into a modern-day Johnny Appleseed of sorts, thanks to a glorious vine growing rampant in his rear courtyard, a rare plant he dearly loves to share. "I planted along the patio a cypress vine, for which I have an excessive enthusiasm," he laughs, "and I

must say tourists are somewhat shocked as I press into their hands a packet of seeds. But then I get thank-you letters from all over the country, and as these vines flourish and bloom, these people tend to think fondly of Natchez."

But seeds are not all they take home, nor are memories and photographs. Many visitors, especially those who are themselves collectors of fine antiques or owners of historic houses, take home 18th- and 19th-century furniture or silver, hand-painted china or delicate crystal, estate jewelry or artworks, clocks or other collectibles purchased from the antiques dealers of Natchez and environs, and it would be hard to find a more knowledgeable or more helpful group of experts.

There could certainly be no more appropriate souvenir of a visit to the Old South. Natchez in particular, according to Garner, "like Williamsburg, has a tendency to conjure up a particular style of furniture as well as a way of life to people, if not from all over the world then at least all over the nation. That style is usually a little later than actual Natchez history; it's the early days as interpreted through the Victorian, and Natchez had its own particular interpretation of Victorian, a bit different."

This is a subject on which Garner can offer a thoughtful historical assessment, based on his years as an antiques dealer and decades spent in the careful restoration and reclamation of such historic homes as the Wigwam, Brandon Hall, Wyolah, Lagonia and The Cedars, Gloucester, Boscobel, and others.

Says Garner, commenting on the birth of the first truly indigenous American style after years of colonial classical dependence, "It surprises me that while I sense a Natchez style, I cannot pin it down as one can, say, a Charleston style. Natchez defies pinning down; it's all echoes and transitions and inspirations. Our most charming houses here have evolved against all odds and are radically different one from the other. Greek Revival was the nearest they ever came to any cohesiveness, and in the 1840s and 1850s, when Greek Revival flowered, bits and pieces of that style were superimposed on homes of earlier periods, and somehow in Natchez it worked."

The Greek Revival style, favorite of the rich cotton kingdom just before the Civil War, had an influence in Natchez "not defined by set boundaries, but more like a mood, drifting out like a mist for miles around," and everything taken with a grain of salt to give it that endearing Natchez slant, the great houses sometimes tipping the hat to Greek Revival but coyly withholding the full curtsy.

Besides actual antiques, however, there is now the Historic Natchez Collection, a licensing program in conjunction with the Historic Natchez Foundation, making available carefully selected reproductions and adaptations of some furnishings and accessories from over 40 famous antebellum homes of Natchez. The collection includes fabrics, wall coverings, and carpets made by Schumacher, lamps, mirrors and decorative items from Paul Hanson, ceramics and brass from Mottahedeh, and silver plate hollow ware and jewelry boxes made by Reed and Barton.

Eventually this collection will include everything from tea caddies to tester beds, wallpaper to writing desks, all with that distinctive Natchez charm and warmth of style. The Historic Natchez Collection is important not only as a means of reproducing perishable original pieces but also as a way to make accessible to people who couldn't afford the originals a special taste of Natchez history all the same.

It's one more way to share with the world the special style of Natchez and the South, a unique blend of historical periods and styles with personal echoes and transitions somehow melding into something special and unique, a creative individuality of expression laden with heritage, rich with character, and as hard to pin down as the morning mist rising from the mighty Mississippi.

Persimmon Pudding

2 persimmons
1 cup sugar
1 cup flour
1½ tsp. baking powder
2 tsp. baking soda
Pinch salt
1 tbsp. melted butter
½ cup milk
1 tsp. vanilla extract

Allow fruit to ripen until very soft, then remove 1 cup pulp. Mix and sift dry ingredients. Mix other ingredients and add with the dry to the fruit. Put in well-buttered mold, dusted with sugar. Can use a small coffee can, as if making plum pudding. Cover with wax paper. Let steam over 1" water for 3 hours. Pudding will double in size. Slice to serve.

Strawberries Romanoff

1 cup fresh strawberries
1 tbsp. sugar
1 orange
1 lemon
2 scoops French vanilla ice cream
½ cup whipped cream
1 oz. Cointreau
1 oz. kirschwasser (cherry liqueur or cherry herring)
2 slices orange for garnish, peel left on

Wash and stem berries. Put berries into mixing bowl and add sugar. With a fork, mash berries coarsely. Peel orange and lemon, discarding fruit but keeping peel intact. Add ice cream to berries. Mix with fork. Fold in whipped cream. Add peels of orange and lemon. Mix well. Add Cointreau and kirschwasser. Chill. When ready to serve, remove peels and spoon into 8-oz. stem glasses. Garnish each with orange slice. Serves 2.

Butter Pecan Turtle Bars

2 cups flour
1 cup light brown sugar
½ cup butter, softened
1 cup chopped pecans
⅔ cup butter
½ cup light brown sugar
1 6-oz. pkg. semisweet chocolate chips

Combine flour, 1 cup sugar, ½ cup butter, and ½ cup pecans in a mixing bowl. Mix at medium speed until mixture becomes fine particles. Pat firmly into ungreased 9x13x2" pan. Sprinkle with remaining pecans. Prepare caramel layer by combining ⅔ cup butter with ½ cup sugar in saucepan; cook over medium heat, stirring constantly, until mixture begins to boil, then boil ½ to 1 minute. Pour caramel over pecans and crust. Bake at 350 degrees for 18-22 minutes. Remove and sprinkle immediately with chocolate chips. Allow chips to melt slightly and swirl, leaving marble effect. Cool. Cut into bars. Makes 3-4 dozen.

Betty Sessions' Crème de Menthe Brownies

½ cup butter or oleo, softened
1 cup sugar
4 eggs
1 cup all-purpose flour
½ tsp. salt
1 16-oz. can chocolate syrup
1 tsp. vanilla extract
¼ cup butter or oleo, softened
2 cups sifted powdered sugar
2 tbsp. crème de menthe
1 6-oz. pkg. semisweet chocolate chips
¼ cup butter or oleo

Cream ½ cup butter; gradually add 1 cup sugar, beating until light and fluffy. Add eggs, one at a time, beating well after each. Combine flour and salt. Add to creamed mixture alternately with chocolate syrup, beginning and ending with flour. Stir in vanilla. Pour batter into greased and floured 9x13x2" pan and bake at 350 degrees for 25-28 minutes. Cool completely. (Don't worry; brownies are supposed to shrink from sides of pan as they cool.) For filling, cream ¼ cup butter. Gradually add powdered sugar and crème de menthe. Spread over cooled brownie layer. For top layer, combine chocolate chips and last ¼ cup butter in top of double boiler; bring water to boil, reduce heat, and cook until chocolate melts. Spread over crème de menthe layer. Cool and chill for at least 1 hour. Cut into small squares. Makes 36 or more brownies.

Eola Hotel

The elegant Eola Hotel in historic downtown Natchez was long the center of social life for the entire surrounding area until modern bypass motels and a declining inner city drew away its patrons and its lifeblood. But now the hotel has been completely renovated and its surroundings rejuvenated as well, restoring the possibilities of a more gracious and unhurried way of life for the discriminating traveler.

At seven stories the highest structure downtown, the Natchez Eola was opened in 1927 to great acclaim and named for the daughter of the head of the controlling Natchez Investment Corporation. Before long, though, the stock market crash brought hard times contributing to the decline of the hotel business, and the corporation defaulted on its mortgage.

The Eola, complete with contents, was sold to the Natchez Eola Hotel Corporation headed by Clarence Eyrich, who with his two sons saw the hotel through both the best and worst of times. The best times came with the advent in 1932 of the immensely popular annual Natchez Spring Pilgrimage, drawing crowds of tourists and hotel patrons from across the country to share the incredible architectural richness of Natchez and relive the glories of "the Old South."

The Eola, long pilgrimage headquarters, was "the" place to go for Mississippi society, its all-night coffee shop drawing crowds around the clock,

its open rooftop "Top of the Town" the scene of many a gracious gathering, and its convention and banquet facilities hosting clubs and parties of all types. Movie stars like Elizabeth Taylor and Montgomery Clift and Tom Mix stayed there, as did politicians, authors, musicians, Miss Americas, and movie directors.

By the 1960s the Eola was showing its age, however, and renovations were considered too expensive. The grand old hotel closed its doors in 1974. Rumors of its demise proved premature, however, and by the late 1970s a group of investors, headed by Texas oilman Norman Germany, who had stayed at the Eola weekly for a 30-year period, began carefully planning its restoration.

Since it reopened in 1982, the Eola, with its courtyards and fanlight windows, its ceiling fans and balconies overlooking the Mississippi River, blends creatively and comfortably with its surroundings in historic downtown Natchez, which is experiencing a similar rebirth. It is now owned by Baton Rouge entrepreneur Bob Dean, but the recipes given here are from the Eyrich era.

Eola Shrimp Remoulade

½ cup minced green onions
¼ cup minced celery
⅛ cup or 1 tbsp. minced bell pepper
1 qt. lite or regular mayonnaise
1 small jar Creole mustard
Dash Tabasco sauce
1 tsp. Worcestershire sauce
A little garlic or garlic powder (optional)

Mix all ingredients. Boil shrimp according to favorite recipe, peel, and place on bed of lettuce. Top with remoulade sauce. Garnish with hardboiled eggs, tomatoes, pickles, and olives. Should serve 12 nicely.

Natchez Pecan Pie

1 cup sugar
1 tsp. flour
3 eggs, beaten
1 cup Karo, light or dark
1 tsp. vanilla extract
1-2 tbsp. butter or oleo
1-2 cups pecans
1 10" pie shell

Mix sugar, flour, eggs, Karo, vanilla, butter, and pecans and place in pie shell. Bake for 1 hour at 350 degrees. Serves 10. The flour keeps the middle of the pie from being soft without requiring overcooking.

Eola Apple Dumpling Cobbler

½ cup sugar
½ cup brown sugar
1¼ cups warm water
½ stick oleo
1 tsp. vanilla
¼ tsp. cinnamon
2 apples
2 tbsp. oil or melted oleo
½ cup sugar
1 cup milk
1½ tsp. baking powder
1½ cups all-purpose flour
Pinch salt

Mix ½ cup sugar, brown sugar, water, ½ stick oleo, vanilla, and cinnamon in saucepan; boil for 8-10 minutes. Peel and dice apples, add to mixture, and boil for 2 minutes more. Make dumplings by mixing 2 tbsp. oil or melted oleo with ½ cup sugar, milk, baking powder, flour, and salt. If using self-rising flour, eliminate baking powder and salt. Pour sauce in 10x10" baking dish. Spoon in dumplings evenly and bake at 350 degrees for 45 minutes. Serve hot with ice cream, or serve cold with whipped cream.

Goat Castle Murder

The year of 1932 was an auspicious one, for it was then that the first Natchez Spring Pilgrimage was held, drawing visitors from across the country anxious for a look at the authentic Old South with its elegant mansions and graceful lifestyle. Nowhere could they see this better than historic Natchez, with its astounding quota of hundreds of impressive antebellum structures. Ever since that year, the pilgrimages have grown in scope, popularity, and profits, providing at least some of the all-important means for preservation.

But if 1932 saw the birth of the vital tourist industry in Natchez, it also marked the date of a brutal murder here that shocked the world and gave the city some unwanted publicity in newspapers and periodicals across the country and throughout the capitals of Europe.

The major characters in the murder story came from prominent families, though in their later years all had fallen into secluded lifestyles noted more for eccentricity than elegance. Murdered was Jane Surget Merrill, aristocratic and wealthy spinster familiarly known as Miss Jennie. Raised abroad while her father served as President Grant's ambassador to Belgium, she was famed as a real beauty of her time, was presented to Queen Victoria at the Court of St. James, and finally, after the death of her father, settled at Glenburnie in Natchez, where she clung to outdated styles, hoarded her money, and received only one caller, her beloved second

cousin Duncan G. Minor, who faithfully arrived on horseback each evening for more than 30 years to pay his respects.

Descended from Stephen Minor, early governor-general of Natchez, handsome Duncan was said to resemble Clark Gable and was called one of the richest men in Natchez, but was also said to be as parsimonious as his cousin Jennie, so much so that some accounts report the family cook of necessity holding an umbrella over her head while preparing meals for the family in rainy weather. It was Minor, 69, white-haired and white-mustached, erect in the saddle at a time when most others drove automobiles, who had the misfortune of discovering the murder when he arrived for his customary evening call on August 4, 1932.

The finger of guilt was soon pointed, erroneously as it turned out, next door to Glenwood, the crumbling mansion where Dick Dana and Octavia Dockery lived in poverty.

Richard Henry Clay ("Dick") Dana was the son of the late respected rector of Trinity Episcopal Church in Natchez, who prior to moving South had been rector of Christ Episcopal Church in Alexandria, Virginia, where he presented Robert E. Lee for confirmation and became such a close friend that he was given many Lee family antiques and books to furnish his Natchez home. A Dana

cousin served as Lincoln's undersecretary of the treasury, another cousin wrote *Two Years Before the Mast,* and a third cousin was the artist who immortalized his wife as the Gibson Girl. Orphaned early, Dick Dana studied piano in New York until a freak accident, a falling window that crushed several fingers, ended his ambitions as a concert pianist.

Dana inherited Glenwood and returned to Natchez around 1890, living a life of gaiety, in much demand socially, surrounded by fine artworks and literature and Lee furniture. One of his friends was the widowed Nydia Dockery Forman, a cousin of Varina Howell Davis, wife of the Confederate president. On her deathbed Mrs. Forman begged her friend Dick Dana to provide for her 28-year-old sister Octavia, who lived with her. At the time only 22 and jobless himself, Dana nevertheless agreed, thus mingling treasured Jefferson Davis furnishings with Robert E. Lee family heirlooms in the house at Glenwood.

Octavia Dockery was born in 1865, the beautiful daughter of Confederate brigadier general Thomas Paine Dockery, captured during the war but released by Grant, who later became a friend. When both families ended up in New York after the end of the war and Grant's presidency, General Grant would escort 16-year-old Octavia, resplendent in a fashionable and costly Worth evening gown, to a ball there. She soon became a successful writer but moved to Mississippi to be near her sister.

When hard times and death interceded, Octavia would write that she had decided to establish a chicken farm on Dana's property in an attempt to make a living. She would eventually have cows, pigs, ducks, geese, and goats as well; she would also have no running water, clothing made of gunny sacks, a fire in the marble-manteled drawing-room fireplace to cook meals over, and bedsprings stretched across a smudge fire in a bedroom fireplace to smoke strips of goat meat.

Disappointment and deprivation seem to have driven Dana to the brink of insanity; unkempt and rambling, he was unkindly known as the Wild Man. Goats and chickens had free run through the crumbling home, nibbling on leather-bound Lee books and stripping the tasty upholstery from finely carved rosewood furnishings.

The goats also frequently crossed the property line onto Glenburnie, where Miss Jennie Merrill got madder and madder at the intrusion until she purchased several guns, became an excellent shot, and stopped not a few four-legged intruders in their tracks. Lawsuits were filed, and animosity grew between the pairs, especially when Duncan Minor bought Glenwood at a tax sale but was prevented from evicting its occupants when Octavia Dockery had Dana declared insane; a law provided that infants and persons judged insane could not legally be deprived of their property for tax debts.

It was only natural, then, once Miss Jennie's death was discovered, to point the finger toward Glenwood, especially when Dick Dana was discovered washing a bloody shirt that he insisted was soiled slaughtering a pig, and when fingerprint evidence indicated a deformation of the hand of the murderer.

Fortunately a black boardinghouse operator came forth to implicate one of her roomers, who also had a deformed hand, in the murder, and it was proved that he had indeed been the guilty party, though before he could be brought to justice he was shot and killed by police in Arkansas while armed with what proved to be the murder weapon. Dick Dana and Octavia Dockery were freed from jail and soon turned Glenwood into a most unusual tourist attraction, the famous falling-down Goat Castle, where the unique tours included piano concerts given by Dick Dana in a white linen suit and poetry readings by Miss Dockery.

Both Dana and Dockery died in the late 1940s and Glenwood was soon demolished to make room for a modern subdivision development, though Glenburnie still stands, restored and often on pilgrimage tours. The story of the Goat Castle Murder has been preserved in a fine little book by Sim C. Callon and Carolyn Vance Smith, complete with astounding old photographs telling the story more movingly than words alone ever could (*The Goat Castle Murder,* Plantation Publishing Co., P.O. Box 17842, Trace Town Station, Natchez, MS 39120).

Mr. Joe Daniel's Barbecued Goat

1 wether (steer goat) with 2" horns
Water
2 qt. vinegar
3 boxes crab boil
8 onions
8 cloves garlic
1 5-oz. bottle Worcestershire sauce
1 small bottle hot pepper sauce
Handful salt
Small handful black pepper
12 lemons, cut up
Hickory chips
Barbecue sauce

Start with goat weighing about 70 or 80 lb. on the hoof; butcher as usual. Cut goat meat into pieces weighing from 2 to 5 lb. Put meat in pot and cover with water, vinegar, crab boil, onions, garlic, Worcestershire, hot pepper sauce, salt, black pepper, and lemons. Boil until goat begins to get tender. Turn off heat and let soak for 30-45 minutes. Remove goat from pot and place on barbecue pit over plenty of hickory chips for fire. Baste frequently with your favorite barbecue sauce. Cook on pit for 1 hour, covered. Should serve 30.

Mammy's Cupboard

Coming into Natchez from Louisiana via U.S. Highway 61, you know you're in the Old South when you spot Mammy's Cupboard, 28 feet tall and just itchin' to please.

Built of brick in 1940 by Henry Gaude, whose family members are still the owners, Mammy's Cupboard is reminiscent of the days when American highways sprouted pop-art buildings advertising by their shapes just what was being offered inside . . . gigantic oranges, enormous hot dogs, or colossal coffee cups.

And what better symbol of that good old-fashioned Southern hospitality and good old down-home Southern cookin' than *Mammy,* so enormous she wears a becoming 5-foot chain as a necklace and horseshoes as earrings.

Inside her 20-foot skirt, painted bright red like her turban, is the reception area of the restaurant; most of the tables are in an attached room to the rear. Together the rooms can accommodate up to 50 diners comfortably, and those diners come from around the world, always expressing amazement upon entering and often waxing nostalgic about visits to Mammy's remembered from childhood.

For years, Mammy dispensed from beneath her voluminous skirts Southern staples like fried catfish, long a Mississippi tradition, whether the fish themselves were purchased fresh from one of the state's many catfish farms, or hooked on lines strung across flooded backwater low spots, or caught while "hand-grabbing," submerging oneself into the murk of cypress lakes or swamps and reaching into hollow logs and other likely spots to actually grab the fish by hand.

Now, however, Mammy's fare is a little more health conscious, thanks to a mother-daughter team who specialize in gourmet sandwiches on homemade bread, fabulous mile-high meringue pies, and multilayer cakes, with everything made fresh daily. Restaurateur Doris Kemp began with a little gift shop, peddling homemade jams and jellies in an attempt to deal with the copious harvest from her acre of blueberry bushes. As customers clamored for food, the gifts took a backseat to the homemade soups and sandwiches and salads and all those wonderful desserts. Lunch is served daily Tuesday through Saturday, featuring at least one hot specialty like chicken pot pie and broccoli cornbread, and diners can take a little taste home with them by way of the house cookbook, available by telephoning Mammy's Cupboard at (601) 445-8957 or by writing Mammy's Cupboard, 555 Highway 61 South, Natchez, MS 39120.

Broccoli Cornbread

1 stick butter, melted
4 8-oz. boxes Jiffy Corn Bread Mix
2 cups chopped raw broccoli
½ cup minced onion
4 eggs, well beaten
1 8-oz. carton cottage cheese
1 14⅔-oz. can cream-style corn
12 drops Tabasco sauce

Oil a large cast-iron skillet or oblong baking pan. Mix all ingredients and bake at 350 degrees for about 40 minutes, or until firm and golden brown.

Mile-High Meringue

5 egg whites
¼ tsp. cream of tartar
⅛ tsp. salt
½ cup sugar
1 tbsp. cornstarch
1 tsp. extract (depending on type of pie: lemon, coconut, vanilla/almond for chocolate pie)
2 tbsp. hot water

Beat egg whites until foamy; add cream of tartar and salt. Add sugar, cornstarch, extract, and water. Beat until stiff peaks form. Swirl over unbaked pie and bake at 325 degrees until meringue is browned evenly.

Chocolate Cream Pie

1½ cups sugar
½ cup flour
½ cup cocoa
Dash salt
3 cups milk
4 egg yolks, beaten
2 tbsp. butter
1 tsp. vanilla extract
½ tsp. almond extract
1 9" baked pie shell

In a thick-bottomed saucepan, mix dry ingredients. Scald milk in microwave for 4 minutes and slowly stir into dry ingredients, beating with wire whisk. Place saucepan over medium heat and stir constantly to avoid sticking and scorching. When custard begins to thicken, remove 1 cup and whisk into egg yolks. Add to cooking custard and continue cooking until custard is thick and creamy. Add butter and flavorings. Turn off heat and whisk until custard is smooth. Pour into pie shell. Top with meringue. Bake in 325-degree oven until browned nicely. For more chocolate flavor, add ½ cup chocolate chips when adding the butter and whisk until chips are melted and blended into custard.

Aunt Freddie

Historic downtown Natchez is so absolutely filled with picturesque Victorian structures that you can drive around for hours and still be fascinated with the varied architectural styles, imaginative trims and color combinations, quaint courtyards, and lush landscaping all right in the middle of town.

But one house always stood out, an enormous columned, turreted, and bay-windowed structure that was home to several venerable Natchez institutions. For four decades this house had been home to the shop called Tot & Teen & Mom. It was also home to Aunt Freddie's Pepper Jelly. And most especially was it home to Aunt Freddie Bailey herself, renowned artist in the kitchen and aunt of the famous New York designer and author Lee Bailey, until his death one of his aunt's biggest fans and boosters.

In this home, Aunt Freddie said, "we have good food and lots of fun," and she had two cookbooks published to prove it, the smaller *Freddie Bailey's "Favorite" Southern Recipes* and nephew Lee's marvelous *Aunt Freddie's Pantry*. Aunt Freddie has gone on to that big kitchen in the sky, but the devotion to her pepper jelly continues undiminished.

Aunt Freddie's pepper jelly was famous around the world, divine on ham, heavenly on cheese and crackers, and, in Aunt Freddie's own words, "just plain different" on meats and vegetables. Everyone who's ever *made* pepper jelly will tell you it's a whole lot easier to *buy* it, and Aunt Freddie shipped hers by order, along with hot mustard sauce, preserves and jellies, chutneys and pralines. Some of her appreciative customers included Bob Hope and Lucille Ball, and she was featured in such national gourmet magazines as *Bon Appetit* and *Food and Wine*.

Her colorful and creative artistic soul shone through not just in her cooking but in her writing as well. Her description of the stained-glass bay window in her home was enough by itself to make you want to visit: "The center depicts *Paul et Virginie,*" she wrote, "a romance by Bernardin de Saint-Pierre, first published . . . in 1787. The author called it a *pastorale,* but it is a tale of passion with didactic digressions.

"Paul and Virginie, two fatherless children, are brought up in poverty and innocence, far from society and its corruption, amid the tropical scenery of the Ile de France (Mauritius). They love

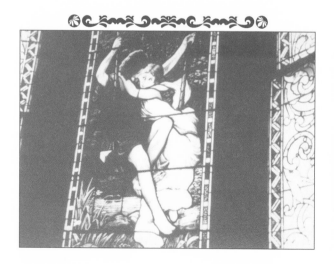

one another from their infancy. Virginie, to the despair of both, is recalled to France by a harsh and wealthy aunt. There she is miserable, and after two years returns to the Ile de France. But her ship is wrecked on the island and she herself is drowned before the eyes of Paul. (She could have been saved if she had been willing to strip her clothes off and jump into the raging sea with the naked sailor who tried to rescue her, but she repulsed him with dignity and awaited inevitable death with *'une main sur ses habits, l'autre sur son coeur.'*) Paul dies of a broken heart two months later, a melancholy moral of the imperfection of human life when it departs from nature."

Aunt Freddie Bailey's Hot Pepper Jelly

¾ cup sliced, seeded bell pepper
¼ cup sliced, seeded hot pepper
6½ cups sugar
1½ cups cider vinegar
1 bottle certo

Put on rubber gloves to slice peppers and remove seeds. Grind peppers together. Add this to sugar and vinegar in large pot. Bring to a full boil. Add certo and bring again to a boil. Pour into sterilized hot jelly glasses. Recommended ways to use include as a glaze over scored ham, topping cheese or cream cheese and crackers, with meats and vegetables, or in cranberries.

Aunt Freddie Bailey's Hot Pepper Fruit Salad

1 env. green lime gelatin
1 cup boiling water
1 jar green hot pepper jelly
1 can fruit salad
Lettuce
Mayonnaise

Dissolve gelatin in water. Add jelly and fruit salad. Pour into molds and allow to set. Serve on lettuce with mayonnaise. A "zesty" taste, says Aunt Freddie.

Aunt Freddie Bailey's Stuffed Mushrooms with Crabmeat

12-18 large fresh mushroom caps
2 tbsp. butter
3 tbsp. chopped mushroom stems
2 tbsp. minced garlic
2 tbsp. chopped parsley
2 tbsp. chopped green onion
1 full cup crabmeat
½ cup unseasoned breadcrumbs
3 oz. dry white wine (Sauterne)
Mild white cheese

Sauté mushroom caps in butter until tender. Set aside and save butter stock. In another pan, sauté mushroom stems with garlic, parsley, and green onions. Cook over low heat 5 minutes. Add crabmeat and stir constantly. Sprinkle in breadcrumbs to make filling more solid. Add wine and butter stock. Stuff mushroom caps with mixture and place on foil in pan. Garnish with cheese cut in strips. Broil until cheese melts.

Muscadine Winery

Muscadines have been used for winemaking in the southeastern United States ever since the French Huguenots settled here in the earliest years of our country's development; even before that, the Indians supposedly knew the secret.

Early settlers, of necessity, used what they had at hand, making their own muscadine wines at home from the bountiful harvest of wild fresh fruit, turning the final product into one of America's most popular wines before the 1940s. Records show there was a scuppernong winemaker producing delightful results in Natchez from 1835 to 1848, and the works of early American writers describe in glowing terms the abundant foliage and fruit of the vines growing along the Gulf Coast. Even later Southern writers like William Faulkner refer far more often to such homemade varieties as scuppernong wine than to the supposedly more famous mint juleps.

Some muscadine vines were brought from South Carolina to Mississippi in the early 1800s by the ancestors of Dr. Scott O. Galbreath, Natchez veterinarian turned vintner and owner of Old South Winery, one of the few muscadine wineries in the South today.

Dr. Galbreath began making his own muscadine wine at age 15 after learning the process from a "good German wine-drinking grandmother," and now grows some 15 varieties of muscadines, buying additional fruit as needed. He says muscadines are today cultivated only in the region from the Louisiana-Texas border to South Carolina in a production process that has been mechanized just like soybeans or cotton.

Visitors in late summer and early fall are lucky enough to observe and taste the fresh fruit right off the vine before being taken on a tour of Old South Winery. Dr. Galbreath tells the story of America's first billionaire, whose funds were made from muscadines cultivated and turned into wine where Dulles Airport sits today. He also relates how, after investing $200,000 to start his own winery in 1979, he found that Mississippi law at that time prohibited the advertising of alcoholic beverages. "Here I was trying to take something uniquely Southern, like fried chicken, and do something with it, and I found I couldn't tell people about it. What I had to do was try to make a wine people would break our door down for."

He did just that, and more than one. Old South Winery produces a dozen or so muscadine wines, ranging from dry whites to semisweet reds and sweet roses, each with the delightful essence of muscadines. Then Galbreath found that Mississippi was ranked 51st among all the states in wine consumption. "The main thing we've tried to do," he says of his strategy since then, "is to add a little more personal touch."

Which is why you'll often find the good doctor personally conducting enthusiastic tours of his winery, followed by wine tasting for which he proudly pours and explains each wine's strong points. His winery has the capacity to handle 5 tons of muscadines an hour; after the dejuicing and pressing, the juice is cooled and fermented, stabilized in his recreated European cellar, bottled at 24 bottles a minute, then marketed to an appreciative public from all around the world.

Muscadine wine, Galbreath says, sells well in south Louisiana to go with crawfish, but he offers no specific advice on what variety to drink with what foods. "Drink the one you like" is all he says. "You're going to take just so many mouthfuls of food before you leave here, so you'd might as well enjoy it."

With all the current emphasis on the need to lower cholesterol and live our lives in a style doctors call "heart healthy," Galbreath prescribes his wines as just what the doctor ordered (and not just what the vet ordered, either), citing one area heart specialist who recommends that his patients drink a certain amount of muscadine wine daily.

"It is important that people understand how to change their lifestyles now," Dr. Galbreath says, "and wine tranquilizes you, slows you down a little bit. There's something in the grape pigment which dilates the blood vessels and lowers the cholesterol. Wine flushes the face and warms the hands and feet, you know, because it brings blood to the peripheral vessels. Cholesterol accumulates in the vessels and slows the blood flow, while dilating the vessels increases the blood flow. Drinking wine moderately is one of the best things you can do to increase your life span."

So, cheers! Here are some of Dr. Galbreath's favorite muscadine recipes. To order wine or the winery's new muscadine nutritional supplement, contact Old South Winery at 65 S. Concord Ave., Natchez, MS 39120, or order online at www.old-southwinery.com.

Dr. Scott Galbreath's Baked Muscadine Catfish

Catfish fillets
Paprika
Lemon pepper
Lemon juice
¾ tbsp. rose or semisweet blush muscadine
    wine

Put catfish in baking dish and "turn red" with paprika. Sprinkle on lemon pepper and lemon juice to taste. Pour wine over fish. Bake at 350 degrees for about 20 minutes or until the fish is dry. Dr. Galbreath, who says he is "on a diet all the time," recommends this as a healthy and low-calorie dish.

Dr. Scott Galbreath's Muscadine Cake

1 box butter pound cake mix
Sweet white blend muscadine wine
Brown sugar
Pecans
Dash nutmeg

Make pound cake according to package directions, except substitute muscadine wine for the liquid. Can top with mixture of brown sugar, pecans, and nutmeg if desired.

Natchez Santa Claus Club

It would take a lot, even in the best of times, to fill out that roomy, red, fur-trimmed suit and polished black boots.

And when times are hard, it simply boggles the mind to picture a single Santa Claus granting the multitudinous Christmas wishes of eager children everywhere.

It's a good thing, then, that there isn't merely one single Santa in Natchez, Mississippi.

There are, in fact, more than *300* of them!

It all began back in 1928 when a small group of gentleman friends bemoaned the fact that there were far too many needy children in town whose faces would hold no joy the next Christmas morning. From that meeting, the Santa Claus Club was born, its original and continuing purpose being the distribution of toys and gifts to children in need.

The club is still going strong with over 300 members ranging in age from wet-behind-the-ears

to way up into the 90s. Club membership is a valued legacy passed from father to son, be he plumber or physician or banker, and select members of the younger generation are recruited to carry on the tradition.

Well in advance of Christmas each year, club members choose one of their own to reign as the annual Santa Claus, a coveted but expensive honor. Each year's Santa must have the financial wherewithal to fulfill obligations ranging from dispensing quarters from his own pocket to children to hosting at his own expense an elegant evening bash with band for all club members, spouses, and several hundred other friends and invited dignitaries.

Santa must also have the stamina to survive a long and grueling Christmas Eve day beginning near dawn, when he prays for cool clear weather and straps on plenty of padding under his hot red suit and itchy beard, until the wee hours of the

following morn as he hurriedly readies his own home hearth for Christmas.

As one former Santa, banker Richard Durkin, says, "It's quite an honor, being Santa Claus. It gives you a warm feeling. The kids believe in you and touch your heart. But it's like being born; you want to do it, but you only want to do it once. It takes plenty of money to be Santa Claus. Of course, I'd do it again in a New York minute if somebody else would pay for it!"

The program is financed through campaigns conducted by the local newspaper and with Santa Claus Club funds; annual dues enable the club not only to provide gifts for needy children but also to make contributions to the local children's home and to a foster child program, as well as to make special grants for childhood illnesses. A committee of local ladies purchases the gifts, and there are usually 300 or 400 youngsters signed up to participate.

Regardless of the numbers, there's something under the Christmas tree for every child in need. "That's what it's all for, the children," Durkin says, "but *we* get more out of it than they do." The experience is indeed moving for the club members. Durkin recalls the year one gentleman was so overcome by the touching orphans that his wife found him filling pillowcases with the household silver to increase the children's gifts, and another member rushed home and loaded up all the presents waiting under the tree for his *own* children and distributed them to the needy!

Christmas Eve for the Santa Claus Club begins early with breakfast at a local restaurant, followed by organization into a motorcade for the trip along a route designed to encompass as much territory as possible so the spirit can be shared with the greatest number of onlookers.

Santa hurls candy from a gaily decorated convertible, police cars lead the way, and with sirens blaring and horns honking, candy flying and smiles blazing, the motorcade is completed by the other 300 or so members of the Santa Claus Club.

First stops on Santa's itinerary include several "hospitality houses," where club members are hosting Christmas parties. Santa dispenses quarters and hears whispered requests from the children present as other club members refresh themselves. Then it's off to one of the local auditoriums where needy children have their chance to whisper in Santa's ear before receiving a bagful of toys, the only Christmas most of them will have.

After a traditional oyster po' boy lunch, Santa and his boys head for a few more parties at the homes of club members, dispensing cheer along the way, and then as dusk falls, it's off to Santa's own big party, called "something to let the ladies be involved in after the men have been running around all day!"

The Santa Claus Club is self-supporting and receives no governmental funding, yet its program reaches hundreds of needy children each year and spreads cheer throughout the entire community. Here are a few specialties from "hospitality house" parties visited by Santa on Christmas Eve as he makes his rounds; these, furnished by Eleanor Young, wife of Santa Claus club member Dr. John Young, and her sister Elizabeth Lehmann, were enjoyed at The Hedges.

Boursin Cheese

2 tbsp. butter, softened
½ tsp. pressed garlic
¼ tsp. dill, basil, or any herb you prefer
⅛ tsp. thyme
2-3 tbsp. chopped fresh parsley
1 tbsp. chives or minced green onion
8 oz. cream cheese, softened

Combine all ingredients until smooth. If it gets too soft, refrigerate until firm enough to roll into large ball. Roll into ball, then roll in coarsely ground black pepper or mixture of black pepper and paprika. Cover with plastic wrap and refrigerate. This is best if made 1 or 2 days in advance of serving.

Cheese Crispies

2 cups flour
2 packed cups grated sharp cheese
2 cups crisped rice cereal
2 sticks butter
Hot pepper sauce, salt, and paprika to taste

Mix all ingredients together well. Drop by teaspoonful onto ungreased cookie sheet. Press down with fork. Bake until firm, about 15 minutes at 350 degrees. Can be frozen.

Cocktail Sausage with Sweet and Sour Sauce

2 tbsp. cornstarch
½ cup sugar
½ cup cider vinegar
1 cup pineapple juice
2 tbsp. soy sauce
Cocktail sausage
1 cup pineapple chunks
½ cup bite-size bell pepper chunks
Cherry tomatoes

Mix cornstarch and sugar well in pot. Add vinegar and juice. Add soy sauce. Bring to a boil, stirring constantly, until thick. Pour over cocktail sausage, fruit, peppers, and tomatoes. The sauce is also good for egg rolls and wontons.

Homemade Mustard

4 oz. dry mustard
1 cup vinegar
2 eggs
¾ cup sugar

Beat mustard and vinegar. Add eggs and sugar. Beat over low heat until thick, about 15 minutes. Serve with tiny homemade biscuits or rolls filled with slice of ham.

Marinated Mushrooms

12 tbsp. red-wine vinegar
6 tsp. salt
3 tsp. freshly ground black pepper
3 cloves garlic, slivered
Dash Tabasco sauce
6 tsp. sweet basil
3 tsp. dried parsley
9 green onions, sliced
18 tbsp. olive oil
1 1-lb. can whole button mushrooms
3 tsp. dried parsley

In large jar, put vinegar, salt, pepper, garlic, Tabasco, basil, and 3 tsp. parsley. Put on lid and shake until salt is well dissolved. Add onions and olive oil. Drain mushrooms and add. Shake well. Let stand at room temperature for 4-5 hours. Refrigerate and marinate by shaking occasionally until ready to serve. Serve sprinkled with 3 tsp. parsley.

Peggy Peabody's Party Chicken

4 large chicken breasts, split, skinned, and boned
8 slices bacon
1 4-oz. pkg. chipped beef
1 can condensed cream of mushroom soup
1 cup sour cream

Wrap each breast with strip of bacon. Cover bottom of flat greased baking dish with chipped beef. Arrange breasts on beef. Mix undiluted soup and sour cream; pour over chicken. Cover and refrigerate. About 3¼ hours before serving time, heat oven to 275 degrees. Bake chicken, uncovered, for 3 hours. Serves 8.

Stone-Ground Cornmeal

Across the river from Natchez are two young brothers who've taken a long (10 generations!) and proud family history of farming and given it a new twist. Or maybe it's an old twist.

It all began one day during the fall harvest season, when brothers Patrick and Jesse Calhoun sat in the middle of 1,400 acres of corn and devoured the dinner their mom, Bobbie, had brought them . . . corn on the cob, cornbread, and several other old Southern staples based on corn.

It struck Patrick that corn played an enormously large part in the family diet, yet strangely enough, most of the corn they baked or fried with came from the supermarket. While the family farmers produced plenty of corn as their major cash crop, most of it was sold to grain elevators, feed mills, and an ethanol plant.

The brothers decided to do something about it, using their own resources and promoting a local agricultural product at the same time. They purchased a stone burr mill and set about the business of turning their Calhoun Bend corn into stone-ground cornmeal for marketing across the South.

The corn they use in their finished product is a pioneer hybrid, a yellow field corn that makes better meal than sweet corn. They soon expanded their inventory to include a cornbread mix and fish fry, with white cornmeal and old-style grits planned for later, all grown and processed right in Calhoun Bend on Black River Lake south of Vidalia, on the Louisiana side of the river just across from Natchez.

Patrick Calhoun says the concept of stone-grinding corn into meal has changed very little since the first settlers arrived on American shores and thanked their lucky stars upon discovering the multitude of swift-running streams and creeks capable of supplying power to turn gristmills.

Diverting the waters' flow toward the mills, the pioneers used this natural source of energy to turn giant wooden paddlewheels, which in turn rotated millstones to grind whole-kernel corn seed.

Waterpower has today been replaced by electricity, but modern cooks and bakers are rediscovering what the old-timers knew all along, that old-fashioned whole-grain stone-ground meals and flours produce delicious crusty breads rich in natural flavor, high in fiber, unaffected by chemical preservatives, and nutritious without synthetic vitamin substitutes.

The Calhoun Bend cornmeal contains the hull, endosperm, and germ of the corn seed, which improves the flavor and nutritional value of the end product. By using all the parts of the corn seed, unlike processed cornmeal, the stone-ground variety is all natural, low in sugar and sodium, and high in starch, fiber, and calcium. (Direct inquiries for mail ordering stone-ground cornmeal to Calhoun Bend Mill, 3615 4th St., Jonesville, LA 71343; telephone 318-339-9090.)

Bobbie Calhoun's Cornbread

1 cup stone-ground cornmeal
1 tsp. salt
¾ cup flour
1½ tsp. baking powder
2½ tsp. sugar
1 egg
1 cup milk
1 tbsp. melted butter

Mix dry ingredients. Add egg, milk, and butter. Stir until completely moist. Mix well. Cover bottom and sides of iron skillet with bacon drippings and sprinkle bottom of skillet with 1½ tsp. cornmeal to prevent sticking. Pour in batter. Bake at 425 degrees for 25 minutes or until golden brown.

Batter Bread

1 pt. milk
½ cup yellow cornmeal
½ stick butter or oleo
Cream, for thinning if needed
3 eggs, separated
1 tsp. sugar
¼ tsp. cream of tartar
½ tsp. salt

Scald milk. Stir in cornmeal until all lumps have disappeared. Drop in butter, mix, and allow to cool. Thin with cream if too thick. Beat in egg yolks one at a time, beating mixture well after each. Beat whites until stiff and add the sugar, cream of tartar, and salt. Fold two mixtures together. Pour into greased casserole dish. Set in pan of cold water and bake in 350-degree oven about 40 minutes. This bread is served with a spoon and should be about the consistency of corn pudding.

Patrick Calhoun's Favorite Apple Corn Muffins

2 cups flour
¼ cup yellow cornmeal
⅓ cup brown sugar
1 tbsp. baking powder
½ tsp. salt
1 cup milk
1 egg, lightly beaten
4 tbsp. unsalted butter, melted
1 large Granny Smith apple, peeled and
    coarsely chopped

Preheat oven to 425 degrees. Lightly grease 12 muffin cups. In large bowl, blend flour, cornmeal, sugar, baking powder, and salt. In another bowl, combine milk, egg, and butter. Add milk mixture and apple to flour mixture and fold lightly until just combined; the batter shouldn't be perfectly smooth. Fill muffin cups about ⅔ full. Bake about 30 minutes until tops are golden brown.

Gertrude Veal's Cornbread Oyster Stuffing

Cornbread
2 eggs
Turkey or chicken gizzards
½ bunch green onions, chopped
Fresh parsley, chopped
2 stalks celery, chopped
Butter
¼-½ lb. ground meat
Fresh oysters

Make cornbread according to favorite recipe, using 2 eggs. Boil turkey or chicken gizzards (discard livers) until soft, then chop; save juice from boiling. Sauté green onions, parsley, and celery in butter with ground meat. Add cornbread, oysters, and gizzards to the sautéed mixture and mush to desired consistency, adding gizzard water as needed. Heat before serving with roast turkey or goose.

Natchez Humane Society Barbecues

Fund-raising in Natchez is probably much like anywhere else . . . the better the food offered, the better the turnout and the more profitable the occasion.

Consequently, when the board members of the local humane society contemplate their fund-raisers, plans usually center around barbecues or box suppers for enormous numbers of paying guests. Society board members can tell you it's no picnic feeding the multitudes!

"Horrors!" shouted one friend at the prospect of a chapter in this book entitled "Natchez Humane Society Barbecues." "Call it something else, for heaven's sake! Just think what people will figure is being barbecued!" So to prevent any misunderstanding, let's get it straight right at the outset that the humane society barbecue menus usually consist of barbecued chicken (store-bought chicken, at that), supported by mountains of marinated vegetables and mounds of pork and beans.

Because the humane society is privately supported, it always seems to be in debt, according to one board member. But the hundred or so animals on its rolls on any given day desperately need help, and when the local governmental animal-control officer has worked his 9-to-5 hours and gone home, only the humane society will send out someone at all hours of the night to help with animal problems. Besides, there are educational pet-care programs to be put on at schools and youth groups, and there are visits to be made to the elderly in nursing homes to share the joys of loving pets.

That's part of the motivation (count the number of pets originating from the humane society shelter at any board member's house, and you'll understand the rest of the motivation) that accounts for finding one board member up to her elbows mixing mounds of marinated vegetables for the salad, another struggling with the mind-boggling computations required for revising a recipe that serves 12 to accommodate 150 people, and another stirring pork and beans all through the night with a boat paddle in a big institutional pot on the gas grill.

It's all for a worthy cause.

Humane Society Pork 'n' Beans for 400

14-16 gal. pork 'n' beans
48 oz. dehydrated onion
1 6-oz. jar yellow mustard
4 lb. dark brown sugar
2½ 10-oz. bottles Worcestershire sauce
Salt and black pepper to taste

Mix all ingredients and heat very slowly for a long time to meld the flavors.

Marinated Vegetable Salad for 150

2 gal. canned whole green beans
2 gal. canned English peas
2 gal. shoepeg white corn
24 cups chopped celery
6 cups chopped onion
2 28-oz. cans chopped pimientos
4 lb. sugar
12 tbsp. salt
4 tbsp. black pepper
12 cups vinegar
12 tbsp. paprika
6 cups oil

Drain vegetables well. Mix seasonings with oil and refrigerate until chilled. Mix vegetables and dressing together and refrigerate together for at least 1 day. This recipe requires an awfully large container. To make only 12 servings, reduce portions to 1 15- or 16-oz. can of each vegetable, 2 cups celery, ½ cup onion, and 1 4-oz. can pimiento; make dressing by combining 1 cup sugar with 1 tbsp. salt, 1 tbsp. black pepper, 1 cup vinegar, 1 tsp. paprika, and ½ cup oil.

The Pig Out Inn

Its location may have something to do with the success of this family operation, across from Canal Street Depot housing some wonderful little specialty shops and pilgrimage headquarters in the restored train station, at the second busiest intersection in Natchez, just up from the river and in the thick of the action for the balloon festival and other special riverside events.

But mostly it's the food, ranging from down-home finger-licking-good barbecue to gourmet catering. Archie Willetts used to live in Dallas, where he was a produce broker; his wife, Anne Vidal, worked as a florist. But her family had been in Natchez for what Archie describes as "270 years," and home was calling. When they moved back to Mississippi, they combined the best of both worlds, opening a little 45-seat hole-in-the-wall eatery specializing in the best BBQ this side of heaven . . . or this side of Dallas, which is where Archie learned to smoke succulent meats from his best friend, who owned four BBQ joints there.

Now the Pig Out Inn specializes in slow-smoked meats cooked right there: pork shoulder, beef brisket, pork ribs, chicken, hot sausage links, and whole boneless turkey breast, plus homemade side dishes like baked beans, potato salad, slaw, fresh corn on the cob cooked in the husk on the smoker, and black bean and corn salsa.

The restaurant serves lunch and dinner daily except Sunday, and does it fast: Archie Willetts says eating at the Pig Out Inn is faster than fast-food outlets, since everything is ready, and the meat is sliced right in front of the customer. The Willettses also do BBQ catering for picnics and informal gatherings, as well as elegant gourmet catering for formal affairs.

If you can't come on in and pig out with Archie, you can do it at home with his favorite recipes.

Archie Willetts' BBQ Sauce with a Bite

2½ oz. Cajun seasoning mix
1½ pt. water
4 lb. catsup
5 oz. brown sugar
2 tbsp. vinegar

In a large saucepan, mix Cajun seasoning mix with water and bring to a boil. Lower heat to simmer. Add remaining ingredients and cook slowly until temperature reaches 180 degrees. Do not bring to a second boil.

Anne Vidal Davis Willetts' Dad's Pork and Beans

1 lb. ground beef
½ lb. bacon
3 medium onions, chopped
1 large bell pepper, chopped
3 large cans pork and beans
¾ cup dark brown sugar
½ cup yellow mustard
1 tbsp. black pepper
1 tbsp. mustard seeds
Salt to taste

Sauté beef; drain and set aside. Fry bacon, crumble, and set aside, saving drippings. In a heavy Dutch oven, sauté onion and bell pepper in bacon drippings. Add all the other ingredients and cook in oven at 250 degrees for at least 2 hours or in smoker for at least 3 hours.

Archie Willetts' Smoked Turkey

1 turkey
1 cup dry spice rub, such as Tony Chachere's
Several sprigs fresh rosemary

Clean bird and apply dry spice rub to skin. Stuff cavity with fresh rosemary. Place more rosemary in pan with water in bottom of smoker. Burn coals to white embers, and place water-soaked wood chips, such as hickory, mesquite, or pecan, on coals. Allow smoke to accumulate, and place turkey in smoker. Cover and allow 30 minutes per pound. Skin should be dark and meat should be juicy.

WOODVILLE AND THE WILKINSON COUNTY AREA OF MISSISSIPPI

Pinckneyville

In the kudzu-draped pastoral reaches of the southwest corner of Mississippi just across the Louisiana state line, Pinckneyville is such a quiet little community today it's hard to visualize the rowdy days when it was nearly wall-to-wall saloons.

But the historic little town had a lively past, beginning when it was settled right on the banks of the Mississippi River at the spot where foot-sore flatboaters crossed onto American soil from Spanish territory, cause for celebration as they made their dangerous way back home after selling cargoes and vessels in New Orleans.

And celebrate they did, accounting for the proliferation of saloons in early Pinckneyville. But after steamboats replaced flatboats, leaving no need for return trips upriver by foot, another blow was struck by the Mississippi River when it picked up and moved away from the town, changing course just enough to strand Pinckneyville high and dry.

By then, cotton plantations had been established in the area and a different way of life began. In 1814 to one of these plantations retired a wealthy merchant named Oliver Pollock. Having arrived in this country a penniless young Irish immigrant, Pollock over the years amassed such wealth and established such vital trading ties with Spanish authorities that he would go down in history as the largest single financial contributor to the American Revolution, supporting with his entire fortune and invaluable personal contacts his beloved adopted country's war for independence.

Pollock backed George Rogers Clark's expedition

to conquer territory now comprising Illinois, Indiana, and Ohio, supplied thousands of pounds of gunpowder for the colonial army, and forged friendships with Spanish authorities in Old New Orleans and Havana, which helped oust the British from West Florida and paved the way for the Louisiana Purchase.

Called "the forgotten founding father," Pollock is buried in Pinckneyville on lands once part of Cold Spring Plantation, where the house dates from the early 1800s and has exterior walls a full foot thick and narrow vertical porch railings that originally extended all the way to the upstairs gallery to keep out wild animals. It was around the time of the Civil War that one daughter of the family here languished so long at an upstairs window, pining away for an unworthy suitor sent packing by her father, that the image of her face was said to be graven forever upon the glass.

A later occupant, driven to desperation by unwanted visitors attracted by tales of the face in the window, finally smashed the glass, but couldn't do a thing about Cold Spring's other resident ghost, that of the home's builder, who was occasionally heard rocking in his basement wine cellar. His death wish had been that his friends lay him to rest only after consuming his entire stock of fine wines, but after gamely fulfilling his wishes, they had trouble recalling exactly where they had buried him, and only when heads cleared was he located and given a proper burial where he belonged.

Nearby Desert Plantation, built in 1810, was originally such an extensive cotton plantation that it took a mile-long row of quarters to house the slaves needed to cultivate its fields; it is still a thousand-acre working plantation. Filled with fine antiques, including many from the Brandon family, which furnished Mississippi's first native-born governor and other notable early leaders, Desert now hosts guests by advance arrangement; some of the late Mrs. Williams W. Brandon's favorite recipes follow.

Catherine Brandon's Salted Pecans

1 qt. pecans
1-2 tsp. sugar
1 tsp. salt or more to taste
3 tbsp. melted butter

Wash and dry pecans in colander. Spread on cookie sheet and heat in oven at 300 degrees until pecans are very hot. Mix sugar, salt, and butter. Spread over pecans and stir well until evenly coated. Continue cooking in oven until pecans break with a sort of pop. Turn off oven but leave pecans in to continue drying out until oven cools.

Catherine Brandon's Cheese Crispies

2 sticks oleo
2 cups flour, sifted
½ tsp. salt
⅓ tsp. cayenne pepper
2 cups grated sharp cheddar cheese
2 cups crisped rice cereal

Allow oleo to reach room temperature, then add flour, salt, and pepper. Add cheese and cereal. Roll into small balls and place on ungreased cookie sheet, flattening with fork to make ridges on top. Bake at 300 degrees for about 10 minutes; do not brown. Keep in airtight container.

Rosemont and Jefferson Davis Pie

In 1810, a full year before the town of Woodville was chartered as Mississippi's third oldest, Samuel and Jane Cook Davis settled just east of town on a plantation that would become known as Rosemont for Jane Davis's beloved rose gardens. A fine example of Federal architecture adapted to the Mississippi frontier, Rosemont is a planter's cottage with personal touches like the Palladian window over the front gallery, added to remind the Davises of previous homes in South Carolina and Kentucky. A captain in the Continental Army, Davis had been lured south by reports of fortunes to be made in cotton and sugar.

The youngest of the Davis children was named for a man much respected by Samuel Davis, the great statesman Thomas Jefferson. This child, who was two years old when the family settled at Rosemont, would one day rival Jefferson in statesmanship and service to his country.

Jefferson Davis would always refer to Rosemont as the place where his memories began. After graduating from West Point, he helped tame the western frontier and was decorated as a military hero in the Mexican War. He would later serve in both houses of Congress representing Mississippi, and for four years was secretary of war under Pres. Franklin Pierce, during which time he modernized the Federal army, developed the Minié ball, brought camels to the U.S. for transporting overland freight in the west, and instituted the medical corps in the army.

In 1861 Davis followed his state into secession and accepted involvement in a war he didn't want, unanimously elected president of the Confederacy, in which post, "without money, without supplies, without resources, without industry, Jefferson Davis made a nation," in the words of Queen Victoria's prime minister William Gladstone.

Meanwhile the Davis family continued to live at Rosemont for five generations. When Jefferson's young nephew Isaac Stamps was killed at Gettysburg in 1863, he issued a presidential pass so Isaac's grieving wife, Mary, could cross enemy lines in a wagon to recover her husband's body from the battlefield and bring him home to Rosemont for burial alongside other family members.

Rosemont's present owners have completely restored the plantation home and its extensive grounds, opened the plantation for periodic tours, and also very generously made it available for the regular gatherings of descendants of the Davis family, who in 1989 marked the centennial of the death of Jefferson Davis. The family association supports related educational and commemorative projects and plans a museum.

When they get together each June, one of the Davis family members' favorite culinary treats is this special pie, made from a recipe furnished by the Mississippi Division of the United Daughters of the Confederacy.

The story told by the UDC is that the pie was created in Missouri during the War Between the States by a spirited plantation cook. When Union officers requested dinner, the plantation master, who was decidedly pro-Confederacy, cautioned his family and servants to refrain from talking politics. The family cook produced this delectable pie and served it in silence to the blue-uniformed soldiers, but when they devoured it with gusto, praised it to the skies, and asked what she called it, she could resist no longer. "Jefferson Davis Pie!" was her smug reply.

Jefferson Davis Pie

½ cup butter
2 cups light brown sugar
4 egg yolks
2 tbsp. flour
1 tsp. cinnamon
1 tsp. nutmeg
½ tsp. ground allspice
1 cup cream
½ cup chopped pecans
½ cup raisins
½ cup chopped dates
1 10" pie shell
Whipped cream

Cream butter and sugar together. Beat in egg yolks. Sift flour and spices into mixture. Add cream, pecans, raisins, and dates. Brown crust in 450-degree oven for 5 minutes, then add filling. Cook until set at 350 degrees. Serve topped with whipped cream.

Woodville Red Recipes

The good cooks of Woodville, Mississippi, take the traditional definition of Southern hospitality—"disposed to receiving and entertaining guests generously and kindly"—and give it a Christian twist and a physical embodiment.

Then they share it all in the cookbook called *Woodville Red Recipes,* prepared by the group of young churchwomen belonging to the service organization known as The Tabithas. The book's name derives from the *Woodville Red* camellia, thought to have been imported from France via the New Orleans French Market and thence to the Woodville area sometime prior to the Civil War.

A quiet little town rich in beauty and history, Woodville's picturesque buildings, oak-shaded courthouse square, and relaxed way of life have been so remarkably well preserved that a Harvard University study named it as the place best typifying the traditions, customs, and culture of the antebellum South. Its historic homes dispense a unique brand of hospitality that many attribute to the predominant Christian influence here.

The strength and longevity of this influence are demonstrated by the age of the little town's church structures, three of which are more than 150 years old; a fourth is over a century old. St. Paul's Episcopal Church dates from 1823, Woodville Baptist from 1809, St. Joseph's Catholic from 1873, and the Woodville United Methodist Church, dating from 1824, is the oldest church building of its denomination in the state.

This religious heritage has had a pervasive influence on the community as a whole. Births, marriages, baptisms, deaths, accomplishments and crises, celebrations and tragedies are all shared, and the tradition of the town is to express heartfelt caring through the sharing of food as well.

The time-honored recipes for good old country cooking in The Tabithas' cookbook, then, represent a lot more than just food on the table; whether handed down through the generations or brought into the community by newcomers who were quickly absorbed into life there, all these recipes have at one time or another been used to represent neighborly love. *Woodville Red Recipes* is available by mail from The Tabithas, Box 488, Woodville, MS 39669.

Helen Ashley's Eggplant Dressing Casserole

1 onion, chopped
1 bell pepper, chopped
3 stalks celery, chopped
½ stick oleo
1 small square cornbread
1 cup cooked rice
2 slices white bread
2 eggs
1 can chicken broth
2 eggplants, peeled, cubed, and cooked in
    salt water
1 cup grated cheddar cheese

Sauté onion, bell pepper, and celery in oleo. Mix in cornbread, rice, white bread, and eggs with enough chicken broth to make moist. Add drained eggplant. Add cheese. Bake for 1 hour at 350 degrees.

Robert E. Lee Cake

9 eggs, separated
2 cups sugar
2 cups all-purpose flour
½ tsp. salt
1 tbsp. lemon juice
2 lemons
3 oranges
2 cups sugar
Grated rinds of lemon and orange
1 cup grated coconut
Grated coconut

Beat egg yolks very lightly, then slowly beat in 2 cups sugar. Fold in well-beaten egg whites. Sift in flour with salt and mix lightly together. Stir in 1 tbsp. lemon juice. Pour into 3 ungreased layer pans and bake at 300 degrees for 25-30 minutes. To make filling, squeeze the juice of lemons and oranges over 2 cups sugar and flavor with a little of the grated rinds. Add 1 cup coconut and blend. Put between layers and on top, then sprinkle cake with coconut.

Honey Gross's Ambrosia Bavarian

1 3-oz. env. orange gelatin
2 tbsp. sugar
¼ tsp. salt
1 cup boiling water
1 cup orange juice
1 8-oz. can crushed pineapple
1 16-oz. container frozen whipped topping,
    thawed
½ cup flaked coconut

Dissolve gelatin, sugar, and salt in the water in medium bowl; stir in orange juice and syrup from pineapple. Chill until as thick as unbeaten egg white. Beat until light and fluffy. Stir in whipped topping until well blended. Fold in pineapple and coconut. Pour into a large serving bowl. Chill several hours or until firm.

Mable Clark's Mamma's Homemade Rolls

¾ cup milk
¼ cup sugar
2¼ tsp. salt
4½ tbsp. shortening
1 pkg. yeast
¾ cup lukewarm water
4½ cups sifted all-purpose flour
Melted shortening

Scald milk. Stir in sugar, salt, and 4½ tbsp. shortening. Cool to lukewarm. Sprinkle yeast in the water in a bowl; let stand until dissolved; stir. Add lukewarm milk mixture. Stir in 2¼ cups flour; beat until smooth. Stir in remaining flour. Turn dough out onto a lightly floured board; knead. Place in greased bowl and brush top lightly with melted shortening. Cover with clean towel. Let rise in warm place free from drafts until doubled in bulk, about 1 hour and 25 minutes. Punch down dough. Form rolls. Let rise until double in bulk, about 1 hour and 25 minutes. Bake at 425 degrees for 20 minutes.

Mrs. A. W. Treppendahl's Wild Duck

2 sticks butter
½-1 cup olive oil
3 stalks celery, coarsely chopped
1 large onion
1½ cups water
1 tsp. Worcestershire sauce
1 tsp. garlic salt
Ducks
¼ apple per duck
1 slice onion per duck
½ stick butter per duck
Salt to taste
¼ cup sherry per duck

Melt 2 sticks butter in bottom of roaster and add olive oil. Add celery. Slice onion and brown in butter and oil. Add water, Worcestershire, and garlic salt. Clean ducks and dry thoroughly. Inside each duck, place apple, onion, and butter. Salt each duck well. Place ducks in roaster, breast-side down. Cover and cook 1 hour at 400 degrees. After cooking 1 hour, turn ducks over and pour on sherry. Continue cooking, covered, for 1 hour or longer, basting often. Turn ducks breast-side down to cool. Remove ducks from broth. Strain broth to make gravy.

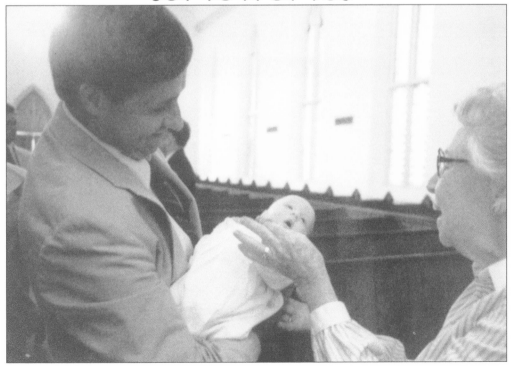

Pond Store

After the Civil War, an influx of carpetbaggers and Jewish families swept across the South, the carpetbaggers leaving mostly a bad taste but the Jewish merchants establishing successful commercial ventures, endowing synagogues and schools, and leaving a mark of a different and longer-lasting nature.

One such commercial establishment was the Pond Store in southwest Mississippi, built by Barthold and Karl Lehman in an auspicious location, the last flat spot on the road to the port at Fort Adams, where cotton from across the central part of the state was hauled for shipment on paddlewheelers to factors in New Orleans.

The teamsters hauling the huge bales of cotton to the river usually stopped to camp overnight at this flat spot, resting their stock before tackling the steep and treacherous hill straight down into Fort Adams. The county built a stock pond on the spot for the convenience of the teamsters in watering their oxen, mules, or horses, and to satisfy the other needs of these men, the Pond Store was built nearby.

When the first store and post office were destroyed by fire, the present wood-frame building was erected in 1881, its raised porch surrounding the living quarters behind the store proper.

The Pond Store was soon taken over by an extremely interesting gentleman named Julius Lemkowitz, a Russian Jew who fled the Bolshevik Revolution and emigrated to the United States in the 1920s. Lemkowitz was a modern-day Renaissance man who read law and passed the bar, then studied medicine and became a fine doctor.

He was a voracious reader with an extensive personal library of rare volumes, many still in the store. He also edited the Natchez newspaper at one time and helped select the books for that city's libraries. Lemkowitz even found five mistakes after reading completely through *Webster's Unabridged,* and was duly thanked by the publishers for reporting them.

Lemkowitz, who subscribed to newspapers from Hong Kong, Paris, and Berlin, spoke a number of languages fluently and was also known to speak to

deceased members of his family, or try to, holding seances with the crystal ball still on display in the store.

Not long after Lemkowitz took over the Pond Store, his need of a clerk drew a young man named Carrol Smith to the store, where he remained for half a century; his daughter and her husband are the present owner-operators.

Smith's wife, Josephine, recalls that, when she first came to "The Pond" in 1924, Lemkowitz and his wife indulged in the European custom of afternoon tea. After the kitchen was cleaned and lunch dishes put away, a table in the dining room or parlor was covered with a large white linen cloth and set for tea, then covered with another cloth until tea time at 4 o'clock. After setting the table for tea, the ladies retired for naps, then arose and dressed in their best clothes, with Mrs. Lemkowitz usually in black taffeta or, during summer, perhaps a silk pongee.

Refreshments for this tea would consist of blackberry wine or a homemade root beer chilled in the cistern, and always hearty exotic teas, plus several kinds of small cakes or cookies like Russian tea cakes, lebkuchen, and cream puffs (Mrs. Smith's recipes follow). After tea, everyone sat on the porch

in the cool of the afternoon and visited until time to close the store and eat supper.

It's still a fine place for sitting in the cool breeze and visiting, and there are groceries to be bought, but the Pond Store mostly trades on nostalgia these days, with displays of vintage farm implements, tools, and old store fixtures. In display cases shining above well-worn wood floors are items like the store's 1916 inventory list, including one bedroom suite of dresser, armoire, and washstand for $17.50, and an iron bed for $1.50. The living quarters include some nice late Victorian pieces from the old inventory as well.

The county stock pond, just across the road, overflows with ducks and geese these days; the donkeys grazing freely on its banks provide rides for children. Also across the road is the entrance to the hiking trails in Clark Creek Natural Area, with its famous waterfalls, and the entire surrounding area is a veritable hunter's paradise.

Chilly fall days find hikers and hunters along with the occasional tourist and traveler drawn up around the Pond Store's old wood stove, where hospitality and history lessons are dispensed as freely as the canned beans and cold beer.

Russian Tea Cakes

1 cup butter
½ cup powdered sugar
2¼ cups sifted flour
¼ tsp. salt
1 tsp. vanilla extract
¾ cups chopped nuts
Powdered sugar

Cream butter and ½ cup sugar. Add salt to flour. Add flour mixture to creamed butter and sugar, work in well with hands, and blend in vanilla and nuts. Chill. Form into 1" balls. Bake 14-17 minutes at 350 degrees, then roll in powdered sugar.

Lebkuchen

⅔ cup honey
1 cup sugar
⅓ cup butter
1 egg
⅓ cup water
4 cups cake flour
1 tsp. baking soda
½ tsp. salt
1 tsp. cinnamon
1 tsp. ground cloves
⅔ cup chopped nuts
⅓ cup chopped citron
Powdered sugar
Water

Boil honey, sugar, and butter together for 5 minutes, then cool. Beat egg and add to ⅓ cup water. Mix and sift flour, soda, salt, and spices. Alternate adding sifted dry ingredients with the liquid ingredients to the honey mixture. Add nuts and citron last. Chill. If the dough is allowed to ripen for several days before rolling out, the flavor improves. Roll out about ¼" thick and cut the size of playing cards. Bake in a moderate oven, about 350 degrees, until a very light brown. Ice with sugar glaze made of powdered sugar with just enough water to make it the consistency of thin cream.

Cream Puffs

5 tbsp. shortening
1 cup water
1 cup flour
¼ tsp. salt
4 eggs
1½ cups evaporated milk
½ cup water
2 egg yolks
½ cup sugar
⅛ tsp. salt
2 tbsp. cornstarch
2 tbsp. vanilla extract
Powdered sugar

Put shortening in saucepan, add water, bring to boil, and quickly add flour and ¼ tsp. salt. Stir with wooden spoon until mixture leaves sides of pan. Remove from heat, cool, but do not chill. Add eggs, one at a time, beating thoroughly. Set in cool place for 1 hour, then spoon out onto cookie sheet to make individual balls (the dough is too light to actually shape). Bake on greased cookie sheet at 375 for 40 minutes. In the last 10 minutes, lower heat in order to crisp. To make filling, scald evaporated milk diluted with ½ cup water in double boiler. Pour over egg yolks, sugar, ⅛ tsp. salt, and cornstarch that have been beaten together. Return to double boiler and cook until thick, stirring constantly. Cool, and add vanilla. Slice puff pastry and fill, then dust with powdered sugar.

Crawfish Etienne

You can take a Cajun out of the bayou, but you can't take the bayou out of the Cajun, which might explain what a nice south Louisiana schoolteacher with the Gallic maiden name of Edine Lemoine was doing up in Woodville, Mississippi, whipping up an elegant crawfish dish.

It helped, of course, that her husband, Stephen Seal, local tractor-dealership owner, had been raising crawfish in ponds near Lake Mary for years, having whet his own appetite for the tasty crustaceans while a KA at LSU and then working with LSU Cooperative Extension Service specialists on innovative ideas for pond design and crawfish production, costs, and competition.

When Stephen Seal began to take note of the way his wife's crawfish dip was always the first bowl emptied at parties, the result was the birth of Crawfish Etienne, a rich crawfish dish with a cream base that the couple, with several friends, marketed already prepared and frozen to be served over fettuccine or rice, in patty shells, or as a dip. Its advent was timed just right to cash in on the Cajun cooking craze sweeping the nation.

The parent company, Craw Daddies, also marketed Crawfish Fat Tails, 1-lb. bags of peeled crawfish meat with the fat still on, helping make available year round a product that went a long way toward sharing the rich culinary heritage of this area with the entire country. The company is no longer in business, but the recipes live on to serve the same purpose.

Crawfish Etienne

1 lb. peeled crawfish tails
1½ sticks butter or oleo
1 small bunch green onions, chopped
½ cup chopped parsley
3 tbsp. flour
1 pt. half & half
3 tbsp. sherry
Salt and cayenne pepper to taste

Using paper towels, gently wipe as much of the fat off the crawfish tails as possible. In skillet, sauté crawfish tails in ½ stick butter or oleo. In another skillet, sauté green onions and parsley in 1 stick butter or oleo. Blend in flour and gradually add cream, stirring constantly to make a thick sauce. Add sherry, then add crawfish tails. Season with salt and pepper. Freezes well. Can be served in chafing dish as a hot dip, or served over fettuccine noodles or rice, or served in patty shells, or even as an elegant finishing sauce over steak.

Margaret Lemoine's Individual Crawfish Pies

½ cup chopped onions
¼ cup chopped celery
¼ cup olive oil
2 tbsp. butter or crawfish fat
1 lb. peeled crawfish tails
2 tbsp. cornstarch
¾ cup water
5 green onions, chopped
2 tbsp. chopped parsley
Salt and cayenne pepper to taste
9 individual prepared pie shells

Sauté onions and celery in olive oil. Add butter and crawfish tails. Cook 10 minutes. Dissolve cornstarch in water, add, and cook until thick. Add green onions and parsley. Season with salt and pepper. Put into pie shells and bake at 350 degrees for 30 minutes. Cool 5 minutes before serving.

Margaret Lemoine's Seafood Casserole

2 boxes long-grain and wild rice
1 cup chopped onions
¼ cup chopped green onions
½-1 stick butter or oleo
1 lb. peeled crawfish tails
1 lb. crabmeat
2 cans cream of mushroom soup
1 cup mayonnaise
1 can mushrooms

Cook rice according to box directions. Sauté onions and green onions in butter. Add crawfish and sauté. Add crawfish, crab, and other ingredients to rice. Bake at 350 degrees until bubbly and hot.

Marinated Crawfish

1 lb. peeled crawfish tails
⅔ 8-oz. bottle remoulade dressing
½ bottle Italian dressing

Mix all ingredients and let marinate at least 24 hours. This makes a good appetizer and is delicious served on a bed of lettuce for a light lunch.

Crawfish Fettuccine

3 large onions, chopped
2 bell peppers, chopped
3 stalks celery, chopped
3 sticks butter or oleo
3 lb. peeled crawfish tails
2 heads garlic, chopped
4 tbsp. chopped parsley
2 pkg. crawfish fat
1 pt. half & half
1 lb. jalapeno cheese, cubed
¼ cup flour
Salt and black pepper to taste
Parmesan cheese
Catsup
1 12-oz. pkg. fettuccine (egg) noodles
Seasoned breadcrumbs

Sauté onions, bell peppers, and celery in butter. Add crawfish, garlic, and parsley. Cook 15 minutes. Add fat, cream, jalapeno cheese, and flour. Simmer 30 minutes. Season to taste. Add Parmesan and a few drops of catsup to taste. Boil noodles, drain, and add to mixture. Pour into casserole, top with breadcrumbs, and bake at 350 degrees until hot and bubbly through and through.

Seafood Fettuccine

3 onions, chopped
4 tbsp. chopped parsley
2 cloves garlic, chopped
2 stalks celery, chopped
3 sticks butter
3 lb. seafood (crawfish, crab, or shrimp)
¼ cup flour
1½ pt. half & half
Salt and black pepper to taste
2 12-oz. pkg. medium noodles or fettuccine, cooked in chicken broth
1 lb. jalapeno Velveeta cheese, melted
¼ cup white wine
½ cup Parmesan cheese

Sauté onions, parsley, garlic, and celery in butter until tender. Add seafood and sauté a little. Mix in flour and half & half slowly and cook for 5 minutes. Season to taste. Mix noodles or fettuccine with Velveeta and wine. Add seafood mixture. Put in casserole dish and top with Parmesan. Bake at 350 degrees for 30 minutes. Serves 20.

NEW ROADS AND THE POINTE COUPEE PARISH AREA OF LOUISIANA

Parlange

Parlange, across the Mississippi River from St. Francisville near New Roads, was built in 1750 by the French marquis Claude Vincent de Ternant, probably a second or third son whose chance of inheritance in the old country was slim under existing French law. He settled in an area first pioneered by French-Canadian trappers and named for a shortcut that Iberville in 1699 used in his explorations. The 22-mile loop of Mississippi River that was cut off by this cut-point (*pointe coupée* in French, from which the parish takes its name) would later be abandoned altogether by the river itself, thus forming False River, on whose banks de Ternant constructed his magnificent colonial home.

Now called Parlange, the rambling West Indies-type structure is completely encircled by broad galleries on both floors and was built of cypress with *bousillage* (mud and moss) insulation and bricks made right on the place. The carved cypress chair railings on interior walls are continued on the exterior along the inner gallery walls, showing that life on the upper gallery outside the main formal living areas, where the cool breezes from the river could be felt, was just as important as that inside the home's recesses.

A National Historic Landmark, Parlange is one of Louisiana's earliest architectural treasures and remains in the original family yet. Since its beginnings in the mid-18th century, when indigo was

raised there under contract with the Prussian Army, which used the blue dye for coloring its uniforms, Parlange has been maintained as a huge working plantation, the main crops being sugarcane, cotton, corn, cattle, and most recently soybeans.

The marquis's son, Marquis de Ternant II, married Virginie Trahan. After his death, she wed Col. Charles Parlange, whose name would endure on the family plantation as well as its occupants. During the Civil War both armies stayed at Parlange, though not at the same time. The Union Army, under the command of Gen. Nathaniel Banks, arrived first. In order to save her home, Madame Parlange and her little son Charles were cordial to the general and gave him the keys to the wine cellar and provision rooms below.

Called back from Paris, where she had a salon and small chateau outside the city and had lived for some years, Madame Parlange had perhaps more of a Frenchwoman's outlook than a purely Southern one, and at any rate was determined to save her home.

Every evening, Madame Virginie served a banquet in the formal dining room for the general and his aide, who slept in the house, as well as his officers, who slept on the galleries encircling the house, while servants prepared a barbecue for the troops out in the gardens, where they were quartered.

After the departure of General Banks and his army, the Confederate forces under the command of Gen. Richard Taylor, son of Zachary, arrived, with Madame Parlange again entertaining them in like manner. Says the current mistress of Parlange, "Of course, after all this, two armies to feed and house, she was dead broke and they had, like the rest of the South, a very tough time of it, but she had saved her home through her finesse." The two generals would later meet at the Battle of Mansfield in north Louisiana, called the last decisive victory for the South.

With his mother, Charles Parlange stayed on at Parlange, never able to return to Paris. As a child he played in the fields and raised bees in the dovecotes, persevered enough to receive an education, and became an attorney, serving as state senator, state lieutenant governor, U.S. attorney, appeals court judge, and federal judge.

The home today is filled with priceless antiques and one of the finest collections of portraits to be seen anywhere. The main salon is dominated by a full-length life-sized portrait of the young Madame Parlange, painted in Paris by court painter Claude Dubufe, who also painted Napoleon.

Virginie's daughter, Marie Virginie de Ternant of Parlange and Paris, married Maj. Anatole Avegno from a prominent New Orleans family, and when he was fatally wounded during the Battle of Shiloh, she took her daughters Virginie and Louise to Paris.

There Virginie, born in 1859, became the subject of John Singer Sargent's masterpiece called *Portrait of Madame X*. This bold portrait, painted in 1883, scandalized society in Paris and Louisiana alike. Perceived as provocative for the figure's décolletage and stance, it now hangs in the collection of the Metropolitan Museum of Art in New York.

With her supportive family, the mistress of Parlange today, Lucy Brandon Parlange, is one of the last of the great Southern hostesses, gracious and warm and hospitable, lending her talents to further preservation efforts, a great patron of the arts, and an even greater lover of life who's just as apt to hitch up her skirts and climb to the top of the hayloft with a visiting child as she is to sit demurely with older guests and pour coffee quite properly and formally from a priceless polished silver service.

It was her mother-in-law, Mme Paule Brierre Parlange, who came up the river from New Orleans as a young bride and first opened the home to visitors in 1918, charging 50 cents per person. One couple climbed the stairs, asked the admission price, and said, *"Fifty cents!* That's too much! Can't you go down on your price?" Madame Paule asked her husband, Walter, who responded, "Tell them it's 49 cents per person," at which point the visitors entered and had a lovely tour.

For many years the family living at Parlange was three-generational. Lucy Parlange, raised on the Brandon plantation called Arcole at Pinckneyville in Mississippi, moved as a young girl to New Orleans; her father, a civil engineer and proud president of the Ancient and Honorable Order of River Rats due to his work with the Corps of Engineers' river and flood control projects, loved the country and farming at Arcole but said he "couldn't make a living on scenery." After attending Newcomb Art School, Lucy married Walter ("Skipper") Parlange, Jr., and moved upriver to Parlange, moving in with his parents, whom she calls "a most delightful pair." Walter Sr. did much of the cooking and insisted upon having soup for every midday dinner, winter and summer. His soup often saved the day, especially when young bride Lucy tried her hand in the kitchen with less-than-perfect results.

The three children, Walter III, Brandon, and Angele, delighted in receiving Bunny Rabbit letters written with childish spelling by the fun-loving Walter Sr. and secreted in hollow places in the Parlange trees. "Dear Mr. Puffin (Walter III)," said one such letter, "I hear you did a fine job pumping out the cesspool. Don't tell anyone you are in this line of business. I am sending you a big half a dollar. Your fren, Bunny Rabbit." Said another, "Dear Mr. Brandon, I hear you climbed way up on that rope. You must be kin to those squirrels in the oak trees. I can't send you much this time as my lettuce crop was short this year. Your fren, Bunny Rabbit."

Now Parlange is so popular with visitors that its present master, Walter Parlange, Jr., has jokingly renamed it "Constant Company," and rare is the day that Lucy is not hosting one of her famous "Banister Brunches" on the front gallery. While the family does indeed eat often in the formal dining room, Lucy says the gallery "is our favorite place to park, sit and talk, and get to know all kinds of interesting visitors, and lots of times we talk the tourists into staying a bit longer and we break bread." One favorite company dish is Coco's Constant Company Carrot Soup, a tasty and refreshing dish made from a recipe given the family by a visiting French girl named Coco, who arrived in a Jeep she called James, just having become an American citizen and having been sent out by her World Banker husband to "discover America."

When the duke and duchess of Argyll of Inverary Castle in Scotland spent a few days at Parlange recently, they delighted in meeting some of Lucy's admirers, who come in all ages and from all walks of life, from the small family friend who expressed disappointment that they were wearing no crowns, to Mr. Claude, the neighbor who calls everyone "Pete" (says he, "It's too hard to remember the names of all the people I know all these years, Pete"). Mr. Claude, presented to the visiting royalty, responded, "How y'all doin', Pete?" On Annie Miller's south Louisiana swamp tour the duchess found the alligators "rather sweet," and both she and her husband thoroughly enjoyed the evening rum punch served in silver tumblers on the upper front gallery at Parlange after each day's excursions; Lucy calls it "Mr. Claude's Sock (Argyll, of course) It to 'em Punch" or "D&D (Duke and Duchess) Delight."

The grown children of the Parlange family return home often with friends on weekends and, after horseback riding or water-skiing on the river or "sometimes having to round up some stray cattle who think the grass is greener on the next plantation," enjoy Lucy's Seafood Casserole.

Mr. Claude's Sock It to 'em Punch or D&D Delight

1 qt. freshly squeezed orange juice
12 oz. unsweetened pineapple juice
4 oz. grenadine
Rum
Ice

Mix everything together except the rum in a half-gallon container. Pour a jigger of rum over ice in a silver tumbler, then fill with punch. Pretty soon, says Lucy Parlange, you'll feel punched out and head for bed. Makes about "a galleryful" of drinks, around 10.

Paule Brierre Parlange's Cornbread

2 cups milk
¼ cup butter
1½ cups cornmeal (home-ground if possible)
2 tbsp. baking powder
1 tsp. salt
2 tbsp. sugar
4 egg yolks, beaten
4 egg whites, beaten

Bring milk to a boil; add butter. When melted, add to the dry ingredients and mix. Then add the egg yolks. Mix well and fold in the egg whites. Pour mixture into a well-greased pan and bake in preheated oven at 450 degrees until browned.

Coco's Constant Company Carrot Soup

8 cups chicken or turkey broth, or water seasoned with 4 chicken bouillon cubes
3 cups peeled, sliced carrots
2 cups peeled, sliced Irish potatoes
1 large onion or 2 bunches green onions
4 cloves garlic, pressed
2 cups milk
Few dashes Tabasco sauce
1 shake Tony Chachere's Creole Seasoning
Parsley flakes

Boil broth (or seasoned water, letting cubes dissolve). Add carrots and potatoes. Chop onion or green onions and add. Add garlic. Boil for 20-25 minutes, until you can mash vegetables with fork. Turn off the heat. Pour in milk. Puree in blender. Season with Tabasco, Tony Chachere's, and some parsley.

Parlange Seafood Casserole

4 lb. shrimp, cooked and peeled
1 lb. crabmeat
6 cups cooked brown rice
1 qt. mayonnaise
3½ cups chopped onions
2 bell peppers, chopped
6 tbsp. Worcestershire sauce
Several dashes garlic powder
Several dashes Tabasco sauce
Several big dashes Tony Chachere's Creole Seasoning
Olive oil

Mix ingredients except oil. Pour a little oil over all. Put in pan and cover with foil. Cook in 350-degree oven for 35-40 minutes. Remove foil for last 5 minutes of cooking.

Walter Parlange Sr.'s Soup

1 large smoked ham hock
12 cups water or broth
10 tomatoes, peeled
3 stalks celery, chopped
3 large onions, chopped
4 cloves garlic, pressed
6 carrots, peeled and chopped
1 cup fresh snap beans
1 cup fresh butter beans
1 cup corn, cut fresh off cob if possible
4 Irish potatoes, cut up
1 small head cabbage, sliced
2 bell peppers, chopped
2 tbsp. olive oil
1 cup okra
Several shakes Tony Chachere's Creole
    Seasoning
3 dashes Tabasco sauce
2 beef marrow bones

Wash ham hock, put in a big kettle in the water or broth, and cook over medium heat. Add tomatoes, celery, onions, and garlic. Cook about 1 hour. Add carrots, snap beans, butter beans, corn, potatoes, cabbage, bell peppers, and olive oil. Cook for 30 minutes. Add okra and cook 10 minutes more. At this point, you might have to add a little more water. Put in the seasonings; can substitute seasoned salt or Mrs. Dash. Put in a big soup tureen or ladle into large soup bowls.

JACKSON AND THE EAST FELICIANA PARISH AREA OF LOUISIANA

Open-Fire Cooking from East Feliciana

The area called West Florida, bounded on the east by the Pearl River, west by the Mississippi, north by the Mississippi state line, and south by the coast, was governed by France from 1717 to 1763, Britain until 1779, and Spain until 1810, when its settlers revolted against Spanish rule, declared the area an independent Republic of West Florida, and after 74 heady days joined the United States. Parts of this originally immense area were syphoned off for inclusion in the states of Alabama and Mississippi, as well as the Louisiana parishes of St. Tammany, Washington, St. Helena, and Livingston, leaving the parish of Feliciana with only that territory that is now East and West Feliciana.

The town of Jackson was in 1813 declared the seat of justice for the original parish of Feliciana, as it was already becoming a center for learning and culture. Its settlers were a hardy lot, willing to brave severe hardship to wrest from the wilderness farms and great plantations. The hilly Felicianas were considered far more healthful than low-lying areas like New Orleans, where malaria, cholera, and other epidemics wiped out great numbers of the populace with tragic regularity.

One particularly picturesque memoir of the early pioneer days was penned by the elderly Mr. H. Skipwith, who described himself as on the shady side of 70 and consequently feared his writings might be dismissed as "the tedious twaddle of a garrulous old man."

Among Skipwith's memorable portraits of pioneer Feliciana life is the story of the courageous young fellow who arrived in one early wave of immigration from the original colonies, sent out from the family homestead in the Carolinas in 1802 and charged with exploring and obtaining a Spanish land grant to a homeplace so that the rest of the family, its slaves, and herds of livestock might soon join him. At night, after a full day cutting cane and

commencing a hatchet clearing along the creek bank, this same prudent young fellow would "retire up in the forks of the trees, from which secure but uncomfortable roost he would calmly observe the gambols, wrestlings and fights of bears, panthers and wolves."

Another young settler, one Eli White, described pioneer life in 1807 near Clear Creek: "I never tasted meat, except bear, venison and an occasional panther steak, until I was a good-sized boy. The only milk I ever tasted was my mother's, until my

father returned to South Carolina and brought out with him one of grandfather's old cows. The dairy utensils my mother used were old-fashioned, big-bellied gourds, sawn in two. My only clothing until I reached twelve years of age was a long shirt of coarse cotton cloth woven on mother's hand loom. I always went barefooted, summer and winter, and my first pair of pants were obtained from mother, after pleading long and persistently. They were of the fruits of the same old hand loom, made in the old style with broad flap in front, a mile too big in the waist, and couldn't be kept up without suspenders. Our farm in those days was a two-acre patch which we planted in corn and sweet potatoes and cultivated with a little pony and a scooter plow with a wooden shovel board."

Within the next few decades, many of the early settlers had prospered sufficiently to construct fine homes for growing families. The home Judge Thomas W. Scott built in 1827 was in the style called "Carolina I" for its popularity in his home state of South Carolina. Now surrounded by ancient live oaks, the house has a wide front gallery, with rows of windows both above and below the gallery roof. One particularly noteworthy aspect of this home, called Oakland, is the two-story brick structure that houses its formal dining room and outside kitchen, separate from the house, where period kitchen equipment is used in the immense (5x7x3') cooking fireplace.

Attorney Bill McClendon, Oakland's owner shown here, with his wife is deeply dedicated to preservation efforts in the area and has made a special effort to master open-hearth cooking, learning the hard way that one doesn't cook 50 chickens on a grill right over the flames (unless one wants to have to hose down with the garden hose before being able to get close enough to turn them in the intense heat, as he had to do on that first fateful attempt).

Having often singed off his eyebrows, he has now acquired skills sufficient to cook even delicate butter beans on trivets on the hearth, adding and removing hot coals to control the temperature during cooking, and has had andirons specially forged by a West Virginia craftsman expert in recreating colonial cooking tools so that he could attach a spit to rotate venison.

His helpful hint for anyone interested in cooking as the pioneers did: have patience. "The biggest problem I have found about any open-fire cooking," Bill says, "is that you always seem to start cooking too soon—the fire always seems to be perfect for cooking just *after* you've finished. An easy solution is to cook some *andouille* or venison sausage or hoecakes, or some other *hors d'oeuvres* (and have another drink), when you would normally begin doing your major cooking." The two open-fire recipes following are Bill's.

Oakland Open-Fire Hoecakes

1 cup yellow cornmeal
1 cup flour
1 egg
4 tsp. baking powder
¼ cup oil, melted shortening, or bacon drippings
1 cup + a little milk
Handful chopped green onions
1 tsp. oregano leaves
1 tbsp. thyme leaves
½-1 tsp. Tabasco sauce
Bacon drippings

Combine cornmeal, flour, egg, baking powder, and oil. I prefer bacon drippings. I do not add salt, because of the later use of Tabasco. Add milk very sparingly so that the mixture is not soupy but is the consistency of thick cane syrup. Add a liberal amount of green onions. Firmly mash, that is, grind up, the oregano and thyme in the cupped palm of your hand. Add these herbs and Tabasco to the mixture. You need a hot fire and a black skillet close enough to the fire so that if you held your hand in the same relative position you could comfortably hold it there only for the count of "1." Grease the skillet with bacon drippings, and then cook your hoecakes the same way you would pancakes. It is rare that the first 2 or 3 turn out OK, so those are reserved for the dog or the chef. I prefer the hoecakes dark and crisp, and I use the bacon drippings liberally. These hoecakes, when hot and with a little butter applied, should be eaten with Scotch or bourbon, or a cold beer.

Super-Seasoned Pecan-Flavored Chicken

Chicken, cut up as desired
Black pepper to taste
Tabasco sauce
¼ lb. oleo
Squirt vegetable oil
2 good squirts or 1 tbsp. yellow mustard
1 good squirt or 2 tbsp. catsup
⅓ of a beer
Liberal handful chopped green onions
1 tbsp. fresh-ground thyme
1 tbsp. fresh-ground oregano leaves
5 good squirts or 1 tsp. Tabasco sauce
About 4 tbsp. Worcestershire sauce
Juice of 2 lemons
Rind of 1 lemon, chopped in about 8-10
   pieces

The secret to grilling chicken over an open fire is to wait until you have a mature fire in which there is only some slight flame, with a good bed of coals. I prefer to use wood consisting of about 70 percent pecan and about 30 percent oak, depending upon the time of year and how hot you want your fire (the more oak you use, the hotter the fire will burn, but the pecan gives the wonderful aroma and flavor). Liberally use black pepper on both sides of the chicken (do not use salt; this is important). As soon as you put the chicken on the fire, liberally douse the coals immediately under the chicken with Tabasco sauce; be careful not to smell the smoke right after this is done! I always prefer to start cooking chicken on the bony side until I have a feel for the fire. Initially, the fire should have a heat equivalent to the count of "1 and 2" before you have to pull your hand away. After the chicken has cooked 5-10 minutes on each side, in order to sear the chicken, it should then be cooked about 1 hour, turning it occasionally and basting with a sauce. The secret to the sauce is not to use any sugar or salt; this is important. To thicken the sauce you will note that I use beer. To make the sauce, mix the remaining ingredients. Bring to a boil only once, and then let it simmer while it's being used. The best kind of pot for the sauce is a three-legged trivet pot so you can set it right near the coals. During this second cooking period the heat from the fire should be reduced either by raising the chicken above the fire or by spreading out some of the coals under the chicken so that the temperature is approximately equal to the count of "1, and 2, and 3, and . . . 4." While cooking the chicken and basting it during the second stage, be careful that you don't allow the fire to flame up. Apply the sauce only during the second stage of cooking. A little sauce, together with the cooked lemon rinds left in the sauce, can be added to the top of the chicken after it has been taken off the fire and just before serving. You should count on about half a chicken per person, and serve without knives and forks.

Oakland Toffee Cookies

Graham crackers (approximately 12 whole)
2 sticks butter
1 cup dark brown sugar
1 large pkg. milk-chocolate chips
1 cup minced pecans

Line large jellyroll pan with graham crackers broken into finger sections. Melt butter, add sugar, and bring to a boil. Simmer 3 minutes. Pour over graham crackers and bake in 400-degree oven for 5 minutes. Immediately pour chocolate chips on top and spread as they melt. Sprinkle with pecans.

Bear Corners

Legend has it that in the closing years of the 18th century, the Jackson, Louisiana, area was an untamed wilderness region teeming with wildlife and originally called Bear Corners for the great numbers of wild black bears crossing nearby Thompson Creek by way of its wide raised sandbars.

Then it was called Buncombe by the founders of the town, John Ball Horton and James H. Ficklin, for their home county in the Carolinas.

Finally, the immense popularity of military hero Gen. Andrew Jackson, who reportedly encamped with his troops on the creek's banks on his way home from the War of 1812, led to the final renaming of the town for him.

By 1820 some early resident had already constructed the building that would later preserve the town's original name. For years, the tiny Bear Corners Grocery Store served a dedicated clientele right in the middle of town, with half of the building used as a residence for the mom-and-pop grocery operation.

In more recent years, though, the location was too prime to waste on a little corner grocery. Just behind it was the elegant 1830s townhouse called Milbank, attracting visitors for tours and overnight stays, and lots of those visitors were hungry.

The grocery was extensively remodeled into a wonderful restaurant complete with freestanding fireplace, views of the Milbank grounds, and stained and etched glass. Buffets were served from an Indian dugout-type serving piece made from a 300-year-old cypress log rescued from the murk of the Homochitto swamps, where it was handfelled nearly a century ago.

During the peak of popularity, the restaurant was known for chef Mary Booty's incredible desserts; recipes for a couple of the most popular are given here.

Chocolate Obsession

1½ lb. semisweet chocolate
½ cup strong coffee
3 eggs, separated
½ cup Tia Maria
6 tbsp. sugar
½ cup heavy cream
1 23-oz. pkg. brownie mix
2 tbsp. water
3 eggs
½ lb. semisweet chocolate
⅓ cup water

For filling, melt 1½ lb. chocolate with coffee in top of double boiler. When chocolate is completely melted, remove pan from heat. Beat 3 egg yolks until pale yellow and stir in chocolate. Gradually stir in Tia Maria, and cool the mixture. In separate bowl, beat 3 egg whites, gradually adding sugar until stiff. Whip cream. Gently fold whipped cream into the cooled chocolate mixture and then fold in egg whites. For cake, beat brownie mix with water and 3 eggs at medium speed until batter is smooth. Grease an 11x15" pan, line with wax paper, and then grease and lightly flour the paper, shaking off any excess flour. Spread batter evenly in pan. Bake 10-12 minutes at 350 degrees or until cake tests done. Turn cake onto a rack and peel off the paper. Lightly oil a 2-qt. Charlotte mold and line with cooled cake. Cut rounds to fit both top and bottom, piecing if necessary. Spoon chilled filling mixture into mold and top with cake round. Chill 3-4 hours or until firm. Unmold and cover with glaze. For glaze, melt ½ lb. chocolate in ⅓ cup water until smooth. Spread over top of cake and drizzle down sides. Chill again.

Buttermilk Pie

1¾ cups sugar
¼ cup flour
½ cup buttermilk
½ cup butter, melted
3 eggs
2 tbsp. lemon juice
1 tsp. vanilla extract
Pinch salt
1 9" unbaked pie shell

Combine filling ingredients in order. Mix well and pour into pie shell. Bake at 350 degrees for 1 hour or until browned. Filling is set when a light crust forms on top.

Jackson's Miss Bea and Miss Dud

Historic Jackson, Louisiana, was once known as the Athens of the South for its high standards of culture and for the large numbers of Greek Revival structures within its borders.

By 1825 what was to become Centenary College had been founded here, only one of a number of educational institutions in Jackson. At its peak, the hallowed halls of Centenary attracted several hundred students eager to study in its lecture and recitation rooms, chapel, gymnasium, library, observatory, and auditorium. Its curriculum included Greek, Latin, French, Spanish, English, logic, rhetoric, ancient and modern history, astronomy, math, chemistry, music, and natural, moral, and political philosophy, with the reading of eminent religious tracts required as a matter of course.

Discipline at Centenary was strict. Chapel was at daybreak and classes and recitation began by 8 a.m., with every waking hour thereafter to be spent at study. When school was in session, students were forbidden to miss class, leave campus, make noise in the dormitories, play musical instruments, ride horses, hunt, or shout at passersby. Which is not to say that the students didn't find time for mischief anyway, as activities proscribed by the preserved regulations attest: students were not to drink, curse, fight with clubs or knives or bare fists, steal from the townspeople, insult the faculty, or ring the college bell at night.

Besides Centenary College, what's left of it now a restored state historic site, Jackson boasts several antebellum churches and many old homes, one of the loveliest of which is Roseneath, long home of some of the town's most highly prized treasures, the venerable sisters "Miss Bea" Johnston and "Miss Dud" Acosta.

These lovely ladies had a floor-to-ceiling stack of vintage scrapbooks, some dating back even farther than the ones they made as turn-of-the-century children mixing their own paste of flour and water. They had a still wider scope of collections and recollections, which even the three ample stories of pillared Roseneath couldn't begin to contain.

Their congregate memories spanned nearly all of Jackson's 20th century, not to mention the tales of earlier days they recalled hearing as tiny tots. Put them together with history-minded contemporaries and the stories would fly. . . .

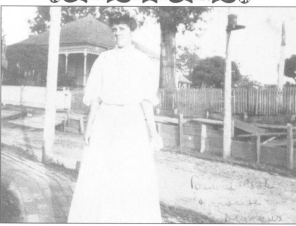

The ladies told of the baby girl who survived a scalping in the Indian attack that wiped out her family. For the rest of her life the poor girl wore caps or bonnets, until she finally drowned swimming her horse across rain-swollen Thompson Creek in a frantic quest for the laudanum to which she'd become addicted due to her constant lingering pain.

Then there was the sorrowful history of the Bride's House, next door to the Old Johnny Jones Store now housing the parish branch library, where grieving Johnny Jones himself waited in vain for his beautiful young bride-to-be. She never came, for she had been tragically swept out of the window by a cyclone.

The stories encompassed births and day-to-day living for a century, and could just as easily be expanded to illuminate death in the little town of Jackson as well; Miss Bea would haul out the journals of the area's first undertaker, detailing the measurements of each corpse and deliveries of tailor-made caskets on a two-horse wagon.

What the stories and memories and scrapbooks showed was the color and charm and character inherent in a little history-conscious spot like Jackson, where there were collectors of stories and memories and scrapbooks like Miss Bea and Miss Dud.

That color and charm and character just couldn't help rubbing off on some of the ladies' pet projects, like the Jackson Assembly, which they helped found and which, a quarter of a century later, they still supported wholeheartedly. When an evening of "Tea and Antiques" was added to complement the Assembly's annual Antique Show one spring, it was to Miss Bea that the show's chairmen turned for refreshments. And Miss Bea, as ever, added just that perfect touch to exemplify the charm and character and color of antebellum Jackson. She whipped up loaves and loaves of her famous Lemon Bread, a delightfully different tangy tea bread that she often used as Christmas presents or bestowed upon the bedridden or sickly (said one town resident, "Receiving a loaf of Miss Bea's Lemon Bread almost makes it worthwhile being sick!"). Miss Bea and Miss Dud are gone but not forgotten, having left a rich legacy of treasures and stories and recipes.

Miss Bea Johnston's Lemon Bread

1 cup oleo
2 cups sugar
4 eggs
3 cups flour, sifted
½ tsp. salt
½ tsp. baking soda
1 cup buttermilk
Grated rind of 1 lemon
1 cup nuts, chopped
Juice of 3 lemons
1 cup powdered sugar

Cream oleo and sugar. Add eggs one at a time; blend. Sift together flour, salt, and soda. Add alternately with buttermilk, lemon rind, and nuts. Pour into 2 greased 9x5" loaf pans and bake 1 hour at 350 degrees. While bread bakes, combine lemon juice and powdered sugar. When bread is baked, pour lemon syrup over hot bread. Can be frozen.

Roseneath Cheese Wafers

½ lb. sharp cheddar
½ lb. butter
2 cups flour
1 egg
50 pecan halves
Salt to taste

Cut cheese and butter into flour. Blend well. Roll out ½" thick and cut into rounds. Brush tops with beaten egg. Top each with pecan half. Bake at 425 degrees for 12 minutes. Remove from oven. While hot, sprinkle with salt. Makes 50.

Milbank

Elegant Greek Revival Milbank, with its massive 30-foot Doric columns and double galleries, stands on Bank Street right in the heart of Jackson, Louisiana, redolent with history and romantic charm.

The oldest commercial structure in town, its site was once owned by Jackson founders John Horton and James Ficklin. Early banking house for the Clinton-Port Hudson Railroad (1836), Milbank over the years would be used not only as a private home but also as Union troop barracks during the Civil War, public assembly hall, apothecary, millinery shop, hotel, ballroom, and newspaper publishing house.

Now furnished with fine antiques, it is once again accessible to the public through tours, receptions, special parties with meals, and Bed & Breakfast operations.

This Blueberry Banana Nut Bread is a special treat prepared for overnight guests at Milbank, who are served a full plantation breakfast in the main dining room. Milbank's curator says the abundance of blueberries grown locally ensures that this tasty bread is a regular feature on the B&B breakfast menu.

Blueberry Banana Nut Bread

3 cups all-purpose flour
2 cups sugar
1 tsp. baking soda
1 tsp. salt
1 tsp. cinnamon
1 cup chopped pecans
3 eggs
1½ cups vegetable oil
3 cups mashed bananas
1 cup fresh or frozen blueberries
1 tsp. vanilla extract

Combine dry ingredients. Stir in nuts and set aside. Combine remaining ingredients and add to dry ingredients, stirring just until batter is moistened. Spoon batter into 2 greased and floured 9x5x3" loaf pans. Bake at 350 degrees for 1 hour or until done. Cool 10 minutes before removing from pans. Remove to wire racks to cool completely. Freezes well.

Linwood

One of East Feliciana Parish's most historically significant homes, Linwood was built between 1836 and 1848 by prominent planter and retired military man Gen. Albert Gallatin Carter to duplicate the galleried Greek Revival family seat in South Carolina. An early agricultural center, it was ideally situated for the shipment of its produce, located just 3 miles from the important river port of Port Hudson, which connected its population and produce with the steamboats plying the Mississippi, and was also directly on the line of the old Clinton-Port Hudson Railroad.

During the 48-day siege of Port Hudson, as the Confederate forces struggled to keep open their last remaining gateway to the world and Union forces struggled just as determinedly to capture that remaining link of the Mississippi River, some of the bloodiest action of the Civil War took place.

With Linwood so close to the fighting, it was only natural that it should almost continually fly from its front galleries the yellow flag signifying the home's use as a hospital. First the Confederates and later Union forces filled the house and nearby sugar house with wounded and dying soldiers, surgeons operating as best they could on the kitchen table. This usage, plus urgent communiqués from General Carter's brother, a Federal general, saved Linwood from the torch of destruction.

While the area was still held by Confederate forces during the early days of the fighting, Linwood served as a safe harbor for family members fleeing the Federal occupation of Baton Rouge. It was during this period, 1862-63, that a 20-year-old belle named Sarah Morgan (later Dawson) wrote portions of her moving book, *A Confederate Girl's Diary,* while seeking refuge with relatives here. Sarah was one of 7 lone women who watched in terror from the upstairs back windows the "shooting stars of flame" from the river bombardment of March 15, 1863.

After the war, Linwood resumed its peaceful agricultural pursuits, with early crops like sugarcane, indigo, and tobacco being supplanted by cotton and, later, dairy and beef cattle. During the turn-of-the-century occupation by General Carter's innovative grandson, a new 4-gable roof replaced the earlier simpler one and a rare gravity-fed water system provided the unheard-of luxury of indoor running water, while a small gasoline engine ran the water pump, circular saw, corn crusher, cream separator, barrel churn, and grindstone.

For most of the 20th century Linwood was associated with the Dougherty family, whose meals Frances Dougherty recalls as often being made with "delicious rat cheese from Mr. Willie McKowen's store, fresh milk from the dairy, fresh homemade butter, and homegrown vegetables." These teacakes, she says, were favorites at Linwood in the late 1800s and were served at the dedication ceremony for the historical marker there one very hot July not long ago.

Old-Fashioned Teacakes from Linwood

2 sticks butter
1½ cups sugar
2 eggs
1½ tsp. vanilla extract
4 cups plain flour
1 tsp. baking soda

Cream butter and sugar in bowl with large spoon. Add eggs and vanilla. Mix flour and soda, then add to mixture. Let sit about 2 hours. Shape round and refrigerate until ready to bake. Then slice very thin. Spray cookie sheet lightly with cooking spray. Place slices on sheet and bake about 10 minutes at 375 degrees. Wrapped in foil, these will keep for weeks in refrigerator.

Asphodel

It was in the 1830s, that cotton-rich era when courtly planters built stately mansions throughout the antebellum South, that Benjamin Kendrick began Asphodel for his beloved wife, Caroline, calling this flowering of Greek Revival architecture after Homer's "Asphodel meadow of vast extent in the fields of Elysium." When Kendrick died the year the home was completed, Asphodel found a new master in his young daughter's husband, one Colonel Fluker.

Tragedy struck again with the Civil War several decades later, bringing the death of Fluker and Yankee soldiers spreading out from the nearby Battle of Port Hudson in search of food, setting the house afire after Mrs. Fluker and the children barricaded themselves in the library. They could only pray that the fire would go out, and it did.

During the years of genteel poverty following the war, the Misses Smith, spinster sisters, kept the place together, never leaving the grounds, not even at death.

In 1958 the Robert Couhig family moved into Asphodel, sharing the historic home but soon conceiving the idea for an entire Bed and Breakfast visitors' complex elsewhere on the property. Picturesque Asphodel Village opened for meals and overnight guests in 1966, providing urban guests with a taste of the pleasures of a relaxed country lifestyle.

Accommodations were offered in tree-shaded townhouses and quaint cottages, while gourmet meals, always accompanied by the famous home-made Asphodel bread, were served in the historic Levy House, 1830s home of a Jewish cotton merchant that was moved onto the Asphodel property. Nature trails crisscrossed the surrounding wooded acreage, designated as a bird sanctuary, and there were also a swimming pool, hot tub, and stocked ponds for fishing. Additional space was provided by the turn-of-the-century railroad depot moved from McManus Crossing.

This collection of structures somehow blended into East Feliciana's best established country inn, a special place to relax and prop your feet on the gallery rail, listen to the birds calling, and watch the fireflies lighting the gathering darkness . . . a place for the harried city dweller to restore his soul. Now under new ownership, Asphodel continues to offer the same hospitality.

The late Marcelle ("Nootsie") Couhig was a dynamic personality whose recipes were as scattered with humorous asides as was her daily conversation. She was always traveling at a hundred miles an hour, so it's no wonder that the home-made bread for which Asphodel was so famous was made according to a recipe containing some short-cuts. She always said the recipe evolved because "I was too lazy to go through all the kneading, turning, twisting that it takes to really make bread. Besides, I always think of it too late. So here is a fast easy bread that turns out to be pretty good."

Asphodel Bread

5 cups biscuit mix
4 tbsp. sugar
½ tsp. salt
2 tbsp. or env. yeast
2 cups warm milk
4 eggs
¼ tsp. cream of tartar

Sift into a very large bowl the biscuit mix, sugar, and salt. Soften yeast in milk; make sure milk is only warm, as too much heat will kill the yeast. Beat eggs with cream of tartar until thoroughly broken up. Combine milk and eggs; pour into dry ingredients. Stir until well mixed. This is a heavy, sticky mixture, so be sure it's well blended. Cover with damp dishtowel or seal with plastic wrap and set aside in warm place. A yeast mixture rises best at about 80 degrees. When double in bulk, stir down and fill oiled loaf pans about halfway. Again double the size before baking at 350 degrees about 20 minutes. Serve very hot. This bread freezes quite well, but remember to allow to completely thaw before reheating, or you may be serving a beautifully heated exterior with a nasty frozen inside.

Asphodel Corned Beef Hash

1 pkg. dry Irish potato granules (about 1 cup)
1 can corned beef, chopped
1 cup minced green onions including tops
Salt and freshly cracked black pepper to taste
Butter

Reconstitute the potatoes according to box directions. Add other ingredients and stir well. Pat into cakes. Dredge in flour and fry in butter. Try this with poached egg on top. Instead of frying, this may be pressed into buttered ramekins; bake in hot oven until edges begin to brown, then drop a raw egg in center and return to oven until egg reaches desired doneness.

Asphodel Coq au Vin

½ lb. bacon
2 fryer chickens or 1 large hen
Salt and black pepper to taste
2 tbsp. flour
1 large bunch green onions, chopped
3 cups Burgundy wine
3 cloves garlic, pressed
1 tsp. dried thyme leaves
¼ cup chopped parsley

In heavy Dutch oven, fry bacon and set aside, keeping fat in pot. Cut chicken into serving-size pieces. Salt and pepper chicken. Brown chicken in bacon fat. Set aside. If you still have a good bit of bacon fat, pour some off, leaving enough to brown the flour for the roux. Add flour and stir constantly until nicely browned (that's a roux). Add green onions and mix well. Add wine and stir until thickened. Crumble bacon and return to pot along with chicken, garlic, and thyme. Cook until tender. If you need more liquid, add water; you have enough wine already. About 5 minutes before serving, taste for salt and pepper and add parsley.

Asphodel Dirty Rice

3-4 strips bacon
1 cup chopped onions
6 chicken livers, cleaned and chopped
1 cup raw long-grain rice
½ cup chopped green onions including tops
2 cloves garlic, minced
½ tsp. dried thyme leaves
¼ cup chopped parsley
3 cups water
Salt
Pepper, preferably cayenne

In heavy Dutch oven or skillet, fry bacon and set aside, keeping fat in pot. Over low heat, fry onions in bacon fat until just turning brown. Add chicken livers and stir around until not wet looking. Add rice and cook, stirring, until rice acquires a nutty, light-brown color. Add green onions, garlic, thyme, parsley, and water and cook until rice is done. Add salt and pepper to taste. Be careful of overcooking. It should fall apart on the fork just as well-cooked rice without seasoning does.

Jackson Assembly Antique Show

Remember back when a visit to Grandma's was pure magic? When there was time to share the blessings and the heartache of everyday life? When the first daffodil of spring was a welcomed occasion for rejoicing? When mealtimes were loud loving intergenerational family gatherings? When there was nothing more pressing to do of a hot summer's day than stretch out on the pond bank with cane pole and can of worms? When giggling cousins met the past draped in musty gowns and ghastly hats from the attic? When the hatching of fledglings from a flower-pot wren's nest marked the culmination of weeks of watchful anticipation, and when a barefoot romp through the twilight to catch fireflies brought to a close another enjoyable day? When snuggling down under a heavy patchwork quilt in a 4-poster bed to listen to stories of past childhoods in the flickering firelight was a final moment to treasure in a day filled with the memories of a lifetime?

If you remember, then you know what life is like in the little rural town of Jackson, Louisiana, a place to savor the seasons of nature and observe the cycles of life.

One cycle may be observed each springtime, when as surely as swallows returning to Capistrano, antiques lovers flock to this historic little East Feliciana town as soon as the first daffodils poke sunny yellow heads above frosty beds and ripening azalea buds brighten the landscape with brilliant hues.

Every year for more than a quarter of a century, the arrival of springtime has brought another eagerly anticipated event, the Jackson Assembly Antique Show and Sale, featuring the select displays of carefully chosen antiques dealers from across the Southern United States.

The show takes place in late March in two huge historic buildings purchased and restored by The Assembly with funds generated by previous antiques shows. The Old McKowen Store, built in 1835, was once the busy commercial center of antebellum Jackson, supplying the great outlying plantations and eventually expanding into the more recently built Pipes-McKowen Store next door, which dates from 1904.

The Old McKowen Store's upper level, made of cypress and heart-pine, once housed a Model-T

dealership as well as a thriving general mercantile store and post office. In the brick basement, the dirt floor supported displays of wagons and buggies until it became the shop where mechanics kept the area's first automobiles in running order. They also worked on the early airplane flown into the area by a barnstorming young aviator named Charles Lindbergh, who offered adventurous locals the thrill of a ride for $5.

Now this basement area, nestled right into the hillside with floor and walls of old brick and exposed beams of hand-hewn poplar, is set with picnic tables covered by gay red-and-white checkered cloths. After working up an appetite admiring displays of polished mahogany and rosewood, gleaming silver and crystal, delicate china and fine artwork, vintage clothing and jewelry, and collectibles of every sort, visitors can enjoy homemade fare prepared by some of the best cooks around.

Here hungry guests are fed under the watchful eyes of dedicated workers who've been involved since the first antiques show in 1965, when the 10 gallons of gumbo and soup that had been supposed to last all three days of the show were devoured before noon on opening day. Now the experienced cooks prepare food enough for nearly 3,000 visitors, the proceeds providing roughly half the profits from the entire antiques show, used to restore historic buildings and promote tourism and preservation in Jackson.

It takes over 100 gallons of homemade seafood gumbo (that's estimated to be 2½ *barrels,* made in batches using a 20-gallon crawfish pot and boat-paddle stirrer), 15 gallons of vegetable soup, more than 12 gallons of chili, 65 pecan pies, 50 cakes, and 70 chess pies in addition to lots of mouthwatering cookies, candies, and cakes. Some of the most popular recipes are given here.

Carlotta Lindsey's Basic Gumbo

¾ cup flour
¾ cup oil
1 large can tomato sauce
1 lb. fresh okra
1 large bell pepper, chopped
1 cup chopped celery
1 large onion, chopped
1 large clove garlic, minced
½ large can tomatoes
½ cup chopped fresh parsley
1 gal. water
1 jar beef bouillon cubes
Salt and black and cayenne pepper to taste
1 lb. shrimp
½ lb. crabmeat

Make a dark roux with the flour and oil. Add tomato sauce and stir until dark. Put in okra; cook until it integrates. Add other vegetables and cook until soft. To water, add bouillon. Let come to boil. Taste. Add first mixture to this. Bring to rolling boil, then reduce heat and let boil 1½ hours. Add salt and peppers. Add seafood ½ hour before taking off stove. Makes 1 gal.

Velma Connell's Chili

5 lb. ground meat
10 tbsp. flour
10 tbsp. oil
3-4 bay leaves
5 large onions, chopped
2½-3 bell peppers, chopped
10 cups water
10 tbsp. chili powder
5 cans tomato sauce
5 cans tomato soup
5 tsp. cumin or oregano
10 cloves garlic, chopped
Salt and black pepper to taste

Cook meat until it turns gray. Add flour and mix well. Cook 10 minutes. Add all other ingredients. Continue cooking until desired consistency. Check seasonings and add more salt and pepper if needed. Makes 2 gal.

Viola Roberts' Fig Cake

1 cup butter (do not substitute)
2 cups sugar
3 eggs
1 tsp. baking soda
⅔ cup buttermilk
2¼ cups flour
1 cup chopped fig preserves
1 tsp. cinnamon
1 tsp. nutmeg
1 tsp. ground cloves
1 tsp. ground allspice
1 tsp. salt
1 cup chopped pecans

Cream butter and sugar. Add eggs, one at a time, beating well after each addition. Stir soda into buttermilk. Add alternately with flour to butter mixture. Add figs, seasonings, and nuts. Pour into well-greased tube-cake pan. Place in 350-degree oven for 1 hour. Do not open door until time is up. Cool on wire rack.

Lucille Giroir's Peanut Butter Fudge

¾ cup sugar
2 tbsp. instant cocoa
½ stick butter or oleo
Enough evaporated milk to dissolve, about ¾ cup
2 tsp. vanilla extract
1 jar marshmallow creme
1 18-oz. jar peanut butter, creamy or crunchy

Cook sugar, cocoa, butter, and milk in saucepan until soft ball forms. Add vanilla and marshmallow creme. Add peanut butter. Mix well. Pour into buttered pan. Cut into squares when cool.

Claudia Connell's Nutmeg Cookies

2 eggs
2 cups sugar
5-5½ cups flour, measured before sifting
1 cup oil and 1 stick butter, heated and mixed
½-1 whole nutmeg, grated
1 tsp. vanilla extract
2 tsp. baking soda
½ tsp. salt

Beat eggs, add sugar gradually, and add about 1 cup flour. Mix. Add hot shortening. Then add the rest of the flour, nutmeg, and vanilla. While dough is warm, place in cookie barrel press. Using bar, press out long rows on greased cookie pans. Bake in 400-degree oven until light brown. Remove from oven and cut into desired lengths while hot before they harden. Store in airtight containers.

Glencoe

Girdled with galleries and topped by turrets, gables, and dormers like so many candles on a flamboyant birthday cake, Glencoe has been called the finest example of Queen Anne Victorian Gothic architecture in the state of Louisiana. Now a private property, for years it was a country inn operated by an innkeeper just as amusing and flamboyant as the house itself.

Set on more than 1,000 acres in the gently rolling hills of East Feliciana Parish, the house was originally constructed in 1870 by Robert Emerson Thompson, a progressive agriculturist who was among the first to raise cattle instead of cotton and row crops, and who had his own pepper mill to cure peppers raised for the hot sauce industry. He also served as agent for the 101 Ranch in Oklahoma City, purchasing livestock for the ranch and supplying horses for troops during the Spanish-American War with fellow agent Tom Mix, the famed silent movie star who visited at Glencoe.

Just 28 years after the Glencoe house was built, Thompson and his family were visiting friends at Oakland Plantation nearby. The year was 1898. They returned home to find Glencoe completely destroyed by fire.

Thompson promised his grieving wife he'd exactly recreate the home on the same foundations, and this he had done by 1903, with this exception: the original home had been covered with cedar shake shingles, but he promised to shingle the new one with "silver dollars," explaining the present roof's galvanized shingles.

Five different shapes of fish-scale shingles decorate the house walls, and Victorian fretwork and trim abound. The front entrance is adorned by 36 columns of Doric style, trimmed with Ionic capitals; side galleries have colonettes and more fanciful trim.

Former innkeeper, the late W. Jerome Westerfield, as innovative in the kitchen and bar as ever Robert Emerson Thompson was in the agricultural field, provided some recipes closely associated with Glencoe, taken from Ina Scott Thompson Smitherman's 1925 book, *The Louisiana Plantation Cookbook*. Mrs. Smitherman was one of six Thompson daughters who called Glencoe home, and her cookbook was a treasure trove of recipes and kitchen hints running the gamut from the proper way to cut up a chicken to the distasteful necessity for boiling crawfish alive. Her niece, Margaret Carruth Ross Evans, recalled riding by carriage from her own home to Glencoe not long after the turn of the century, and always being greeted by her grandmother Martha Emily Scott Thompson with a slice of freshly baked pound cake served with a hot lemon sauce; the only girlchild among 9 grandchildren, "Miss Marnie" lovingly referred to her grandparents as "Mama Cake" and "Daddy Thompson."

Glencoe Plantation Lemon Sauce

1 tbsp. flour
½ cup sugar
½ pt. water, boiling
Grated rind and juice of 1 lemon
1 egg, well beaten

Add flour to sugar; mix in saucepan and add boiling water. Stir until boiling. Add the lemon rind and juice. Pour, while hot, into egg, beating all the while. Orange or vanilla may be used in place of lemon, and for rich puddings, add 1 tbsp. butter, at the last.

Glencoe Scotch Scones

2 cups flour
1 cup milk
1 egg
1 tsp. salt
1 tbsp. butter
2 tsp. baking powder

Mix ingredients. Take teaspoon and drop small bits on a buttered pan or aluminum board and bake. The lightest of all breads. Bake in quick oven and serve with afternoon tea.

Glencoe Crawfish Bisque

1 gal. large live crawfish
2 spoons lard
2 spoons flour
Seasonings to taste
1 tbsp. butter
⅓ loaf bread, grated into crumbs
Green onions, chopped
Parsley, chopped
Celery, chopped
1 egg yolk
1 tbsp. butter

Wash crawfish in salt water 4 times, then place them in boiling water and boil them alive; very cruel but the only way to kill. They will turn red when done. Cool and break off the tails, peel like shrimp, and crack claws to remove meat. Chop fine. Place all heads and cracked claws back on heat to boil and extract the fat from heads. Boil well and strain and set aside, reserving liquor. Make a thick roux of lard and flour; when it is well browned, pour into this enough of the boiled liquor to make a bisque, season highly, and let boil again for 2 hours. Take the heads and see that they are clean inside. Place in a skillet 1 tbsp. butter and pour into this the crawfish meat and juice. Soak breadcrumbs in water and squeeze dry. Add to crawfish. Add green onions, parsley, celery, a little water to thin the dressing, egg, and 1 tbsp. butter. Stuff every head and float on bowls of the bisque just before serving.

Feliciana Peach Festival

In 1982 an early-summer festival was started to celebrate East Feliciana's coveted crop of succulent homegrown peaches. Also celebrated were the hardworking peach farmers, hardy survivors who persevered in the face of late frosts and untimely freezes nipping tender buds at just the wrong time.

Several days of family fun at the Feliciana Peach Festival included beauty pageants, poster contest, sports, midway games and rides, runs, live bands and other entertainment, and arts and crafts.

But center stage was always held by the plump and juicy Feliciana peach, with peach dishes to sample after the cooking contest was judged, area growers furnishing fresh fruit from booths, and plenty of refreshments like peach cobbler, peach ice cream, peach tarts, peach pies, and even peach daiquiris.

Now, Louisiana State University has its experimental peach farm still functional in the area, but many of the privately owned farms fell upon hard financial times and are no longer in business.

Here are some of the prize-winners in past festival peach cooking contests.

Nelwynne Tynes' Peach Ice Cream

3 cups sugar
6 tbsp. flour
6 eggs, beaten
1½ qt. milk
1 pt. whipping cream
2 pt. half & half
1 tbsp. vanilla extract
3 cups pureed peaches

Mix sugar and flour. Add eggs and mix well. Stir in milk, cream, and half & half and mix thoroughly. Pour mixture into a granite pan, place over water, and cook until velvety. Stir constantly while cooking. Remove from heat and cool; best if cooled in refrigerator overnight. When ready to freeze, pour into freezer bucket and add vanilla and peaches. Follow directions for freezing ice cream.

Connie Landry's Frozen Fruit Salad

1 can condensed milk
1 8-oz. pkg. cream cheese, softened
12-oz. container whipped topping
1 cup shredded coconut
1 cup walnut pieces
2 cups sliced peaches
2 cups sliced strawberries
2 bananas, sliced
1 large can crushed pineapple, drained
8-10 cherries, chopped

Mix condensed milk, cream cheese, and whipped topping. Stir in remaining ingredients and freeze overnight.

Juliana Delee's Peaches-n-Cream Pie

1 can condensed milk
¼ cup lemon juice
3 cups peeled, sliced peaches
8-oz. container whipped topping
Graham-cracker crust
Peach slices

Mix milk and lemon juice well. Fold in 3 cups peaches. Add whipped topping and pour into crust. Decorate with peach slices. Chill. Serves 6.

James Soileau's Cajun Jubilee

⅓ cup flour
1¼ tsp. salt
1 tsp. black pepper
1¼ tsp. marjoram
2 tbsp. chopped fresh parsley
4 deboned chicken breasts, cut into small chunks
½ cup milk or cream
2 tbsp. butter
¼ cup oil
¾ cup chopped onion
¼ cup lemon juice
1 tbsp. honey
1 cup peach syrup
3 canned peach halves, pureed in blender

Mix flour, salt, pepper, marjoram, and parsley. Dip chicken in milk and roll in the seasoned flour. In a large skillet, heat butter and oil, and brown chicken until crisp. Transfer to a 2-qt. baking dish in 1 layer. Sauté onion and sprinkle over chicken. Add remaining seasoned flour to skillet and brown. Add lemon juice, honey, and peach syrup, cooking 5 minutes or until thickened. Pour peaches and the sauce from the skillet over chicken. Bake 45 minutes at 350 degrees.

ST. FRANCISVILLE AND THE WEST FELICIANA PARISH AREA OF LOUISIANA

Plantation Country Cookbook

The culinary practices and recipe files of any particular place reveal a great deal of the history and influences of that area. And when the history and influences are as varied and as fascinating as those of West Feliciana Parish in Louisiana, a cookbook based on local recipes, like the Women's Service League's *Plantation Country,* is bound to be just as interesting, its recipes reflecting the diverse cultural influences that converged during the formative years and were enriched with each new wave of immigrants.

Originally a rowdy shantytown that grew up among the riverbank willows to offer shelter to the flatboatmen navigating the perilous Mississippi River during the 1700s, the settlement called Bayou Sara grew and prospered as cotton was grown in immense quantities on inland plantations and transported after 1832 aboard America's first standard-gauge railroad line for shipment from the port there. Inns, taverns, and then fine hotels with equally fine dining rooms sprang up to cater to the needs of steamboat travelers and businessmen, serving not just local produce but the finest foodstuffs of the world fresh off the sailing ships and sent upriver from New Orleans.

By 1850 Bayou Sara was the largest Mississippi River port between New Orleans and Memphis. Packet steamers and cargo vessels laden with the produce of the entire Mississippi Valley docked at Bayou Sara's wharves, taking on immense cargoes of cotton for shipment to factors in New Orleans and discharging all the fine furnishings and finished goods the wealthy planters imported to beautify their surroundings. A regular fleet of luxurious steamboats picked up Feliciana folk bound for New Orleans and thence the world, and dockside warehouses stacked with bales of cotton stretched along the riverbanks for one solid mile.

The determination of the early residents rebuilt the settlement after such devastating tragedies as an 1855 fire that destroyed more than 50 mercantile establishments and, less than a decade later, destructive shelling by Union soldiers who torched the town during the Civil War. Old-timers still recall the tragic day in 1912 when the levee protecting Bayou Sara broke and the river waters, swelled beyond their banks by melting snow and ice upriver, rushed into town with a great roar, sweeping away most of the houses; this and subsequent

floods and fires would be the death of Bayou Sara, now just desolate flat floodplain swept clean by floodwaters still.

The town of St. Francisville would prove more permanent after it developed just above Bayou Sara atop the bluffs, where the first lots were sold in 1807. Its muddy thoroughfares were strewn with stumps and clogged with cattle drives and other obstacles to wagon traffic, but soon teemed with trade as well.

This oldest town chartered in the Florida Parishes quickly became the social, cultural, religious, and commercial center for the surrounding cotton-rich plantation country and would have both a newspaper and library by 1812. It could also boast of having its own fine hotel, built in 1809 by public subscription and serving as legislative chamber of the short-lived independent Republic of West Florida the following year; hotel management advertised splendid dinners complete with "flasks of wine, with a Turkey, Beef, and other Trimmings," served with Malaga grapes and oranges and marzipan.

Grand tours of the Continent broadened home-grown tastes, while the homelands of other early settlers lent lasting culinary influences too, as German, English, Irish, Scottish, Creole, French, and Italian dishes found their ways onto dinner tables in both Bayou Sara and St. Francisville. Family plantations in the nearby country furnished home-grown staples for many a townhouse table, supplemented by hothouse fruits and vegetables forced out of season and by fresh game and seafood supplied by the intrepid hunters and fishermen of each family.

Reflecting all these varied influences, the *Plantation Country* cookbook lives up to its introductory promise as truly a "celebration of memories and experiences, adventures and introductions," and is available by mail from the Women's Service League, Box 1010, St. Francisville, LA 70775. The proceeds are used by the Women's Service League to finance a variety of worthwhile community projects, including a playground, public landscaping, disaster assistance, annual Christmas parade, and summer story hour for small children.

To introduce new editions of their popular cookbook, the Women's Service League members have often held Tasters' Teas featuring prepared foods from the book. Here are some favorites.

Martha Jones' Spinach Crabmeat Dip

1 10-oz. pkg. frozen chopped spinach
1 bunch green onions and tops, chopped
4 tbsp. butter
⅓ cup grated Parmesan cheese
2 7-oz. cans crabmeat

Cook spinach and drain well. Sauté green onions in butter. Mix all ingredients, heat, and serve in chafing dish with crackers or large corn chips.

Janet Rinaudo's Chicken-Almond Casserole

Salt and black pepper to taste
10 chicken breasts, deboned and skinned
½ cup flour
½ cup oleo
½ cup white wine
1 10¾-oz. can cream of celery soup
1 10¾-oz. can cream of mushroom soup
½ cup grated Parmesan cheese
¼ cup slivered almonds

Salt and pepper chicken, coat with flour, and brown in oleo. Remove chicken to 9x13x2" baking dish. Pour wine mixed with soups over chicken. Top with cheese and almonds. Bake at 350 degrees for 40 minutes.

Joan C. Newton's Walnut-Sweet Potato Torte

½ cup California walnuts
1 cup sifted all-purpose flour
¼ cup packed brown sugar
⅓ cup butter
1 3-oz. pkg. cream cheese
1 large egg
1 1-lb. can sweet potatoes, mashed
1 14-oz. can sweetened condensed milk
1 tsp. pumpkin pie spice
½ tsp. salt
1 cup hot water
Whipped cream
California walnut halves to decorate

Chop walnuts medium fine. Combine flour and brown sugar. Cut in butter until mixture resembles coarse meal; add walnuts. Press firmly in an even layer over bottom of 6 ¼x10x1 ¼" baking dish. Bake at 350 degrees for about 20 minutes, until lightly browned. Meanwhile, soften cream cheese. Beat in egg. Add sweet potatoes, milk, spice, and salt. Beat until smooth. Stir in water. Pour into baked walnut crust and return to oven. Bake about 50 minutes longer, until filling is barely set in center. Cool thoroughly before cutting. Decorate each piece with a swirl of whipped cream and walnut half.

Hattie Carmenia's Squash with Crawfish

6 medium yellow summer squash, sliced
2 eggs
½ cup chopped green onions
⅓ cup chopped celery
3 tbsp. butter
½ cup milk
1 cup peeled crawfish tails
About 1 cup breadcrumbs
Salt and black pepper to taste

Boil squash in unsalted water until tender. Drain and mash well. Add eggs and mix well. Sauté onions and celery in butter until soft. Add milk, crawfish, and breadcrumbs and mix well. Season with salt and pepper. Put in casserole dish and sprinkle top with breadcrumbs. Bake at 350 degrees until brown.

Marsha Lindsey's Cranberry Wine Sauce

1 tsp. cinnamon
Grated rind of 1 lemon
¼ tsp. ground cloves
½ cup port wine
Dash nutmeg
3 tbsp. sugar
1 1-lb. can whole cranberry sauce

Combine all ingredients except cranberry sauce and simmer about 5 minutes. Add cranberry sauce, stir with wire whisk until smooth, and heat thoroughly. Serve as sauce for baked or roasted lamb. Makes 1 pt.

Ellen Bennett's Hummingbird Cake

3 cups all-purpose flour
2 cups sugar
1 tsp. salt
1 tsp. baking soda
1 tsp. cinnamon
3 eggs, beaten
1½ cups oil
1½ tsp. vanilla extract
1 8-oz. can crushed pineapple, undrained
1 cup chopped pecans
2 cups mashed bananas
1 8-oz. pkg. cream cheese, softened
½ cup butter or oleo, softened
1 16-oz. pkg. powdered sugar
1 tsp. vanilla extract
½ cup chopped pecans

Combine flour, sugar, salt, soda, and cinnamon in large mixing bowl; add eggs and oil, stirring until dry ingredients are moistened. Do not beat. Stir in 1½ tsp. vanilla, pineapple, 1 cup pecans, and bananas. Bake in greased and floured Bundt or tube pan at 350 degrees for 45-60 minutes. Frost with frosting made by combining cream cheese with butter and creaming until smooth. Add sugar and beat until light and fluffy. Stir in vanilla and pecans. If making layered cake, double icing recipe.

Catholic Church

I t was the high bluffs safe from the marauding floodwaters of the mighty Mississippi that first attracted the Spanish Capuchin monks from Pointe Coupee to the other side of the river where St. Francisville sits today. Here on the towering headlands, the brothers came together, acquired a personal grant of land from the king of Spain, and established a short-lived monastery and a long-used burial ground. The date of the land grant, where the old Catholic cemetery remains, is set between 1773 and 1785.

After the site was claimed by the Capuchins, the king of Spain sent Irish priests to minister to the Catholics among the predominantly English speaking settlers of West Florida. By the 1850s the ecclesiastical parish of the Felicianas had been established, with Jackson the priests' residence and St. Francisville a mission visited only at intervals.

West Feliciana's early Catholics met for mass conducted by missionaries or visiting priests in Bayou Sara's Market House until it was burned during the Civil War, after which they met in private homes, the parish courthouse, or rented rooms. It was not until 1871 that land was acquired by the congregation, and even then the high spot on what is now called Catholic Hill was purchased from J. F. Irvine for intended use only as a cemetery.

A visit that same year by the archbishop of New Orleans inspired the congregation to erect its own church building. Plans were drawn by Civil War general P. G. T. Beauregard and executed by English architect Charles N. Gibbons, who also built nearby Grace Episcopal Church.

Dedicated under the patronage of St. Mary of Mount Carmel, the simple frame structure was built of native woods, with immense towering pillars and beams of solid longleaf pine and doors of cypress.

118

It was its location, set atop bluffs towering more than a hundred feet high in places, that attracted the area's first permanent settlers, but that same location in recent years gave Our Lady of Mount Carmel Catholic Church its share of problems as well, with erosion increasing and huge chunks of earth sloughing off the bluffs upon which the church sits.

Thus was born Festival in the Country to "save the hill," a weekend of family fun sponsored by the church several years in a row to raise funds needed for re-grading and drainage work. Besides lots of rides, games, crafts, and the like, the bulk of the proceeds were usually raised at an auction, at which an eclectic collection of donated items was auctioned off to the highest bidder in lively fashion.

And every year at the auction, there was one item that always commanded a staggeringly high price, and with good reason. That was the crawfish dinner prepared by Betty Rinaudo, locally famed as a marvelous cook always ready to turn her talents toward helping others, whether cooking tempting treats for the sick, preparing refreshments for receptions and all kinds of gala get-togethers, or furnishing items for charity bake sales.

Betty Rinaudo's crawfish dinners often went for as much as a thousand dollars; one year her dinner for 11 couples brought a staggering $1,100 to benefit the restoration effort. Included on her menu were before-dinner drinks, seafood gumbo with crawfish, fried crawfish tails, crawfish étouffée on rice, yellow squash cooked with crawfish tails, Sensation Salad, green beans, buttered rolls, strawberry roll, amaretto freeze, and wine. The dinner required a good 15 to 20 pounds of crawfish tails alone. The verdict from the guests? Worth every penny, and then some!

Betty Rinaudo's crawfish recipes follow, as well as one concocted by one of her protegees, young attorney Bob Butler, who has often cooked with Betty for special events; his recipe is similar to hers, though it includes a few short-cuts gleaned from other versions of étouffée preparation.

Betty Rinaudo's Fried Crawfish Tails

1 lb. peeled crawfish tails
Salt to taste
Tabasco sauce
1 cup buttermilk
2 cloves garlic, minced
2 cups flour
Black pepper to taste
Oil

Season crawfish with salt and Tabasco. Add to buttermilk and garlic; soak at least 1 hour. Season flour with salt and pepper in a paper bag. Put in crawfish and shake well to coat. In deep-fat fryer, heat oil to 350 degrees and add crawfish when hot. Fry until golden brown, about 1 minute.

Betty Rinaudo's Yellow Squash with Crawfish

1 cup chopped green onion
½ cup chopped bell pepper
1 stick butter
4 cups sliced yellow squash
Salt and black pepper to taste
Tabasco sauce
½ cup dry white wine
½ lb. peeled crawfish tails

Sauté onion and bell pepper in butter. Add squash and seasonings. Boil for 5 minutes, then add wine and crawfish tails. Simmer for 5-7 minutes or until squash is tender. Serves 4.

Betty Rinaudo's Crawfish Etouffée

1 stick butter
4-6 tbsp. flour
1 tbsp. tomato paste
¾ cup chopped bell pepper
1 cup chopped onion
¾ cup chopped celery
2 cloves garlic, minced
2-3 cups chicken broth
½ can Ro-tel tomatoes, chopped in blender
Salt to taste
Cayenne and black pepper to taste
Tabasco sauce
1 lb. peeled crawfish tails
½ cup chopped green onions
½ cup chopped parsley

Melt butter in a heavy pot and add flour. Make a light roux. Add tomato paste, bell pepper, onion, celery, and garlic. Cook, stirring, about 5 minutes. Add chicken broth and tomatoes. Add salt, peppers, and Tabasco. Simmer about 30 minutes. Add crawfish and simmer about 10 minutes. Then add green onions and parsley for brief period. Serves 4-6.

Bob Butler's Crawfish Etouffée

1 stick oleo
6 tbsp. flour
4 green onion bottoms, chopped
½ onion, chopped
2 tbsp. chopped bell pepper
½ 10-oz. can Ro-tel tomatoes, pureed
2 cups water
2 lb. peeled crawfish tails
Juice of ½ lemon
4 green onion tops, chopped
Fresh parsley, chopped
2 pinches sweet basil leaves
4 tsp. sugar
Salt to taste

Melt oleo and make a roux with the flour. Add green onion bottoms, onions, and bell pepper; cook until clear. Stir in tomatoes, water, and crawfish. Bring to boil, but don't scorch. Turn heat to low and stir occasionally while cooking 20 minutes. Add lemon juice, green onion tops, parsley, basil, sugar, and salt for the last 10 minutes of cooking. Serve over rice or in patty shells.

Family Reunions

Alexander Stirling was born in 1753 in North Britain but within the next several decades would be serving under Spanish general Don Bernardo de Galvez in that portion of Louisiana then known as West Florida. Young Stirling was described in military records promoting him to under-lieutenant as "Scottish of nation, man of good education and very zealous for the service of his majesty."

His wife's father, John Alston, by some accounts traced his ancestry back to Alfred the Great of England but had moved his family from North Carolina to the Mississippi territory and obtained a large land grant from the British near Natchez.

Both families would ironically be instrumental in furthering American control of the area after wresting it away from both British and Spanish regimes.

When the Spanish governor of Louisiana, with help from West Florida planters, perhaps including Alexander Stirling, ousted the English, Alston and others took the Spanish fort at Natchez in 1781 in hopes of bringing the District of Natchez under American control. When the British flag was raised instead, Alston fled in fear of his life.

Sending his wife and three small children overland to safety, Alston was captured and sentenced to life imprisonment. His wife was killed when her horse fell during the flight, but the children were hidden in a one-room cabin in the swamp on the plantation of a family friend, cared for by a faithful servant, Mammy Pratt or Pat.

Additional assistance came from one Alexander Stirling, then acting as plantation manager. By 1784, the 31-year-old Stirling had fallen in love with Alston's 17-year-old daughter Ann and married her. Her sister Lucretia would eventually become mistress of Oakley Plantation and mother of Audubon's pupil Eliza Pirrie.

John Alston, meanwhile, languished in prison until a visit by England's Prince William Henry in 1783 led to his release, but only after Galvez imposed the condition that under no excuse should "the Chief of the Natchez Rebellion and his accomplices" return to the Territory of Louisiana.

The young Stirlings, Alexander and Ann, settled in what was then New Feliciana, now West Feliciana, near Thompson's Creek, where they had a store. They later moved to a place they called Egypt.

Alexander received Spanish land grants and purchased other tracts totaling some 10 square miles. Serving as an *alcalde* to help make and carry out political and civil regulations, Stirling was also a successful planter.

He and his wife had 12 children, their second son, Lewis, becoming one of the leaders of the West Florida rebellion against Spain when he called together over 500 other patriots in 1810 to set in motion the chain of events that led to the capture of the Spanish fort in Baton Rouge, the creation of the independent Republic of West Florida, and the eventual inclusion of the Florida Parishes in the United States of America some time after the rest of the Louisiana Purchase had been annexed.

Lewis Stirling served in the Battle of New Orleans, married Sarah Turnbull, and began the fine Greek Revival home Wakefield in 1834. The young couple then set off on a year-long buying expedition by boat and stagecoach to furnish the house, visiting Philadelphia, New York, and other cultural centers.

While it's fairly common for old houses to have been added to by succeeding generations, according to the dictates of finances and family size, Wakefield had the distinction of actually being physically divided in 1877, when Sarah and Lewis's heirs raised the roof, removed the top floor, and then lowered the roof onto the remaining story and a half to settle the estate.

Other descendants of Alexander Stirling gather once every 50 years for full-scale family reunions complete with nametags color-coded to show line of descent. In 1934 some 230 Stirlings attended, while planners of the 1984 gathering invited relatives from 31 states and 4 foreign countries.

The 650 or so who gathered at Wakefield on May 26, 1984, some having attended the first reunion, enjoyed a full day of baptisms, picture taking, mule-drawn wagon rides, children's activities, bagpipe music (the gathering of the clan, of course), visits to family cemeteries, and displays of treasured personal mementos. There was even a videotaping session so attendees could say a few words for posterity and future reunion gatherings.

The catered lunch served under the big tent and enjoyed by cousins on quilts and blankets spread across the lawns included jambalaya, barbecued chicken, corn on the cob, salad, and French bread, with hamburgers and chips for the children. Relatives living closest provided their specialty desserts for family members to sample, and one entire tent was filled with tantalizing slices of cakes, pies, cookies, and other goodies.

The reunion was so popular that descendants decided not to wait 50 years before getting together again, and some 700 gathered in 1999.

Beverly Stirling Robinson's Coconut Pound Cake

1 cup shortening
2 cups sugar
5 eggs
2 cups flour
1½ tsp. baking powder
1 tsp. salt
1 cup buttermilk
1½ tsp. coconut flavoring
1 can flaked coconut (frozen, preferably)
½ cup water
1 cup sugar
1 tsp. coconut flavoring

Cream shortening and 2 cups sugar together. Add eggs one at a time, beating well after each. Sift flour, baking powder, and salt and add alternately with buttermilk. Add 1½ tsp. coconut flavoring and coconut. Bake in a greased and floured pan at 350 degrees for 50 minutes to 1 hour. Glaze with glaze made by boiling for 1 minute water and 1 cup sugar, then adding 1 tsp. coconut flavoring. Brush over cake while still hot.

Dot Stirling Yerby's Delicious Bread Pudding

1 loaf stale French bread
1 qt. milk
3 eggs
2 cups sugar
1 can fruit cocktail, drained
2 tbsp. vanilla extract
1 cup raisins
3 tbsp. oleo, melted
1 cup sugar
1 stick oleo
1 egg, beaten
Whiskey

Break bread into small pieces and soak in milk. Add 3 eggs, 2 cups sugar, fruit cocktail, vanilla, and raisins. Pour melted oleo into 9x13" baking dish, pour in pudding, and bake at 375 degrees until firm, about 35 to 45 minutes. Combine 1 cup sugar with 1 stick oleo in double boiler and cook until hot and dissolved. Add 1 egg and whip together. Cool slightly, then add whiskey to taste. Pour sauce over pudding and place under broiler about 30 seconds.

Dot Stirling Yerby's Coconut Melt Aways

1 stick oleo
2 cups flour
½ cup shortening
1 cup coconut
3 tbsp. sugar
Powdered sugar

Combine all ingredients except powdered sugar and mix well. Roll into small balls. Flatten with fork. Bake at 350 degrees for 15-20 minutes. Remove from oven and sift powdered sugar over warm cookies. Makes about 5 dozen.

Dot Stirling Yerby's Chocolate Delights

1 egg yolk
½ cup oleo
2 tsp. water
1½ cups flour
1 tsp. sugar
1 tsp. baking powder
1 12-oz. pkg. chocolate chips
2 eggs
¾ cup sugar
6 tbsp. oleo, melted
2 tsp. vanilla extract
1 cup chopped pecans

Beat together egg yolk, ½ cup oleo, and water. Stir in flour, 1 tsp. sugar, and baking powder. Press in a 9x13" pan. Bake 10 minutes at 350 degrees. Sprinkle at once with chocolate chips and return to oven for 1 minute. To make topping, beat eggs until thick. Add ¾ cup sugar. Stir in melted oleo, vanilla, and pecans. Spread on top and bake at 350 degrees for 30-35 minutes. Cool and cut into squares.

Marian Spann's Goo Cake

1 stick oleo
2 eggs
1 box yellow cake mix
1 8-oz. pkg. cream cheese, softened
1 box powdered sugar
2 eggs
Powdered sugar

Beat oleo until creamy. Add 2 eggs and cake mix. Spread into 9x12" greased and floured pan. For topping, mix cream cheese with 1 box sugar and 2 eggs until very "soupy." Pour this over the top of the cake mixture. Bake at 350 degrees for 40 minutes. For a more cakey, less moist square, cook for 45 minutes. Edges will be brown. Top swells, but do not puncture; it will fall. Center will be good and gooey. Sprinkle powdered sugar on top after cake has cooled. Cut into 1" squares.

Rosale

For nearly two centuries there had been a Robert Hilliard Barrow in West Feliciana Parish, each generation exhibiting characteristic innovative leadership at home in peaceful pursuits or military valor and distinguished honorable service in wartime, often a combination of the two. It was no wonder, then, that the fifth-generation Robert Hilliard Barrow, General, U.S. Marine Corps (retired), would feel the pull of history drawing him home to restore Rosale Plantation after 41 years of active military service all over the world, including 7 tours of duty in the Far East and 4 challenging years in Washington, D.C. as commandant of the Marine Corps.

Now several hundred acres of sweeping vistas, its manicured green pastures punctuated by groves of live oaks and large lakes dotted with geese, Rosale was initially part of the immense 1795 Spanish land grant made to Alexander Stirling. Originally called Egypt, according to some sources it was the site of a secret formative meeting of planters plotting the overthrow of the Spanish in 1810, a move that culminated in the independent Republic of West Florida followed by annexation to the United States.

Stirling's son Lewis was one of those daring pioneers; another leader of the rebellion was William Barrow of Highland Plantation, whose son, the first Robert Hilliard Barrow, eloped with the beauteous 16-year-old Eliza Pirrie, whom artist John James Audubon had come to the Felicianas to tutor in 1821.

Young Barrow was 28 at the time of the elopement; he would not live to see 29. His gallantry in carrying his charming young bride across the flooded Homochitto Bayou on their honeymoon resulted in the pneumonia that would prove fatal 6 weeks later. The union nevertheless bore fruit, for Barrow's son, the second Robert Hilliard Barrow, was born posthumously.

This Robert Hilliard Barrow would marry a cousin, Mary Eliza Barrow of Afton Villa, and in 1845 acquire the place that would be renamed Rosale for its extensive rose gardens. There was a 2½-story brick house with basement, many brick dependencies, and a 2-story frame schoolhouse, which the carpenter had built to temporarily house his workers as he constructed the main home in 1835.

Barrow was an innovative planter and one of the earliest to import Brahman cattle from India, in 1859 ordering a bull and cow that arrived at the Bayou Sara wharf in deplorable shape after a lengthy and difficult voyage by sailing ship. Their descendants proved Barrow correct in his assumption that crossbreeding would result in cattle better able to withstand the severe summer heat here; subsequent Brahmans adapted so well, in fact, that one Barrow cousin harnessed a crossbred bull to pull his buggy, eliciting plenty of joshing, no doubt, but regularly passing up the horses when the roads were bad.

During the Civil War, Barrow raised and outfitted his own company, the Rosale Guards, its company

flag carefully handsewn by his wife and daughters, and returned from war a colonel.

In 1888 the main house at Rosale burned, so the family moved the frame schoolhouse to the exact spot where the other had been and added onto it to accommodate a growing family. Two more generations passed along, and then there was again a Robert Hilliard Barrow at Rosale, this one a 4-star general who earned some of the highest decorations given by this country and many foreign ones as well.

General Barrow was in China during much of World War II, serving with a Chinese guerrilla force operating extensively in enemy-occupied territory in Central China, and would remain in China for another year after war's end, then return to the Orient as a rifle company commander during the Korean conflict and later as an infantry regiment commander during the Vietnam War.

Mrs. Barrow was herself the daughter of an army officer and spent much of her own childhood in the Philippines and China. From her early years in China, she recalled that military families all had wonderful Chinese cooks and house servants, and as a result became very interested in Chinese food. It was in the 1930s that Mrs. Barrow's mother collected some of the recipes that the family continues to enjoy today.

Moo-She Pork

¼ cup lily buds
¼ cup clouds' ears
4 dried mushrooms, sliced thin
Warm water
1 lb. lean pork
1 tbsp. soy sauce
2 slices fresh ginger, chopped fine
1 clove garlic, chopped fine
1 tsp. sugar
¼ tsp. salt
Pinch monosodium glutamate
1 scallion, chopped fine
½ cup finely shredded cabbage
1 round medium onion, sliced fine
2 eggs, scrambled lightly
¼ cup thinly sliced bamboo shoots
6 water chestnuts, sliced thin

Soak lily buds, clouds' ears, and mushrooms 30-60 minutes in water. Shred pork. Pour soy, ginger, garlic, and sugar over meat and marinate for 30 minutes. Stir-fry meat until it loses its pinkness. Add salt, monosodium glutamate, scallion, lily buds, clouds' ears, mushrooms, cabbage, and onions. Stir-fry 2 minutes over high heat, then cook covered 1-2 minutes over medium heat. Add eggs, bamboo shoots, and water chestnuts. Serve hot. Serves 4-6.

Fried Rice

4 tbsp. oil
1 large onion, shredded
½ cup shredded green onions
4 cups cooked rice
½ cup shredded ham
2 eggs, beaten
1 tbsp. soy sauce
½ tsp. salt
Parsley

Heat pan and add oil. Fry onions for 1 minute. Add rice and sauté for 1 minute. Add ham, eggs, soy sauce, and salt. Mix well. Remove from heat and garnish with parsley.

Pickled Cucumbers

1¾ cups cucumbers
2 tsp. salt
½ cup vinegar
5 tbsp. sugar
2 tbsp. minced fresh ginger
1 tsp. sesame seeds

Pare cucumber, leaving part of it green. Cut in halves. Remove seeds and slice fine. Place in bowl. Add salt, mix well, and allow to stand for 5 minutes. Squeeze off excess water. Mix vinegar, sugar, ginger, and sesame in a pot and allow to boil. Then add to sliced cucumbers. Serve cold as pickles or as garnishes for spareribs.

Peking Meat Dumplings (Chiao Tzu)

1 large head napa cabbage (3½ lb.)
7 cups water, boiling
1 tbsp. sesame oil
1 onion, minced
1 lb. pork or mutton, chopped
2 tbsp. sesame oil
3 tbsp. soy sauce
1 tbsp. salt
1 bunch chives, sliced thin
3 cups flour
1¼ cups water
¼ cup soy sauce
2 tbsp. vinegar

Cut cabbage into 2" pieces. Parboil cabbage in boiling water for 10 minutes. Remove and rinse in cold water. Place cabbage in cheesecloth and squeeze water from cabbage. Chop cooked cabbage finely. Place in large bowl. Heat pan. Add 1 tbsp. sesame oil and sauté onion and pork. Add 2 tbsp. sesame oil, 3 tbsp. soy sauce, salt, and chives. Sauté for 3 minutes. Allow to cool and add to cabbage. Make a stiff dough with flour and water. Knead well and roll out very thin, then cut into rounds with cookie cutter. Fill each round with pork mixture like tarts. Fold over and pinch the edges together. Cook a few at a time in boiling water for 3 minutes; may be steamed as well. Dip cooked dumplings in a mixture of ¼ cup soy sauce and vinegar. Leftover chiao tzu may be fried for cocktails in deep fat until light brown.

Ho Pao Eggs

½ lb. pork, minced
½ lb. shrimp, minced
2 tbsp. minced green onions
10 water chestnuts, minced
2 tsp. sherry
3 tbsp. soy sauce
Salt to taste
⅛-½ tsp. black pepper
Oil
10 eggs, beaten lightly in large bowl

Place pork, shrimp, green onions, and water chestnuts in bowl; add sherry, soy sauce, salt, and pepper. Heat pan, add oil, and sauté the above mixture until cooked. Remove. Reheat pan, add 2 tbsp. oil, then add 1 tbsp. beaten egg at a time, spreading 1 tsp. of the shrimp mixture on half of the egg immediately, then folding over and browning both sides of little omelet. Remove omelet and place on plate. Repeat process, adding oil to pan each time, until all the eggs are used.

Audubon Pilgrimage

The birth of a son in April 1785 to a married French ship captain and an unmarried Creole mademoiselle in Santa Domingo seemed inauspicious enough at the time, yet the child born of this union would go down in history as one of the world's outstanding artists, Jean Jacques La Foret Fougere Audubon. Several decades later, Monsieur Audubon the artist would spend time in both Natchez and the Felicianas, leaving a lasting mark.

Legally adopted and reared in France by his father's wife, young Audubon soon exhibited a marked preference for wandering the woodlands rather than the confinements of formal study. After art lessons in Paris, in 1803 he journeyed to America, leaving behind enough mystery in his early years to lead his own granddaughter, much later, to surmise that he might very well have been the little Lost Dauphin of France, tragic son of the beheaded Louis XVI.

As an adult Audubon retained much of this aura of mysterious charm and was referred to in a 1937 biography as "a gifted artist, quasi-naturalist, sometime dandy, quondam merchant, unkempt wanderer, many-sided human being . . . generally regarded as mad because of his strange self-absorption, his long hair, tattered garments, and persistence in chasing about the countryside after little birdies."

The good-looking and graceful young Audubon had a decided way with the ladies, played the flute as well as flageolet and violin, danced a mean cotillion,

fenced, knew how to plait hair in many more than the usual three-stranded braids, and was partial to snuff and a liberal helping of early-morning grog.

He was also no businessman, as a trail of failed ventures and constant financial hardship attest. Audubon was the first to admit his shortcomings, once writing to his wife with characteristic careless spelling, "But I love indepennence and piece more than humbug and money."

In 1808 Audubon married Lucy Bakewell of Pennsylvania, and to the union were born two sons who survived infancy. After failed attempts to earn a living at trade, flatboating, gristmilling, and store-keeping, Audubon moved his family to Louisville, where he painted portraits, "stuffed fishes" for a museum, and met 13-year-old Joseph Mason, whose special skill in painting floral backgrounds would soon be in evidence in many of Audubon's paintings.

There he conceived the awesome idea of drawing from nature all the birds of the vast territory of America.

In 1820 Audubon set out for New Orleans by flat-boat, without a cent but armed with his trusty gun, flute, violin, bird books, two portfolios of drawings, chalks, watercolors, drawing papers in a tin box, and a record book. He soon met the Pirrie family of Oakley Plantation in West Feliciana, whose need of a tutor for their young daughter Eliza introduced Audubon to the fertile fields and woodlands of an area so rich in wildlife that he would paint more than 80 of his famous bird studies there, 32 at Oakley alone.

The Pirries hired the temperamental Frenchman to teach the beauteous Eliza dancing, music, drawing, math, French, and hair-plaiting.

The arrangement was to leave him with half of each day free to devote to his own paintings and studies, but even his artistic appreciation of his pupil's beauty, which he immortalized in a portrait, did not quiet his chafing under the bonds of practical employment.

Audubon's tenure at Oakley lasted only 4 months, but his appreciation of the natural bounty of the countryside led him to return to the parish several more times throughout the 1820s as he worked on his bird studies and his wife taught at several area plantations.

Oakley, begun in 1799, is now the center of the state-owned Audubon State Historic Site, where visitors can climb the narrow stairs to the tiny quarters off the back porch that the artist shared with young Mason, still cluttered with artist's para-phernalia and naturalist's treasures.

The artist's stay in the area is further commem-orated by the West Feliciana Historical Society's Audubon Pilgrimage each March, when antebel-lum homes and some of the great gardens of the South are opened for touring, including homes once occupied by some of Mme Audubon's pupils, a few still owned by direct descendants of those very same students. Hostesses are clad in elegant award-winning costumes authentically duplicating the clothing of the 1820s.

One particularly popular part of the pilgrimage each year is the food lovingly prepared and served by local churchwomen at Jackson Hall next to Grace Episcopal Church in St. Francisville. Over two decades of pilgrimages, the recipes used for these luncheon specialties have been simplified and refined to perfection, easy to prepare and even easier to consume.

Pilgrimage Pecan Pie

½ cup brown sugar
1 cup light corn syrup
2 eggs
3 tbsp. flour
1 tsp. vanilla extract
1 tbsp. butter
1 cup pecan halves
1 9" pie crust, unbaked

Combine sugar, Karo, and eggs. Add flour, vanilla, butter, and pecans. Pour into pie crust and bake at 400 degrees for 15 minutes. Reduce heat to 350 degrees and bake 30 minutes longer. Filling will appear soft in center. Nine small tarts can be made same way by baking at 350 degrees for 25 minutes.

Pilgrimage Chess Pie

3 eggs
½ cup butter or oleo
1½ cups sugar
2 tbsp. cornmeal
1 cup cream
1 tsp. vanilla extract
1 9" pie crust, unbaked

Separate eggs and beat yolks. Cream butter or oleo with sugar and add to egg yolks. Add cornmeal to cream and add this to egg-yolk mixture. Add vanilla. Beat egg whites and fold into mixture. Bake in pie crust for 50-55 minutes at 325 degrees.

Pilgrimage Coconut Pie

3 eggs
1½ cups sugar
2 tbsp. melted butter
1 tsp. vanilla extract
½ cup milk
1 3½-oz. can coconut
¼ tsp. salt
1 9" pie crust, unbaked

With fork, beat together eggs and sugar until well blended. Mix in all other filling ingredients. Pour into pie crust and bake at 350 degrees for 1 hour.

Pilgrimage Pound Cake

3 cups sugar
1 lb. oleo
9 eggs
3 cups flour
1 tsp. vanilla extract

Cream sugar and oleo. Add eggs and flour, alternating. Add vanilla. Bake for 20 minutes at 325 degrees and then 50 minutes at 350 degrees.

St. Francisville and the West Feliciana Parish Area of Louisiana

Christmas in the Country

I t was the bluffs, high above the reach of flood-waters, that led the first white men to wend their way up to the highlands where St. Francisville is now located to bury their dead in the 1770s, but later permanent settlers were a much livelier lot.

By 1807 the town of St. Francisville had been laid out on a loessial finger ridge so narrow that it has been called, with not complete exaggeration, the town 2 miles long and 2 yards wide. Lots were sold, bordered by streets with such optimistic names as Prosperity and Prospect.

St. Francisville was soon filled with commercial establishments and mercantiles serving the needs of the rich surrounding plantation country. In this period of the mid-1800s, the large planters who harvested immense acreages of cotton, sugarcane, and indigo along the Great River Road from Natchez to New Orleans comprised more than two-thirds of America's known millionaires.

Their large plantations generated immense needs for goods and services, which could not always be supplied by skilled workmen right on the property. Fancy furnishings, the latest fashions, libraries full of rare books, fine artworks, and even some finished building materials were shipped by flatboat or steamer to the riverport landing at Bayou Sara, just beneath St. Francisville's bluffs. Small establishments sprang up to handle the trade and provide such services as blacksmithing and cotton ginning right in St. Francisville itself.

Saturdays found the plantation folk from the surrounding countryside flocking into town by the wagonload or in fine buggies, making their purchases for the week or month, taking care of business transactions, enjoying the excitement of a trip to town, browsing through the latest goods hot off the riverboats, and greeting friends seldom seen in isolated outlying areas.

Add to the anticipation of these Saturday trips a little Christmas magic, and you have an idea of the holiday joy modern-day visitors feel during St. Francisville's festive community-wide celebration of the season called *Christmas in the Country* the first full weekend in each December.

It's a real small-town traditional Christmas, harking back to the time of small mittened fingers clearing frost from storefront windowpanes to dream of china dolls and bright red wagons, of the reaffirmation of a joyous faith proclaimed in voices raised in praiseful carols, of the sense of wonderment and thanksgiving aroused by living nativity scenes, of family gatherings complete with great feasts and shared memories spiced with the pungency of fresh cedar boughs and baking mincemeat pies.

Most of St. Francisville's quaint little gift and antiques shops band together to host this old-fashioned celebration of the season, providing special entertainment, activities for children, and carol singing, all highlighted by the Women's Service League's annual Christmas parade.

Many of these shops are housed in restored Victorian structures, which the shop owners go all out in decorating, transforming the entire downtown historic district into a veritable winter wonderland. Each shop also serves complimentary refreshments; recipes for some specialties, given here, are as varied as these delightful little shops and would add a touch of old-timey magic to any holiday observance.

Shadetree's Mulled Cider

2 qt. apple cider
1 tsp. whole allspice
6 or more cloves
1 stick cinnamon
½ cup honey
⅓ cup lemon juice
½ cup orange juice

Simmer cider with spices and honey about 30 minutes. Add juices and strain. Serve immediately or store in refrigerator for reheating and serving later.

Shadetree's Almond Punch

1 large can frozen orange juice
1 large can pineapple juice
¼ cup honey
1 small can lemon juice
1 large can apricot nectar
½-¾ small bottle almond extract

Mix all ingredients together well and refrigerate before serving.

Old South Antiques' Champagne Punch

4 cups sugar
3 cups orange juice
3 cups lemon juice
3 cups pineapple juice
4 cups water
1 bottle ginger ale
1 bottle champagne

Boil sugar in juices to dissolve. Cool. Add water and ginger ale. Mix. Just before serving, add champagne.

Magearl House Antiques & Interiors' Gingerbread Men

1 cup shortening
1 cup packed brown sugar
1 tbsp. cinnamon
1 tbsp. ground ginger
1 cup dark corn syrup
2 eggs
2 cups flour
1½ tsp. baking soda
3½ cups flour

In large bowl, cream shortening with sugar, cinnamon, and ginger until fluffy. Beat in corn syrup and eggs until well blended. Mix 2 cups flour with baking soda and beat into creamed mixture. Stir in 3½ cups flour. Wrap airtight and chill. Cut with cookie cutter and bake at 350 degrees until golden brown, about 20-25 minutes.

Magearl House Wassail

2 qt. apple cider
1 pt. cranberry juice
2 sticks cinnamon
1 small orange studded with cloves
¾ cup sugar
1 tsp. bitters
1 tsp. ground allspice
2 cups rum

Simmer slowly for 6 hours. Serve warm. Makes 3½ qt., and doubles well.

The Shanty Too's Boston Punch

2 cups sugar
1 large can orange juice
1 cup lemon juice
1 large can grapefruit juice
1 large can pineapple juice
2 cups crushed pineapple
2 cups sliced strawberries and juice
1 1-liter bottle ginger ale
1 qt. gin

Mix sugar and juices together. Add fruit, then add ginger ale and gin. Mix well. Float large chunks of ice in punch before serving. Should serve 75.

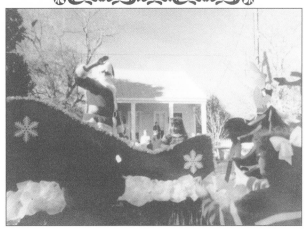

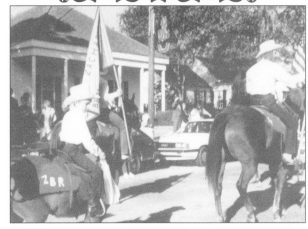

Barrow House B&B

One of St. Francisville's oldest structures, the Barrow House is a 2-story saltbox on a raised lot shaded by a spreading oak. It was built around 1810 by Amos Webb, egocentric theater owner who became postmaster and attempted without success to have the whole town renamed for himself. When he advertised this house for sale in 1812, he called it "well calculated for a store and private family" on a lot "not inferior to any in the Village."

Not long before the Civil War the Barrow House belonged to local lawyer J. Hunter Collins, who added the cottage extension for his law offices; Collins allowed young William W. Leake to read law with him after losing his original partner in the explosion of the steamboat *Princess*.

By 1866 Leake had been admitted to the Bar and had purchased the home for his growing family of 11 children. It was Leake who inspired the heartening effort that stopped the Civil War briefly so that he might bury a fellow Mason, albeit a Union gunboat commander, in Grace Episcopal Church cemetery under flag of truce.

Leake's daughter Camilla married Dr. A. Feltus Barrow of Highland Plantation in 1892 and lived here. Her husband was a real horse-and-buggy doctor, treating patients in town and throughout the surrounding plantation country; eventually he built a sanitarium, complete with screened porches and lots of climbing roses, next door to his home, with offices downstairs and bedrooms upstairs for critical patients or expectant mothers from isolated areas approaching their time of confinement.

Dr. Barrow was a huge man, so large it was said he could slip his wedding ring over the wrist of premature babies, and he had an enormous bathtub installed in a downstairs room next to a window. Always available for medical emergencies, Dr. Barrow made exhausting trips into remote regions

to treat the sick, fording creeks that often rose and stranded him away from home for days, so when he found time to relax, he relished his bath. His niece Camilla Bradley Truax recalls patients dripping with blood being brought by, and the good doctor, soaking in his tub, would lean out of the window and give instructions for admitting them to the sanitarium. He also served as town mayor and was known to occasionally hold court right in the bathtub, the accused waiting outside the window to be pronounced guilty or innocent.

Dr. Barrow would proudly own the second car in West Feliciana Parish, a big red Maxwell with a horn that had to be squeezed, and later he got a Willys Knight, with a shovel, chains, and rope for when he got stuck on muddy lanes.

The Barrow House is now operated as a Bed and Breakfast right in the midst of St. Francisville's extensive National Register-listed Historic District. Owner Shirley Ditloff is a gourmet cook, as evidenced by these special recipes of hers.

Shrimp Salad with Two Sauces

On salad plate place 2 mounds of cooked, peeled shrimp on shredded lettuce. Put 2 tbsp. Sherry Sauce on 1 mound and 2 tbsp. Creole Mustard Sauce on the other. Separate the 2 mounds with 1 parsley sprig or strip of red bell pepper.

Sherry Sauce

1 egg yolk
¼ tsp. salt
¼ cup catsup
¼ tsp. white pepper
3 tbsp. chopped green onions
Tabasco sauce
2 tbsp. dry sherry
1 tsp. Creole mustard
½ cup oil

Place all ingredients except oil in food processor or blender and process 20 seconds. With machine running, add oil in a thin steady stream until smooth and thick. Makes 1 cup.

Creole Mustard Sauce

1 cup mayonnaise
1 tbsp. lemon juice
1 cup sour cream
1 tbsp. wine vinegar
¼ cup minced celery
1 tsp. Worcestershire sauce
¼ cup minced green onions
1 tsp. sugar
½ tsp. minced garlic
⅓ cup Creole mustard
1 tbsp. chopped parsley
Salt and black pepper to taste

Mix all ingredients well and chill. Makes 3 cups.

Cajun Crabmeat Filo Pastries

⅓ cup chopped onion
⅓ cup chopped celery
⅓ cup chopped bell pepper
½ stick butter
½ tsp. onion powder
½ tsp. garlic powder
½ tsp. basil
½ tsp. salt
¼ tsp. white pepper
¼ tsp. black pepper
¼ tsp. cayenne pepper
2 tbsp. flour
1 lb. crabmeat
2½ pkg. (8 oz. each) cream cheese
3 egg yolks
1 box filo dough
3 sticks butter, melted

Sauté vegetables in ½ stick butter for 7-8 minutes. Add spices and flour and cook 2 minutes more. Add crabmeat (shrimp may be substituted) and cream cheese. Stir until cheese is smooth and incorporated. Add egg yolks when cool. Lay out double sheets of filo (may do several at a time), keeping rest of dough covered. Brush filo with butter. Cut dough in half from long end, and then again in half to make 4 strips. Place a spoon of filling in the bottom corner of each strip; take corner, and fold over to other side. Repeat this all the way up the strip until you have a little triangular package. Place on baking sheet and brush again with butter. Bake at 350 degrees for 20 minutes. May be frozen before baking; if so, place frozen on baking sheet, brush again with butter, and bake 30 minutes. Makes 3-4 dozen.

Creole Seafood au Gratin

2 medium onions, minced
1 bell pepper, minced
2 stalks celery, minced
1 stick oleo
1 tsp. paprika
1 tsp. onion powder
1 tsp. garlic powder
½ tsp. dried basil
¼ tsp. dry mustard
½ tsp. black pepper
½ tsp. white pepper
⅛-¼ tsp. cayenne pepper
3 tbsp. flour
1 8-oz. pkg. cream cheese, cut into pieces
1 can mushroom soup
1 8-oz. can sliced mushrooms, drained
1 lb. peeled shrimp
1 lb. peeled crawfish
½ lb. crabmeat

Sauté onions, bell pepper, and celery in oleo until soft. Add spices and sauté another 3 minutes. Add flour and sauté 2 minutes. Add cream cheese; stir constantly until melted. Add soup and mushrooms. Add shrimp and heat until shrimp are barely cooked, then add crawfish and crabmeat. This can be made ahead and refrigerated, then reheated slowly on stove until comes to boil, or put in separate ramekins and heat in 350-degree oven for 25 minutes. Sprinkle with grated cheddar cheese. Serve with basmati rice, an imported Indian rice, which should be soaked for 20 minutes, drained, and cooked as regular rice.

Strawberry Crepes Flambé

1 cup milk
3 eggs
1 tsp. vanilla extract
½ cup flour
¼ cup oil
8 oz. cream cheese, softened
⅓ cup sugar
2 tsp. vanilla extract
3 tbsp. chopped pecans
2 10-oz. pkg. frozen strawberries with sugar
½ stick butter
4 tbsp. strawberry liqueur, Cointreau, or rum
2 tbsp. rum (151 proof)
Whipped cream or topping

Put milk, eggs, 1 tsp. vanilla, flour, and oil in a blender or food processor and mix on high speed for 1 minute. Let stand at room temperature for a least ½ hour. Grease crepe pan or large griddle with butter. Spoon batter into pan or on griddle, making circles 6-7" in diameter; can do more at one time with griddle. Cook until lightly browned, then turn and cook other side. Makes 8-10 crepes. Stack between pieces of wax paper. For filling, cream together the cream cheese, sugar, 2 tsp. vanilla, and pecans. Lay out the crepes and put about 2 tbsp. filling on each. Roll up. Can be frozen. For sauce, heat strawberries, butter, and liqueur in pan large enough to accommodate crepes. Add crepes and heat through. Place in a chafing dish and pour on 2 tbsp. rum. Ignite. When flames die, place 1 crepe on each plate and top with whipped cream.

The Rural Homestead

Corn has been a staple of our diet ever since the pilgrims first set foot on the rocky shores of New England and were saved from starvation by friendly Indians who showed them how to grow the maize or Indian corn that already covered thousands of miles across the Americas.

Reported in the Mayan and Incan empires, corn was so important to the American Indians that it was regarded as a sacred gift from the gods. While modern-day botanists may consider the plant the result of an accidental crossing of several wild grasses, each ancient Indian tribe had its own legends as to the origins of maize. The Navajos, for example, passed down the story of a great turkey hen dropping to earth an ear of blue corn as she flew overhead.

As the first early settlers rode the Mississippi's waters into the South in the 1700s to carve great plantations from the virgin forestlands, they cultivated vast acreages of cotton, cane, and indigo as cash crops, but always reserved sufficient space for growing corn as well. It was an important foodstuff not only for the farmer's family, but for his livestock as well.

While the farm folk feasted on corn in its many varieties—fresh roasting ears, corn pudding, creamed corn, cornbread made of dried cornmeal throughout the year, fritters, cornmeal mush, hoecakes, and batter cakes—the barnyard stock feasted as well, with dried kernels for poultry and small stock, and fodder made of crushed dried cornstalks for huge herds of cattle and the many oxen, mules, and horses needed for farming and transportation. Even the dried cornhusks were soaked until pliable and then skillfully woven by dexterous fingers into durable doormats, chair seats, lacy table mats, mule collars, and dolls to delight tiny pioneer children.

The importance of corn to the daily lives of early settlers is commemorated each year at the West

138

Feliciana Historical Society's Rural Homestead, a recreated farmstead where the daily skills of the farm folk are demonstrated each year during the Audubon Pilgrimage the third weekend in March.

Rural Homestead life centers around the kitchen with its open hearth and shingle roof. Sweet potatoes and cornbread are baked in the oven of the wood-burning stove, with the meal ground right outside the door in a 19th-century steam-powered gristmill. In the yard near the cow pen, vast kettles are stirred over open flames as cracklin's fry in hot lard. The fat is then used to make soap the old-fashioned way, with lye and plenty of elbow grease.

Other simple skills shown to the accompaniment of lively old-time music include riving shingles from cypress logs with a froe, weaving baskets from split-oak strips, carding and spinning wool, horseshoeing near the blacksmithery, carving simple early toys like bamboo whistles, weaving cane chair seats, piecing together and quilting colorful patterned quilts, and plowing the garden with horse or mule power.

The Rural Homestead is a favorite for children and nostalgia buffs of all ages. Visitors find that just watching all the hard work going on stimulates the appetite, making the hot cornbread and sweet potatoes and cracklin's taste all the better. The cooks of the Rural Homestead, who in workaday lives may be lawyers or insurance salesmen or riverboat pilots or farmers or artists or pediatricians or mothers, promise that everything tastes even better when enjoyed in the open air in the midst of the hustle and bustle of a 19th-century homestead.

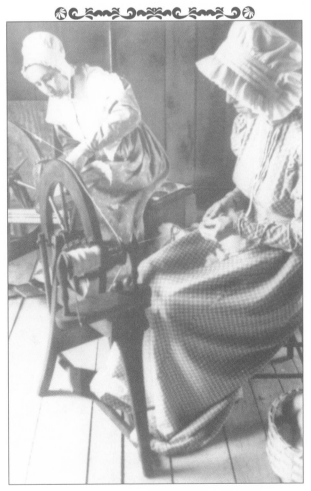

Catherine Rheames' Cornbread

4-5 tbsp. bacon drippings or lard
1 cup cracklin's (optional)
1½ cups yellow cornmeal
2 tsp. baking powder
1 tsp. sugar
½ cup flour
½ tsp. salt

Heat iron cornbread-stick pans on top of a wood stove and coat with bacon drippings or lard rendered from cooking cracklin's. When the cornbread batter is mixed and put into these hot pans, a thin crust forms. Cook cornbread in oven until browned and cooked through.

Cracklin's

Cracklin's are the trimmings of fat removed from butchered pigs before the good meat is smoked or pickled in brine. They are cooked primarily to get the lard, which can be put up for later use. Lard can be used to preserve sausage or bacon, as shortening for cooking, and as flavoring in cornbread. It is also used to make soap. One of the cracklin' master chefs at the Rural Homestead gives this detailed recipe for making this delicacy: "Put 'em in a pot and cook 'em!" It is an inexact science! He uses huge iron kettles over open fires and says the fires must be made of dry oak wood, as other woods smoke too much and the smoke, if it curls into the pot, can discolor the grease. As the cracklin's fry, the grease is released and cooked out slowly. The clear bubbles on top are skimmed off, and that's the clear white lard. As the cracklin's get crisp, they are removed with a slotted scoop and seasoned with a mixture of salt, black pepper, and other seasonings as desired. Are they good? It's not unusual for the Rural Homestead to go through 1,500 lb. of cracklin's during the 3 days of the pilgrimage.

Butler Greenwood Plantation

So well insulated from busy U.S. Highway 61 that not even many West Feliciana residents knew it was there, Butler Greenwood Plantation opened its doors for tours and Bed & Breakfast in 1991 for the first time since the plantation was established in the 1790s. One of 3 early plantations in the immediate vicinity called Greenwood, this is the oldest and is called Butler Greenwood to eliminate confusion.

Butler Greenwood was begun in the 1790s on Spanish land grants received by Dr. Samuel Flower, a Pennsylvania physician who moved here in 1770 to become one of Feliciana's earliest pioneers. Listed on the National Register of Historic Places, the English-style raised cottage was built of cypress and blue poplar, its joints mortised or pegged and interior planks hand-planed, with chimneys and wells of slave-made brick and the plaster mixed in the English method combining river silt with white horsehair and slathered on lathing made of sassafras.

Dr. Flower left the house to his daughter Harriett when he died in 1813; her husband, Judge George Mathews, was one of the justices of the first Louisiana Supreme Court, and during his frequent absences on court duties Harriett ran the plantation, shipping indigo and cotton from her own dock on Bayou Sara, raising sugarcane on other family plantations, and extending the landholdings. It was she who added the Victorian touches to the house in the 1850s. Her meticulous records of nearly a century of plantation life are in the Louisiana and Lower Mississippi Valley Collection of historic papers at Hill Library, LSU, providing

invaluable clues for researchers. The house has remained in the same family since its beginnings, and the current children are the eighth generation.

The formal gardens of Butler Greenwood, dating from the 1840s, were recorded as part of the first Historic American Buildings Survey in Louisiana following the depression. The magnificent summer house has a metal roof and wonderfully detailed trim work. The live oaks shading the grounds came from acorns brought out by a planter's family fleeing the 1799 slave insurrection in Haiti. A sunken garden borders the drive. The 1790s detached kitchen of slave-made brick, with its arches and stepped facade, is one of the parish's oldest structures and one of few extant showing the influence of the Spanish regime, which in this area, once called West Florida, lasted until 1810.

Rare antiques may be found throughout the house, but the magnificent Victorian formal parlor is the real gem, with its 12-piece set of carved rosewood furniture still in the original scarlet upholstery, towering pier mirrors, gilt cornices above lambrequins at the floor-to-ceiling windows, lace curtains parted by rare porcelain calla-lily tiebacks, floral Brussels carpet, marble mantel, and fine family portraits in oil . . . providing in its unchanged state of preservation a matchless mirror of life as it was savored when more than two-thirds of the country's antebellum millionaires were counted among the cultured planters inhabiting the richly blessed region along the Great River Road between Natchez and New Orleans. The family of Butler Greenwood Plantation was very much a part of this society and in the 1820s were well acquainted with the artist Audubon, whose wife tutored several of the girls of the family.

Butler Greenwood Plantation is open for tours daily and also offers Bed & Breakfast in the 8 outbuildings, several of them historic dependencies, overlooking steep wooded ravines or ringing the duck pond where deer often drink in the early mornings. For additional information, contact Butler Greenwood Plantation, 8345 U.S. Highway 61, St. Francisville, LA 70775; telephone (225) 635-6312; e-mail butlergree@aol.com; Web site www.butler-greenwood.com. It is now occupied by the family of busy author Anne Butler, whose most recent books have been significant nonfiction ones on crime and criminal justice, so the long mahogany dining table in the Butler Greenwood dining room is most often graced by cold salads or other quick-fix meals, a couple of which are offered here.

Broccoli Salad

1 bunch broccoli
½ cup raisins
½ cup cashew halves
1 small red onion, sliced in very thin rings
1 cup mayonnaise
2 tbsp. sugar
2 tbsp. vinegar

Wash broccoli and cut into florets. Mix with raisins, cashews, and red onion. Mix mayonnaise with sugar and vinegar, then combine with salad mixture. Serve cold.

Spinach Salad

Fresh spinach leaves
3 eggs, hard boiled and sliced
½ lb. fresh mushrooms, sliced
6-8 slices bacon, crisply cooked and crumbled
1 egg
½ cup sugar
½ cup vinegar
2 tsp. bacon grease

Wash and stem spinach leaves. Tear into bite-sized pieces and mix with eggs, mushrooms, and bacon. Make a dressing by beating egg, then combining egg, sugar, vinegar, and bacon grease in pan. Cook over low heat, stirring, until boiling. Chill, then combine with spinach mixture when ready to serve.

The Cottage

An overnight stay at The Cottage in West Feliciana Parish provides visitors with the quintessential experience of the antebellum South in all its glory, for this lovely old home is the center of a country plantation village dating from the days when such places were nearly self-sufficient. Besides the law office/schoolhouse, milk house, outside kitchen, and laundry room, there are also the commissary, tenant cabins, smokehouse, and carriage house still containing the magnificent state carriage purchased in Philadelphia in 1820, complete with silver handles, silk curtains, velvet lining, and Brussels carpeting.

Guests sleep in antique 4-poster beds and are awakened with coffee served in bedrooms on a silver tray, followed later by a full plantation breakfast in the formal dining room, where it wouldn't be a bit of a surprise to find oneself seated next to the Grand Duke Alexis of Russia, 1872 banquet guest here, or Gen. Andrew Jackson, who stayed overnight at The Cottage much earlier on his way home from the Battle of New Orleans. Jackson's chief of staff was a brother of Judge Thomas Butler and swelling his entourage were 7 other Butler cousins, so taxing the accommodations of even this commodious home that the hosts were reportedly forced to sleep in the pantry.

On land originally granted in 1795 (the Spanish land grant is on display), The Cottage was purchased in 1811 by Judge Thomas Butler, first judge of the Florida Parishes after they became part of the United States in 1810. To the original simple

Spanish structure, additions were so skillfully made over the years as to seem an integral part of the English-style home, a low rambling structure with gable roof and rear bedroom wing, with a front gallery so unusually long that 4 doors and 9 windows open onto it.

For generations The Cottage was home to members of the noted Butler family, the American branch of which began in 1748 when Irish-born Thomas Butler emigrated to Pennsylvania. Of his 12 children, 5 sons became Revolutionary War heroes known as the "5 Fighting Butlers," called by George Washington "Honor's Band." Though 2 of the brothers were mere teenagers at enlistment, they so distinguished themselves that the Marquis de Lafayette wrote, "When I wish a thing well done, I order a Butler to do it."

The second Thomas Butler, a colonel, was immortalized by Washington Irving for upholding the family tradition of tenacity (some might call it stubbornness) in refusing to cut off his queue, symbol of aristocratic wealth and rank, in the face of orders from General Wilkinson; when he succumbed to yellow fever in New Orleans, he still wore it proudly, and there were even hints of a strategic hole being cut in his coffin to make sure everyone knew it!

His son, Judge Thomas Butler of The Cottage, represented Louisiana in the 15th and 16th sessions of the United States Congress; when his grandchildren sold the property in the 1950s, it was opened as a Bed and Breakfast, and continues to offer guests the rare experience of staying overnight in the midst of the 19th century.

A restaurant was operated for awhile in one of the old cabins on the grounds, called Mattie's House Restaurant (some favorite recipes are included here); the outside kitchen has been turned into an antiques shop; and guests from around the world have raved over the breakfast biscuits made according to the recipe of longtime Cottage cook, the late Estelle Munson.

Estelle's Biscuits

2½ cups flour
½ tsp. salt
3 tbsp. sugar
1½ tbsp. baking powder
¾ cup shortening
About ⅔ cup milk

Mix flour, salt, sugar, and baking powder well. Cut in shortening. Add enough milk to hold dough together. Place mixture on floured board, knead a couple of times, and roll to about ¾" thickness. Cut with 2" cutter and place on ungreased pan. Bake in preheated 450-degree oven for about 20 minutes, until golden brown on top. Makes 15.

Catfish with Mushroom Sauce

6 6-8-oz. catfish fillets
1½ sticks butter
1 tbsp. lemon juice
1½ cups sliced fresh mushrooms
3 tsp. minced garlic
3 bay leaves
¼ cup flour
¼ cup chicken or vegetable broth
½ cup heavy cream
2-3 tbsp. Cognac (optional)
½ tsp. salt
¼ tsp. white pepper
½ tsp. Tabasco sauce

Broil, grill, or pan sauté fish until done, about 5-7 minutes. Top with mushroom sauce made this way: In a skillet, melt 1 stick butter and add lemon juice and mushrooms. Stir. Add garlic and bay leaves. Sauté 10 minutes. In a separate skillet over low heat, stir in remaining butter and flour. Cook, stirring, for 5 minutes. To this, gradually add broth, cream, Cognac, salt, and pepper. Simmer for 5 minutes. Discard bay leaves. Stir mushrooms and their liquid into cream sauce. Add Tabasco. Refrigerate sauce until ready to use. Reheat and serve.

Swedish Cream

1 cup sugar
1 env. plain gelatin
2 cups heavy cream
1 pt. sour cream
2 tsp. vanilla extract
2 pt. berries
Whipped cream

Combine sugar and gelatin in saucepan. Add cream and mix well. Heat gently. Stir over low heat until gelatin dissolves. Do not boil. Cool until mixture thickens. When cool, fold in sour cream. Add vanilla. Chill in refrigerator. Top with fruit and whipped cream before serving. Serves 6.

Shrimp Etouffée

2 lb. shrimp
7 tbsp. oil
¾ cup flour
¼ cup chopped bell pepper
¼ cup chopped onion
¼ cup chopped celery
3 cups broth made from shrimp heads
2 sticks butter
1 cup chopped green onions
1 tsp. salt
⅛ tsp. white pepper
⅛ tsp. black pepper
½ tsp. cayenne pepper
1 tsp. basil
½ tsp. thyme
Hot cooked rice

Cook and peel shrimp. Make broth with the heads and strain to get 3 cups broth. In a heavy skillet, heat oil. Add flour and cook 2-3 minutes to make a dark-brown roux. Add bell pepper, onion, and celery. Cook about 3 minutes. Add broth and cook until roux is well dissolved. In a saucepan, melt the butter. Stir in shrimp and green onions and cook 1-2 minutes. Add seasonings. Add all to roux mix, cook about 5 minutes, and serve over rice. Crawfish may be substituted for shrimp.

St. Francisville and the West Feliciana Parish Area of Louisiana 145

Catalpa Tea Parties

When Sadie Fort reached the public school system's mandatory retirement age, she transferred to a private academy for another decade, having spent nearly a lifetime opening her heart to the gap-toothed grins and tousled heads of hundreds of second-graders. Passing on the responsibility for inspiring succeeding classes of students to a younger generation of teachers was not easy, for Sadie loved each and every child.

Her sister Mamie, on the other hand, ever the more adventurous of the two, married and gave her heart to only one child, her own Mary, she of the big blue eyes and bright burnished ringlets. But just as Sadie lost her second-graders to promotion each year, so Mamie lost her Mary to a career in the big city of New Orleans.

For years the two sisters lived on the Fort family plantation Catalpa, just north of St. Francisville, surrounded by treasures handed down over the years by loving hands. A love of history and enjoyment of introducing the past to the present led them to share their home with visitors, and the tour there was surely one of plantation country's warmest and most personal ambles down memory lane.

"There is always such a good time to be had at the Forts," the saying went a century ago, for Catalpa and its surrounding parklands were laid out for pleasure, with wisteria-draped summer houses, a pavilion for dancing, a fishing pond centered by a fountain and an island for fish fries and picnics, a deer park, swans and flocks of peacocks, wrought-iron garden benches, and blossoming plants everywhere the eye might fall. The rare elliptical avenue, lined with moss-hung live oak trees planted by Mamie and Sadie's great-great-grandfather, was lined with enormous pink conch shells in such quantities that there was one servant whose sole occupation was keeping them polished.

The first of the Fort family to arrive from the Carolinas in the very early 1800s had the home built by the expert brick masons and skilled carpenters among his servants, but the pride of Catalpa, especially just before the Civil War, was its huge multi-storied glass greenhouses, in which flourished such exotics as cinnamon, guava, mandarins, tropical plants, tea and coffee, bananas, and orange trees. A central stage brimmed over with flowering potted plants, and fragrant vines hung from the latticework. In brick pits, vegetables were grown out of season, and pineapples, pears, peaches, plums, nectarines, and melons were cultivated in a protected environment. The produce of these hothouses was an eagerly anticipated part of dinner parties at Catalpa.

The Civil War brought the death of William J.

Fort and the gradual ruination of the grounds. As servants fled, roving bands of soldiers tore down fences, loose livestock trampled the gardens, and the greenhouses were destroyed. Though blind in her later years, widowed Sally Fort managed somehow to keep the place intact and raise her family, never losing her love of flowers and taking such solace in fine music as to nearly wear the ivory off the keys of the rare old Pleyel piano in the parlor.

Surrounded by priceless antiques from both Catalpa and restored Rosedown Plantation, home of the sisters' mother, Mamie and Sadie reveled in reliving with visiting children their own idyllic childhoods, country days filled with horseback rides and picnics, fish fries and forays into the cool dark attic, tea parties and pets and playing dress-up in historic costumes from the armoires of the past perhaps once worn by such ancestors as Eliza Pirrie, then nights filled with roasting marshmallows by the heat of the open fireside, chilling ghost stories, and thrilling bedtime books.

When Mamie's daughter Mary was small, the sisters saw to it that she and her contemporaries enjoyed such old-time simple pleasures as well, hosting tea parties for tiny ladies in long gowns and feather boas at diminutive tables set with fine starched linens and flowered china holding frozen mint tea and teacakes and tarts, or sending bare-legged sunbonnetted little girls out onto the grounds of Catalpa with picnic baskets so heavily laden with fancy finger foods that often the gardener had to be dispatched as bearer for the expeditions.

While tea parties and picnics, ice-cream socials and other old-fashioned entertainments centered around the children of the family, the grownups were never neglected either, and the famous Fort hospitality was dispensed undiminished over the years. At one party, the huge sugar kettle on the patio was completely filled with crushed ice, into which were stuck glasses filled with famous Catalpa mint juleps. And each Christmas Eve, the fires blazed in the *faux marbre* fireplaces, the silver gleamed, and the flickering candlelight reflected on polished rosewood and carved mahogany as rich Catalpa eggnog was enjoyed before late services at Grace Episcopal Church.

The legacy of hospitality and history that Mamie Fort Thompson and Sadie Fort shared at Catalpa was more valuable than any of their fine china or clear-ringing crystal, sparkling silver, or Mallard sofas. *"There is always such a good time to be had at the Forts,"* the saying went a century ago, and the same holds true today, with Mamie's daughter Mary hosting tea parties for yet another generation of visiting children.

Famous Catalpa Mint Juleps

Gather a nice bunch of mint. Wash well and break it up. Place generous amount in glasses. Put 1 level tbsp. sugar (per glass) on top of mint and mash together to extract mint juices. Add 2 oz. (per glass) bourbon whiskey on top of that. Mash again, then put through sieve and discard the leaves. Pour liquid into glass, fill with crushed ice, and garnish with a sprig of fresh mint. Don't *dare* add water; on a hot day the crushed ice will melt fast enough.

Another Julep Recipe

Remove stems from mint and wash leaves. Put in quart jar, filling jar ¾ full with mint leaves. Add bourbon to fill. Soak mint leaves overnight in bourbon. Strain bourbon off in the morning. Use a jigger of the mint bourbon with about 2 tsp. simple syrup. Simple syrup is made by filling a small saucepan ¾ full of sugar, then the rest of the way with boiling water, according to sweetness and thickness desired. After adding simple syrup to bourbon, fill glass with crushed ice and garnish with mint.

Frozen Mint Tea

Rinds and juice of 6 lemons
Rinds and juice of 3 oranges
1 big handful fresh mint
2 cups water
Sugar
Fresh mint for garnish

For those too young for mint juleps, this is the perfect tea-party refreshment. Put rinds and mint into water. Boil 15 minutes or so. Add the juices. Throw away rinds and leaves. Sweeten liquid to taste. Put in ice trays with dividers removed or any shallow freezer container. Stir hard several times while freezing. Serve slushy in tall frosted glasses with sprigs of fresh mint for garnish. Makes about 2 qt., and really tastes just as good if you use mint, tea, water, and frozen orange juice with sugar.

Gertrude Veal's Tea-Party Teacakes

2 sticks butter
2 cups sugar
4 eggs
2 tsp. vanilla extract
3 cups flour, sifted
2 tsp. baking powder
1 cup flour

Cream butter and sugar, add eggs and vanilla, then add 3 cups flour and baking powder. Take 1 cup flour and use to roll the dough out on board. Cut out in circles big enough to make about a 3" cookie. Bake at 400 degrees about 10 minutes, until just beginning to brown.

Mary Butler's Teacakes

1 cup butter
2¼ cups sugar
4 eggs
1 tsp. vanilla or almond extract
5 cups flour
5 tsp. baking powder
Pinch salt
⅓ cup milk (optional)

Cream sugar and butter thoroughly. Add eggs one at a time, beating well. Add extract. Add flour sifted with baking powder and salt, alternately with milk if used. Roll to desired thickness. Cut out in circles big enough to make about a 3" cookie and bake at 350 degrees until light brown, about 10-12 minutes.

Mary Minor Butler Hébert's Little Fellow Lemon Pies

½ cup butter
1½-2 cups sugar
4 eggs
1 tbsp. flour
⅓ cup lemon juice

Cream butter and sugar, then add eggs one at a time, beating after each addition. Add flour and mix. Stir in lemon juice. Line muffin tins with rounds of your favorite pastry recipe. Fill ⅔ full with lemon mixture. Bake at 350 degrees for 30 minutes.

Spinach Sandwiches

1 10-oz. pkg. frozen chopped spinach
2 cups mayonnaise
Juice of ½ lemon
½ cup chopped fresh parsley
½ cup chopped green onions
1 pkg. Knorr dry vegetable soup mix
1 tsp. black pepper

Drain spinach well. Mix mayonnaise with lemon juice, add other ingredients, and mix. Chill. Spread on thinly sliced bread from which the crusts have been removed. Cut into shapes if desired. Makes a good dip, too.

Catalpa Spanish Cream

1 level tbsp. plain gelatin
2½ cups milk
½ cup sugar
3 eggs, separated
¼ tsp. salt
Vanilla extract
Whipped cream

Soak gelatin in milk 10 minutes. Place in double boiler over hot water. When dissolved, add sugar. Beat egg yolks. Pour milk slowly over yolks and return to double boiler. Cook until thickened, stirring constantly. Remove from heat. Beat egg whites and add with salt and vanilla. Pour into molds and refrigerate. To serve, unmold and top with whipped cream.

Brer Rabbit Goodies

½ cup shortening
¾ cup sugar
1 egg
½ cup molasses
2½ cups sifted all-purpose flour
¼ tsp. baking soda
1 tsp. salt
1 tsp. cinnamon
1 tsp. ground ginger
1 tsp. ground cloves
Pecan halves (optional)

Cream together shortening and sugar. Add egg and beat well. Add molasses. Sift together flour, soda, salt, and spices. Add to creamed mixture and mix well. Form dough into rolls 2" in diameter or less. Wrap in wax paper and chill ¾ hour or longer. Slice thinly and place on greased cookie sheet. Top each with pecan half if desired. Bake at 350 degrees for 8-10 minutes. Makes about 5 dozen.

Grace Church Dinners

Historic Grace Episcopal Church in St. Francisville was chartered by the legislature in 1827 as the oldest incorporated Episcopal parish in Louisiana, second only to Christ Church in New Orleans. Its present brick structure, replacing a simpler 1829 place of worship, was built in 1858 by master-carpenter Charles Nevitt Gibbons, whose childhood recollections of English country churches contributed to its unadorned Gothic simplicity. Its cornerstone was laid by Leonidas Polk, who would later become known as the Fighting Bishop of the Confederacy.

By the time of the depression culminating in the panic of 1837, however, the church had fallen on hard times, yellow fever rampant and its first rector, the Reverend Mr. Bowman (second husband of Audubon's pupil Eliza Pirrie), dead. A visiting clergyman was aghast to find "the doors wide open, the windows broken, the organ gone, the few prayerbooks torn in pieces, playing cards strewed about, and everything looking like sin and desolation itself."

A new fireball of a rector got things straightened out and the fine new building was completed just in time to be shelled and heavily damaged by Federal gunboats patrolling the Mississippi River during the Civil War siege of Port Hudson; gunners unmercifully trained their sights on the church's graceful bell tower, visible above the trees. One shell entered the church's front corner, dislodging masses of brick, spent its force in the chancel, and lay there unexploded; another passed through the pipe organ, and Grace Church was saved from total destruction only when the rector sent under flag of truce a message that "to fire upon God's House is unthinkable."

When the commander of one of the Union gunboats, John E. Hart of Schenectady, New York, died during the shelling, he was buried during a ceasefire in Grace's cemetery by fellow Masons wearing

Confederate gray, with a monument erected later "in loving tribute to the universality of Free Masonry" preserving in marble this brief moment of brotherhood in the midst of bloodshed. The cemetery surrounding the church is shaded by centuries-old live oaks and filled with quaint monuments, weathered statuary, and wrought-iron fencing.

Inside this picturesque church with its vaulted ceiling is a Bohemian glass door said to have been given by a remorseful Yankee gunner and a Pilcher organ shipped down the river from St. Louis in 1858 as a memorial donation made by the widow of Judge George Mathews and now considered the oldest two-manual tracker-action organ in the country.

Congregation members often gather after church to "break bread" in celebration of special church milestones, with one former rector, the Reverend Kenneth Dimmick, explaining, "Eating together is true Christian fellowship, an act of worship as much as the songs we sing or the prayers we pray, and the planning and preparations for our dinners are an act of worship the same as polishing the brass on the altar, for example. What we are doing is giving God our best in church and also in the dining hall, as we share something of supreme importance with one another. Our church dinners are a celebration of our common life."

Churchwomen provide samplings of their best culinary creations, like those following, which are usually augmented by main dishes like honey-baked ham, garlic cheese grits, and plenty of luscious desserts. One eagerly anticipated offering is always Spinach Madeleine, that regionally famous dish created by one member of Grace Church for the Baton Rouge Junior League's phenomenally successful cookbooks.

Madeline Nevill's Spinach Madeleine

2 10-oz. pkg. frozen chopped spinach
4 tbsp. butter
2 tbsp. flour
2 tbsp. chopped onion
½ cup evaporated milk
½ cup vegetable liquor
½ tsp. black pepper
¾ tsp. celery salt
¾ tsp. garlic salt
½ tsp. salt
Cayenne pepper to taste
1 tsp. Worcestershire sauce
1 6-oz. roll jalapeno cheese, cut in small
   pieces

Cook spinach according to package directions; drain, reserving liquor. Melt butter in saucepan over low heat. Add flour, stirring until blended and smooth but not brown. Add onion and cook until soft. Add liquids slowly, stirring constantly to avoid lumps. Cook until smooth and thick; continue stirring. Add seasonings and cheese. Stir until melted. Combine with spinach. May be served immediately or put into casserole topped with buttered breadcrumbs. May be frozen.

Anne Purnell Jackson's Curried Fruit

1 13½-oz. can pineapple chunks
1 No. 2½ can sliced peaches
1 No. 2½ can sliced pears
1 10-oz. jar Maraschino cherries
1 No. 1 can Bing cherries
1 cup brown sugar
4 tbsp. cornstarch
1 tbsp. curry powder
1 stick oleo
1 tbsp. brandy or sherry

Drain fruit and put into casserole dish. Mix sugar, cornstarch, and curry powder. Sprinkle over fruit. Melt oleo and pour over fruit. Cover casserole and bake 30 minutes in 350-degree oven. Uncover and bake 10 minutes more. Just before serving, add brandy or sherry.

Miss Mott Plettinger's Green Pea Salad

1 can petit pois green peas
2 hardboiled eggs, chopped
1-2 stalks celery, chopped
Sweet pickle relish
Salt and black pepper to taste
Mayonnaise

Gently mix peas, eggs, celery, relish, and seasonings with enough mayonnaise to make it a little bit gooey. Chill well before serving.

Rosedown Housewarming

In a parish so richly endowed with natural beauty that John James Audubon was spellbound when he first arrived in 1821, nationally famous Rosedown Plantation in St. Francisville is an outstanding example of what unlimited time, wealth, labor, and horticultural knowledge, combined with rich loess soil and a happy climate, could produce during the antebellum plantation culture.

A magnificent showplace, Rosedown was built in 1835 by wealthy cotton planter Daniel Turnbull for his wife, Martha Barrow, daughter of Highland Plantation's builder, William Barrow, Jr. Now a museum of the lavish way of life along the Great River Road when cotton was king, Rosedown is approached by an oak alley considered to be one of the most beautiful in the South, its century-old oak trees forming a vaulted canopy above the imported marble statuary along its edges.

On her wedding trip to the Continent, Martha Turnbull fell in love with Versailles and other great European gardens, and wasted no time once she returned home, becoming one of the first to import camellias and azaleas to the South in the late 1830s, setting out roses in the fertile soil, and making her gardens an early proving ground for the exotic flora of the Orient. Keeping meticulous records of nearly 60 years of gardening, Mrs. Turnbull turned 28 acres flanking the house and avenue into one of the great gardens of America, which she struggled to save during the difficult years of the Civil War by paying the help with plantation produce and often working by their sides.

The only son of the Turnbulls, young William, tragically perished young by accidental drowning; their daughter Sarah was famed as "The National Belle" of 1849, a beautiful charmer accomplished in the social graces and a skilled equestrian as well, according to a written account of her visit to West Point, when, attending the drills on horseback, Miss Turnbull was dared by an officer to take a hurdle. *"A Southern girl was never known to refuse a dare, sir,"* responded Sarah with characteristic spirit as she gracefully cleared the obstacle, upon which the cadets saluted her and the band struck up "Dixie." She would return home, however, to give her heart and hand to James Pirrie Bowman, son of Audubon's pupil Eliza Pirrie.

The next generation at Rosedown, the slim Bowman sisters, somehow kept the great house and gardens intact through years of genteel poverty, and enough potential shone through the undergrowth to win the heart of the late Catherine Fondren Underwood of Houston in 1956. The 10-year restoration project she undertook after purchasing Rosedown returned both house and garden to mint condition, admired today by tourists from around the world.

Preserved as a State Historic Site, Rosedown today looks much as it must have when a delighted Martha Barrow Turnbull moved in to begin a family with her beloved husband. It was a gracious time of simple pleasures and grand entertainments, preserved in writings of turn-of-the-century parish historian Miss Louise Butler, who grew up nearby at The Cottage Plantation dating from the 1790s. Fondly recording a day's visit by neighboring plantation aristocracy, she describes the visitors arriving with a touch of *mal de mer* from a rough coach ride and being immediately fortified in proper sequence with cordials, juleps, claret, sherry, champagne, and spirited coffee, so that they depart, the gentlemen especially, with eyes considerably brighter than when they arrived!

During just such a period the charming young bride Martha Turnbull planned a housewarming party to introduce to her relatives and loved ones the fine home her Daniel had built for her in 1835.

Here was the young bride's "grocery list" for a menu planned for the gustatory pleasure of only some 30 expected guests:

6 chickens	12 dozen eggs for cakes
2 turkeys	23 bananas
2 ducks	6 pineapples
1 ham	2 hogshead ice
1 tongue	4 decanters wine
1 roast mutton	4 decanters brandy
1 pig	8 bottles champagne

Old Cake Recipe from the Misses Bowman of Rosedown

1¾ lb. flour, sifted
1¼ lb. fairly brown sugar
¾ lb. butter, creamed
1¼ lb. raisins
¼ lb. citron
1 grated nutmeg
4 eggs, separated
1 pt. milk, slightly sour
1 tsp. baking soda
2 cups water
1½ tsp. cornstarch
1 large spoonful butter
½ cup sugar
Wine (optional)

Mix flour with brown sugar, creamed butter, raisins, citron, nutmeg, separately beaten eggs, and last add milk mixed with soda. Bake in a cake mold almost 2 hours. This cake is delicious served as a pudding with a rich sauce made by boiling water thickened with cornstarch, then adding butter and sugar. Add wine if desired after it cools. This recipe is taken from an early cookbook, *Feliciana Recipes,* published by Grace Episcopal Church.

Black Church Suppers

Among the rolling hills and hollows of this area flourishes a surprisingly bountiful crop of churches. Besides the usual smattering of denominations such as Episcopal, Methodist, Roman Catholic, Presbyterian, and a few more charismatic groups, we have a whopping number of Baptist churches, a great many of the smaller ones with predominantly black congregations.

Boasting such colorful names as Raspberry Number One and Sweet Cherobee, these congregations adhere to a literal interpretation of the Good Book and a basic translation of its ideas into practice.

Baptism in these country churches is therefore a literal washing away of the sins of the white-clad candidates for baptism in the Holy Spirit. While the encroachments of progress have meant in-church baptismal fonts for many of the more prosperous modern congregations, some continue to practice the cleansing ritual with liberal dunkings in farm ponds or creeks. These outside ceremonies follow revivals and prayer meetings and are accompanied by rhythmic chants and time-honored gospel songs like "Amazing Grace" in a joyfully moving ritual of a deep and literal faith.

At West Feliciana's Afton Villa Baptist Church, for example, church member Violet Pate says the number of candidates varies from year to year. "Some years we have good baptizings, 30 to 40 head; other years nobody wants to get religion." Afton Villa used to baptize in ponds on Afton Villa or Catalpa plantations or Spring Grove, but now there's a pool behind the newly bricked church.

Afton Villa Baptist Church is the oldest black church in West Feliciana Parish, beginning in Civil War days when the mistress of

Afton Villa Plantation donated a small piece of land for a school and church to a congregation of several hundred blacks who'd been meeting in a nearby hollow in the woods. The donation was made largely because of a slave brought to Afton as a small child when her Kentucky mistress married plantation owner David Barrow. Named Jenny Lind, no doubt for the "Swedish nightingale" who toured

the United States in the early 1850s to great acclaim, she was raised by Mrs. Barrow and educated at home, so completely considered one of the family that when she married George Tilly on New Year's Day 1867, the ceremony was performed in the formal parlor at Afton Villa.

Now the church, its building modernized over the years but still on the land Jenny Lind's mistress donated because of her commitment to formalized religious instruction and education for blacks, continues to hold services and celebrations of faith in time-honored ways. Besides baptisms, there are wake services the night before burial. In the old days, the deceased was transported to church in a huge black glass-windowed covered wagon pulled by mules, then waked throughout the night. "The old folks," Violet Pate explains, "always sat up with the dead; they said it was the last they could do for them, to wake them right." At the funeral services, marked by music, eulogies, obituaries, and the reading of condolences and cards, the deceased's customary seat is "veiled" and left vacant for 30 days out of respect if he held church office, and funeral programs give highlights of his life and maybe even a photo.

An annual Pastor Anniversary celebration honors the pastor on the anniversary of his calling; Afton Villa's Rev. Sam Johnson came to the church in 1957. Older church members are honored at programs called "This Is Your Life," planned in absolute secrecy to surprise them with the reading of a life history, gatherings of children from far away, and monetary gifts pinned onto the recipient's clothing.

The church anniversary is also celebrated, with donations, the return of old friends and often even descendants of Jenny Lind Tilly, a birthday cake, and the proud recitation of the long saga of the history of the congregation. Recalls Violet Pate of this moving service, "The old-timers really have told us about the old days, how they used to walk to church with lanterns at night, and how they'd walk barefooted along the dirt roads and clean their feet with a rag before putting on their shoes to enter the church." Other special services mark the anniversaries of the choirs, stewardesses, ushers, and deacons; the ushers play a major role in church, seating newcomers, keeping order (no gum chewing), quieting children, passing out water, and seeing to those vigorously seized by the spirit or "shouting."

Stemming from the old days when members had few resources other than the church in time of trouble, Afton Villa's two long-established benevolent societies fill many needs, sitting with the sick, paying for some medical care, and providing burial insurance. An annual homecoming service attracts former members from across the country and is often the occasion for serving some good home cooking from the spacious and spotless kitchen added onto the main church building.

Afton Villa's church suppers are famous throughout the community for fine cooking—platters full of fried chicken or baked hen, potato salad, vegetables, and lots of delectable desserts—and are extremely useful fundraising tools, too. Violet Pate is usually in on the preparations, and shares some of her favorite church supper recipes here (for more of them, order her wonderful *Plantation Recipes,* Box 1252, St. Francisville, LA 70775).

Violet Pate's Pecan Pie

⅔ cup sugar
1 tbsp. flour
3 eggs
1 tbsp. butter or oleo
1 cup corn syrup, light or dark
1 tsp. vanilla extract
1 cup pecan halves
1 9" pie crust

Mix sugar with flour, then add eggs and butter. Add corn syrup, vanilla, and pecans. Pour into unbaked pie crust. Start in oven at 400 degrees for 10 minutes, then lower temperature to 350 degrees for 45 more minutes, or until firm.

Violet Pate's Lemon Meringue Pie

1 cup sugar
¼ cup cornstarch
¼ tsp. salt
1½ cups water
2 tbsp. butter or oleo
3 eggs, separated
⅓ cup lemon juice
1½ tsp. grated lemon rind
1 9" baked pie crust
6 tbsp. sugar

Mix 1 cup sugar, cornstarch, salt, and water; cook until thick. Add butter and egg yolks, lemon juice, and grated rind. Pour into pie crust. Beat egg whites with 6 tbsp. sugar until very stiff. Pour over filling and bake at 350 degrees for 15-20 minutes, until slightly browned on top.

Violet Pate's Bread and Butter Pickles

6 medium cucumbers
4 medium onions
2 bell peppers
½ cup salt
1 qt. water
Ice cubes
3 cups vinegar
3 cloves garlic
5 cups sugar
1½ tsp. turmeric
2 tbsp. mustard seed
1 tsp. celery seed

Slice cucumbers, onions, and bell peppers very thinly. Sprinkle salt over vegetables. Add water and ice cubes; let stand for 3 hours, stirring several times. Drain. Make syrup by mixing vinegar, garlic, sugar, turmeric, mustard seed, and celery seed. Boil about 5 minutes. Add drained cucumbers, onions, and bell peppers to mixture and let come to a boil for about 2 minutes. Pour into jars and seal carefully. Makes about 7 pt.

Violet Pate's Chocolate Glazed Pound Cake

3 cups sugar
1½ cups butter
5 eggs
3 cups sifted flour
½ cup cocoa
½ tsp. salt
½ tsp. baking powder
1 cup milk
2 tsp. vanilla extract
4 oz. German sweet chocolate
1 tbsp. butter
¼ cup water
1 cup powdered sugar
½ tsp. salt
1 tsp. vanilla extract

To make cake, mix sugar, 1½ cups butter, and eggs. Add flour, cocoa, ½ tsp. salt, baking powder, milk, and 2 tsp. vanilla. Bake in tube pan at 300 degrees for 1½ hours. To make glaze, cook chocolate with butter and water over low heat; add powdered sugar, salt, and vanilla. Pour over cake.

Violet Pate's Pecan Candy

1 can evaporated milk
3 cups sugar
1 cup sugar
2½ cups chopped pecans
1 heaping tbsp. marshmallow creme
1 tbsp. butter
1 tsp. vanilla extract

Mix milk and 3 cups sugar; heat over low heat and be careful not to boil. Caramelize 1 cup sugar in skillet. Mix with milk and sugar. Cook until comes to soft boil and "balls" in cold water. Add pecans, marshmallow, and butter. Cook about 10 minutes. When mixture "balls" in cold water and sort of pops like jelly does when it's done, add vanilla. Remove from heat and cool. When it sugars, beat once more and spread in greased pan. Cool and cut like fudge.

Gertrude Veal's Lemon Cake

1 cup butter
2 cups sugar
2 tsp. cream of tartar
3 cups sifted flour
1 tsp. baking soda
1 cup milk
6-7 egg whites
3 egg yolks
⅓ lb. sugar
1½ sticks butter
1 tsp. cream of tartar
Rind of 1 lemon, grated
Juice of 2 lemons

Cream 1 cup butter and 2 cups sugar until light. Add 2 tsp. cream of tartar to flour and sift again. Dissolve soda in milk and add alternately with the flour to the creamed mixture. Whip egg whites until light but not dry, and fold into batter. Pour into 2 pans lined on bottom with wax paper. Bake in moderate oven (350-375 degrees) until cakes leave the sides of pans. Cool. To make frosting, beat 3 egg yolks. Cream ⅓ lb. sugar with 1½ sticks butter. Add cream of tartar, lemon rind, egg yolks, and lemon juice. Cook carefully in top of double boiler until mixture firms to consistency desired for frosting. Frost between layers and on top.

St. Francisville Inn

A quaint country inn that salvaged from total disrepair a picturesque Victorian structure that for years had housed only vagrants and strays right in the heart of historic downtown St. Francisville, the St. Francisville Inn had been built around 1880 by Morris Wolf, member of the town's thriving early Jewish community and owner of the bustling Wolf's General Store and Cotton Gin across the street from his home. A supplier of plantation goods, Wolf sold everything from boots and buggies to coffins, and Saturdays saw the country folk from miles around crowding in by the wagonload to make their weekly or monthly purchases there.

Wolf and his brother Emmanuel built Victorian Gothic homes set side by side, well back from the bustling street traffic and surrounded by live oaks and gardens; Emmanuel's house was eventually torn down, and Morris's was in a sorry state prior to restoration . . . no plumbing, no electricity, no doors, no windowpanes, no sewer system, porches rotting, roof full of holes, plaster fallen, and bay windows sagging.

Now the peaked dormers and gingerbread trim, wrought-iron gallery rail and pleasant porch swings, twin parlors and antique prints, period wallpapers and lace curtains, arched bay windows

and ceiling medallions provide plenty of historic ambiance, and overnight rooms have been added to the rear across the New Orleans-style landscaped brick courtyard with its splashing fountain.

Restored by Dick and Florence Fillet, the inn is now home to a young family and combines the husband's culinary skills with the wife's hotel background to provide a warm and accommodating atmosphere. Pat Walsh was a petroleum engineer in the midst of Louisiana's oil patch when he took early retirement, published a cookbook called *OIL & GAStronomy* (some of his recipes follow), wiped the oil from his boots, and moved his wife and young children from New Orleans to Audubon plantation country. Wife Laurie grew up in the family-owned LaSalle Hotel in the Crescent City, so running a popular B&B plus restaurant was no challenge for her, and the three kids pitched in to help when needed. The whole family is active in community affairs, with Laurie employed as Main Street director for St. Francisville and the inn serving as headquarters and center of activities for nearly every festival and special event in town, located as it is right in the heart of the downtown Historic District next to public Parker Park with its live oaks and Victorian-inspired bandstand.

Cajun Cayenne Toast

2-3 loaves French bread
2½ tsp. cayenne pepper
1½ tsp. sugar
1½ tsp. salt
1½ tsp. onion powder
1½ tsp. garlic powder
1 tsp. paprika
½ tsp. black pepper
1 cup olive oil

Using an electric knife, slice bread about ¼" thick. Place slices in single layers on ungreased cookie sheets. Mix all seasonings and oil in a small bowl. Lightly coat one side of each bread slice. Whisk mixture often so seasonings will not settle to bottom. In a 200-degree oven, dry slices until very crisp, similar to melba toast. Cooking time should be approximately 1 hour. Best served fresh, but will keep several days. Can also be frozen. Serves 8-10.

Trout Meunière with Roasted Pecans

1 cup pecans
5 tbsp. butter, softened
3 tbsp. lemon juice
½ tsp. Worcestershire sauce
3 tbsp. oil
3 tbsp. flour
1 ½ cups fish broth or bottled clam juice
3 tbsp. Worcestershire sauce
½ cup clarified butter
¼ cup chopped parsley
6 tbsp. lemon juice
1 cup flour
2 tbsp. Tony Chachere's or other Creole seasoning
1 tsp. cayenne pepper
1½ cups milk
2 eggs
6-8 trout fillets
8 tbsp. butter, softened

Spread pecans on cookie sheet and bake for approximately 10 minutes at 325 degrees. Put approximately half the pecans into blender with 5 tbsp. butter, 3 tbsp. lemon juice, and ½ tsp. Worcestershire sauce. Blend until smooth. Break the other half of the pecans into various sizes, leaving a few whole. In a heavy skillet, heat oil and 3 tbsp. flour. Stirring constantly, heat until a medium-brown roux about the color of pecans. Add the broth a little at a time, stirring continuously. Bring to a boil, then turn down heat and simmer for 45 minutes. Add 3 tbsp. Worcestershire and the clarified butter, stirring vigorously to blend in the butter. Add parsley and 6 tbsp. lemon juice. Stir in, then remove from heat and set aside. To 1 cup flour, add Tony Chachere's and cayenne pepper. Beat together milk and eggs. Dip trout in egg/milk bath, then dredge through flour. Repeat process if thicker crust is desired. Melt 8 tbsp. butter in a heavy skillet. Sauté fish approximately 2 minutes on both sides over medium heat. Fillets should be golden brown. Serve by spreading the pecan butter onto each fillet, then covering with the meunière sauce, then sprinkling with the pecan pieces. Serves 6-8.

Ice-Cream Socials

St. Francisville's present United Methodist Church, its roof sloping steeply into the overhanging oak trees dripping with Spanish moss, was built in 1899. Today, more than a hundred years later, its congregation still fills the entire downtown Historic District with the sweet sound of Sunday-morning hymns, the songs swelling from the little frame church on Royal Street.

The bell that rings in its belfry was salvaged from the first local Methodist church, built in 1844 right on the bustling main street of Bayou Sara when that community was a busy riverport, its wharves piled high with cotton and the floating palaces they called steamboats waiting to transport the populace to New Orleans and thence the world.

That earlier church had galleries wide enough to accommodate several hundred slaves during services and high enough to shelter many terrified townsfolk from rising river waters in the series of disastrous floods that eventually sounded the death knell for Bayou Sara.

Ever mindful of its long, proud heritage and tradition of community helpfulness, the present congregation hosts late each summer an entertainment that might just as easily be taking place a century ago, a hymn sing and ice-cream social, to encourage continuing community fellowship. After joining friends of many denominations for an evening of singing favorite old hymns (requests are taken), homemade ice cream and from-scratch cakes are served in the parish hall, the perfect conclusion to an evening of old-fashioned spiritual togetherness.

Icebox Vanilla Ice Cream

1 can condensed milk
2 cups light cream
1 cup cold water
1 tbsp. vanilla extract

Combine ingredients in bowl and pour into big flat pan. Freeze until nearly firm. Put in chilled bowl and beat until smooth. Return to pan and freeze until firm.

Katharine Butler's Homemade Chocolate Sauce

1 square unsweetened chocolate
2 heaping tbsp. butter
1 cup sugar
½ cup water

Melt chocolate and butter in saucepan. Add sugar and water, stirring well. Cook and stir over medium heat at a slow boil until quite thick. Pour hot over ice cream. This sauce is supposed to be very gummy, hardening when it touches the cold ice cream.

Loelia's Vanilla Ice Cream

2 tsp. gelatin
¼ cup cold water
¾ cup milk
1 vanilla bean
¾ cup sugar
⅛ tsp. salt
3 cups whipping cream

Soak gelatin in water. Scald milk and vanilla in double boiler. Discard vanilla. Stir in the sugar and salt until dissolved. Stir in the soaked gelatin. Cool and place in refrigerator until thoroughly chilled. Whip whipping cream with a wire whisk until thickened, but not stiff, and fold into the chilled and beaten gelatin mixture. Freeze.

Loelia's Vanilla Ice Cream with Egg Yolks

2 egg yolks
½ cup powdered sugar
¼ cup cream
1 tsp. vanilla extract
1 cup whipping cream
2 egg whites

Beat yolks. Beat in sugar and cream until well blended. Cook and stir in double boiler over hot water until slightly thickened. Chill. Add vanilla. Whip whipping cream until thickened but not stiff. In a separate bowl, whip egg whites until stiff but not dry. Fold the cream and egg whites into the custard and freeze.

Chocolate Ice Cream

1 14-oz. can condensed milk
⅔ cup chocolate syrup
2 cups whipping cream, whipped

Stir together milk and chocolate. Fold in whipped cream. Pour into 9x5" loaf pan, lined with foil. Freeze 6 hours or until firm. Slice or scoop out to serve.

Christmas Desserts

Christmas in this area has always meant a customary gathering together of the clan to celebrate the season according to special and much-loved family traditions.

In Woodville, Mississippi, the late Miss Mary Scott remembered turn-of-the-century Christmases as festive times of long family visits, candles burning in every window, and two separate dining rooms filled with feasts and feasters. Platters of partridges were not uncommon after daily hunts made by the men of the family, and the sideboard groaned under marble cakes, plain cakes, chocolate cakes, pink cakes, ribbon cakes, white fruit cakes, dark fruit cakes, and even a 32-egg cake cooked in a specially designed pan. The *piece de resistance,* however, was the Christmas charlotte russe, all frothy and full of whipped cream.

In West Feliciana, Christmas was just as full of tradition, beginning Christmas Eve after late church services and lots of eggnog. At Catalpa Plantation, cookies and a toddy were left on the mantelpiece for Santa Claus; at Butler Greenwood, eggnog or sherry and fruitcake were the offerings, while at Greenwood Plantation in Weyanoke, Santa was lured with hot chocolate and cake and a sack of pecans, and could always be heard on the roof 4 floors up. At the Plettinger home at the foot of the hill in St. Francisville, children of the family always considerately left oats for Santa's reindeer on the front gallery.

Houses were filled with the pungent scent of fresh-cut boughs of greenery, with mantels decked with cedar, pine, and native holly with bright red berries. Plenty of mistletoe with waxy white berries, shot down from the treetops by the boys of the family, was strung around by girls hopeful of kisses. Family portraits, gilt-framed mirrors, and carved stair railings were entwined with miles of green Christmas vine, the *Southern Smilax.*

The decorated Christmas trees, usually cedars

just cut in the surrounding woods, were lit by hundreds of blazing candles, real fire hazards that were enjoyed sparingly and not seen by the children of the family until early Christmas morning. This excitement was usually followed by firecrackers, a breakfast of quail on toast, church services, and servants hollering, *"Christmas Gift!"*

Christmas dinners were feasts of filé gumbo with oysters or oyster cocktail, fish, turkey and cornbread dressing or roast goose with oyster dressing, sweet potatoes, cauliflower, salted nuts, cranberry sauce, ground artichokes, homemade pickles or relish, and jellies. Oysters were used plentifully, in oyster stew for holiday suppers and in cocktails, dressings, gumbo, and other dishes for Christmas dinner; merchants of the parish in the old days ordered bushels of oysters shipped up from the coast, then gave them away to favored customers during the season.

For dessert, there would be ambrosia, flaming plum pudding with hard sauce liberally spirited with good whiskey, mincemeat pies, and fruitcake. Another favorite old-fashioned dessert was Floating Island.

These Christmas desserts were special treats to which children looked forward throughout the entire year, well worth the time and trouble to concoct. Like children's tea parties and other simpler old-fashioned entertainments, the homemade Christmas dessert tradition shouldn't be allowed to die out, for sadly lacking is the child nourished on the immediate gratification of frozen Sara Lee (however tasty) rather than the mouthwatering anticipation of slowly cranking the ice-cream freezer, or following with wide eyes the progress of the flaming plum pudding to the Christmas dinner table, or marveling at the tiny red spots of currant jelly topping dollops of meringue adrift in a sea of custard in the holiday Floating Island.

Consequently, many of the plantation houses and smaller homes of the area continue to follow these old traditions, taking pleasure in passing down through the generations special family recipes and customs. Christmas Eve, for example, finds revelers toasting the season with eggnog just as in the old days at Catalpa Plantation, always famous for its hospitality, then trooping off to late services at Grace Episcopal Church in St. Francisville just as their ancestors, some of the founding vestrymen, did before them.

Charlotte Russe

¾ tsp. gelatin
¼ cup cold water
⅓ cup scalded milk
⅓ cup powdered sugar
2 tbsp. strong coffee
1 cup whipping cream
Ladyfingers
Custard rum sauce

Soak gelatin in water, then dissolve it in scalded milk. Beat in powdered sugar. Cool. Flavor with coffee and chill slightly. Whip cream until stiff and fold lightly into chilled ingredients. Line a mold with ladyfingers, then pour pudding into it. Chill thoroughly. Unmold and serve with your favorite custard sauce flavored with rum.

Floating Island

1 qt. milk
3 eggs
½ cup sugar
½ tsp. salt
1 scant tbsp. cornstarch
2 tsp. sugar
Vanilla extract
Currant jelly

Heat milk. Separate eggs. Mix sugar, salt, and cornstarch. Add to yolks beaten slightly. Beat whites until very stiff, add 2 tsp. sugar, and beat lightly. Spread on top of hot milk and cook 3 minutes. Lift out with a skimmer onto a plate and set aside. Pour hot milk on beaten yolks. Put this mixture into a double boiler and stir and cook until it thickens to consistency of cream. Don't overcook, or it will curdle. Cool, add vanilla to flavor, and pour into serving bowl. Put cooked whites, in dabs, over top, placing specks of currant jelly on the whites. Serve cold.

Eggnog

6 eggs
¾ cup sugar
1 pt. whipping cream
1 pt. milk
1 pt. bourbon
Nutmeg (optional)

Beat yolks and whites separately. Add ½ cup sugar to yolks while beating. Beat whites stiff and add ¼ cup sugar. Mix whites and yolks. Stir in cream and milk, add bourbon, and stir thoroughly. Top with sprinkling of nutmeg if desired.

Mamie Thompson's Famous Catalpa Eggnog

6 eggs, separated
6 tbsp. sugar
6 jiggers bourbon
1 half-pt. whipping cream, whipped
¾ cup milk (optional)
Nutmeg

Beat egg yolks until very light. Add sugar. Beat. Beat egg whites, then gently fold into yolk mixture a little at a time. Pour bourbon over, to sort of cook the egg whites. You can use half an eggshell as your jigger, said Mamie Thompson, but be sure it's the bigger half! Mix. Add whipped cream, folding in gently. If too thick, add up to ¾ cup milk. Refrigerate until very cold. Top with sprinkling of nutmeg.

Old English Plum Pudding

1 lb. sugar
1 lb. raisins
1 lb. currants
1 lb. beef suet, minced
½ lb. stale breadcrumbs
½ lb. flour
8 eggs, beaten separately
1 wineglass brandy
1 wineglass wine
1 pt. milk
2 nutmegs, grated
1 tbsp. mixed cinnamon and mace
1 tsp. salt

Mix ingredients and boil 4 hours in tin bucket set in water. Lift top to let steam escape before serving. Eat with hard sauce flavored with plenty of good whiskey or brandy. This recipe, from the vintage *Feliciana Recipes,* published by Grace Episcopal Church, was said at the time to have been "brought from Liverpool more than a century ago and age has not lessened its popularity."

Sweet Potatoes

It was Harry Daniel, with the help of Dr. Julian Miller of the LSU Horticulture Department, who initiated commercial sweet-potato production in the Felicianas in the early 1940s. The rich soil proved perfect for growing yams, and for decades many of the area farmers raised potatoes as their main cash crop, selling the produce directly to Princeville Canning Company in St. Francisville.

Daniel's son Ed put in years raising potatoes himself, planting over a thousand acres and employing more than a hundred workers growing yams. When Princeville was sold to Joan of Arc and eventually to Pillsbury, though, the local canning plant was closed and area potato production dropped sharply.

For a time Harry Daniel's grandson Irv, with several sons of his own, got back into potatoes, having learned the hard way not to try to compete with the Corn Belt in the grain market. He made the move only after careful consideration, working with LSU specialists in horticulture, marketing, and finance. The farm plan they made using his resources showed sweet-potato production could indeed still be profitable, and Daniel's Feliciana Yam brand, a refined version of the original Puerto Rican Unit One strain developed by Dr. Miller, hit the market.

Planting several hundred acres in a process that was mostly mechanized, Irv stayed busy from dawn until dusk and got a laugh from his grandfather's diary, recording planting and harvesting data from half a century ago. "Back then," Irv said, "tenants lived on the place and shopped at the little store on the place. It's hard to believe he writes about going off fishing for a few days right in the middle of the season, but back then there was nothing to break and there was a higher level of leisure in management, with tenants farming their own plots and being responsible for their own crops, using their own mules. The only repair work might be a little blacksmith work on plowshares."

The bulk of Daniel's crop was sold for canning under contract with canneries, though about 35 percent was sold in supermarkets as Grade No. 1 potatoes, basically a one-serving potato free of defects, containing only 140 calories and ranking high as a healthful food product.

Rich in vitamin A, carotene, and two types of nutritive fiber, the sweet potato is considered one of the best foods for preventing certain types of cancer. Just one deep-orange-colored yam contains several times the recommended daily allowance of vitamin A and one-third the RDA of vitamin C as well as iron, thiamine, and calcium. Its two types of fiber include both the regular coarseness fiber and a water-soluble fiber that is thought to absorb fats as it goes through the digestive system.

At least partly because of their healthful aspects, sweet potatoes have enjoyed a comeback on

American dinner tables. Said Irv Daniel, "Sweet potatoes have traditionally been a holiday food, served with lots of butter and sugar. But they are just plain delicious steamed the same way you'd steam other vegetables like broccoli. Even served with butter, they have fewer calories than Irish potatoes served with sour cream."

Daniel's "Feliciana Cured" potatoes were planted in tried-and-true fashion by methods improved upon through 4 generations of his family, rotating the sweet-potato crop with pastureland for cattle. Plowed in winter, contoured in late spring to encourage precise drainage, fertilized and sub-soiled and put into beds, the land was ready in March for seed potatoes to be bedded out, taken out of storage, and covered with soil so they'd sprout and produce the slips that were then transplanted into the fields.

Slips are sprouts cut above the ground by hand with a knife and then fed by hand into a trans-planting machine operated by 10 workers. It takes 12,500 slips to plant an acre, set out 1' apart on 42" rows. Ten workers could plant about 8½ acres a day, and planting season lasted until 300 or more acres had been planted.

One hundred thousand or so acres of potatoes are grown nationwide. When the packing houses and cannery were in operation locally, at least 2,500 acres of potatoes were planted right in West Feliciana Parish, but that acreage has dropped considerably. Besides growing and packing his own potatoes, Irv Daniel spent a lot of time developing a market for his product and encouraging other farmers to grow potatoes for him to pack and sell.

Not that he had time on his hands. Planting last-ed through late June, and harvest began in late July, so there was no time for Irv to go fishing! As the potatoes developed in the fields, careful culti-vation was done, and a spraying routine was begun to keep bugs from laying eggs that would become tunneling larvae harmful to the crop.

After the growing season, which ideally lasted 120 days, the vines were removed and a mechani-cal digger, pulled by a tractor, began the harvest. The digger lifted the potatoes out of the soil, shook the dirt loose, and transported the potatoes up to a moving table manned by 12 people, who stood on each side sorting the potatoes right there in the field as the digger slowly made its way through the rows. Daniel kept 2 diggers going throughout most of the harvest.

The potatoes were sorted in 60-bushel bins, then hauled immediately to the curing room in the packing plant. While some planters sell green pota-toes right from the field, Irv took pains to cure his properly so they'd last longer. For 5 to 7 days the harvested potatoes were kept in a controlled atmosphere of 85 percent humidity and 85 degrees, then moved into a room at the same humidity but with the temperature lowered to 60 degrees. Cured that way, the potatoes maintained weight and remained dormant so they could be kept nearly year round if properly stored in a hamper in a cool room (never in the refrigerator).

Besides knowing just about all there is to know about raising potatoes, Irv Daniel knows a good bit about eating them, too, from long years of practice, even though he has now switched to growing hard-wood seedlings for reforestation, after some bad potato crops and constant labor problems. Here are some of his favorite recipes, some sure to please the calorie-conscious eater and others rich enough for the traditional holiday groaning board.

Irv Daniel's Favorite Sweet-Potato Pie

3 oz. cream cheese
1 cup flour
1 stick butter
2 cups peeled, boiled yams
1 cup sugar
2 tbsp. flour
2 tsp. vanilla extract
1 stick butter

To make crust, mix cream cheese, 1 cup flour, and 1 stick butter thoroughly in a bowl. Chill bowl and board. Roll out and shape. Fit into pie pan. Yams will be so soft after boiling that you won't even have to mash them, just push them into the measuring cup. Add sugar, flour, vanilla, and 1 stick butter. Mix and pour into crust. Bake at 375 degrees until crust is browned.

Baked Sweet Potatoes

Bake only cured sweet potatoes. Wash and dry, then trim ends. Rub lightly with oil, place on cookie sheet, and bake in oven preheated to 400 degrees. After 15 minutes, reduce temperature to 375 degrees. Cook until potatoes are soft, about 1½ hours. Sweet potatoes should be baked in a conventional oven, not wrapped in foil or microwaved, to maintain their rich syrupy flavor.

Steamed Sweet Potatoes

Peel potatoes and slice ⅜" thick. Steam until tender with mixed vegetables like broccoli, onion, cauliflower, or whatever else you're steaming. Serve with a little butter and lemon juice. The potatoes will steam as quickly as other vegetables.

Sweet-Potato Crudités

Peel potatoes, slice as you would carrot sticks, and use them the same way, mixed with other raw vegetables in crudités platters or as after-school snacks. Be sure to soak the potato sticks in lemon juice and water so they don't oxidize and turn black.

Leola Metz's Sweet-Potato Pie

1½ cups sifted flour + 2 tbsp.
Pinch salt
½ cup shortening
3 tbsp. water
10 No. 1 medium sweet potatoes
3 tsp. cinnamon
5 eggs
2½ cups sugar
1½ sticks butter, melted
1½ tsp. vanilla extract
1½ cups cream
2 heaping tbsp. cornstarch
1 tsp. nutmeg
1½ pt. whipping cream

To make crust, sift flour and salt in small mixing bowl. Add shortening and work into flour. Add enough water to form a ball. Don't overwork dough. Place ball of dough onto floured wax paper or board. Pat out into a circle and then roll with rolling pin, preferably a frozen rolling pin. Bake crust about 5 minutes before filling. Makes 1 crust (doubles easily). Peel potatoes, rinse in salt water, drain, and cover with water. Cook until tender. Drain potatoes, then mash. Add cinnamon, eggs, sugar, butter, vanilla, cream, cornstarch, and nutmeg while beating. Pour into uncooked pie crusts and bake at 425 degrees for 10 minutes. Turn oven down to 350 degrees and bake for 20-30 minutes more. Serve topped with whipping cream whipped until stiff and sweetened with a little sugar. Makes 2 pies. The filling can be baked in a casserole dish and freezes well, even baked as pie. This is a delightfully rich and delicious dessert or vegetable for a holiday dinner.

Audubon Pilgrimage Sweet-Potato Bread

3 cups sugar
1 cup oil
4 eggs
1 tsp. cinnamon
1 tsp. nutmeg
3½ cups sifted flour
2 tsp. baking soda
½ tsp. salt
⅔ cup water
2 cups cooked mashed sweet potatoes
1 cup chopped nuts (optional)

Combine sugar and oil; beat well. Add eggs; beat. Combine dry ingredients and add to egg mixture alternately with water. Stir in sweet potatoes and nuts. Pour into 3 small greased loaf pans. Bake at 350 degrees for 1 hour.

Sweet-Potato Muffins

1 large potato
1 tsp. butter
½ tsp. salt
½ cup milk
2 eggs, well beaten
2 tsp. baking powder
2 cups flour
3 tsp. sugar

Boil potato until soft, then mash through colander to get 1 cup. Add butter, salt, and milk. Mix thoroughly. Mix in the eggs. Sift dry ingredients; add to the potato mixture. Pour in greased muffin pans and bake in moderate oven. This recipe was contributed by Mrs. Harry Daniel to the wonderful old *Star Hill Cook Book*, published by the Home Demonstration Club in that part of West Feliciana Parish years ago.

Bopotamus Festival

In the rural reaches of the Feliciana Parishes, it's sometimes necessary to make one's own entertainment, and the late lamented little local festival named for the bopotamus was a prime example of just how much fun that could be.

Held in the downtown business district of Star Hill (don't blink, or you'll miss it), the festival celebrated the wily bopotamus, first cousin to the nauga of naugahyde fame. There were enormous cash prizes offered for sightings, a museum complete with purported bopotamus artifacts, children's activities, competitions among volunteer firemen, watermelon-eating contests, live bands and entertainment, arts and crafts, food with such evocative appellations as "Nauga Legs" furnished by local restaurants, and a Miss Bopotamus contest pitting hopefuls against each other who were of such questionable beauty as to assure that the bopotamus would never come out of the woods!

There was also a fund-raising auction to benefit the local fire department substation and a scholarship given annually to needy college-bound students in memory of the late Murphy Dreher, Jr., self-proclaimed mayor of Star Hill and father of the festival.

A notorious prankster whose long-suffering friends often opened the newspaper to find their engagements announced to the lovely Miss Bertha Butts, Murphy's pet pig, Dreher only met his match once, and that was when he received a letter, supposedly from an official wildlife foundation, naming him leader of an expedition to capture the first bopotamus, an elusive little critter sighted nowhere but the rugged Tunica Hills (it actually seemed to range primarily between the Audubon Lounge and the bar at Club South of the Border).

A specially designed bopotamus gun was soon forthcoming, and in an effort to flush out the sender of these missives, Dreher organized the first annual Bopotamus Ball, at which the letter writer was to wear a red carnation. Unfortunately that particular

individual was detained by car trouble and never *did* put in an appearance, but everybody else in the world was at the ball . . . *all* wearing red carnations.

That first ball's Bopotamus Beauty Pageant attracted such varied entries as a lovely lady in her seventies sheathed in a revealing leopard-skin jumpsuit and a gentleman wearing only a loincloth who imbibed a bit too freely and lost his false teeth on the side of the road on the way home, an accident made all the more regrettable because of his pending appearance the following day as best man in his son's wedding; the next year the same gentleman attended the ball in the same attire, with the addition of a pouch around his neck to hold his false teeth as needed.

Held the last weekend in August, the festival was a fitting fling to mark the end of summer fun. It was also the highlight of the social season in the tiny and close-knit Star Hill community, whose good cooks provide some of Murphy's favorite recipes.

Mulla's 1-2-3-4 Cake

1 cup butter
2 cups sugar
3 cups sifted cake flour
4 eggs
4 tsp. baking powder
¼ tsp. salt
1 cup milk
2 tsp. vanilla extract

Mix butter and sugar, creaming until well blended. Add eggs one at a time, mixing well after each addition. To flour, add baking powder and salt. Add to creamed mixture, alternating with milk. Add vanilla and bake at 350 degrees until done, about 30 minutes or more. This recipe seems to have originated with Mrs. T. H. Martin, Sr., but was a favorite of "Mulla," Lorena Dreher, who was Murphy Jr.'s mother. A person who dearly loved people and whose porch was always a favorite stopping spot for anyone passing through Star Hill, she had a wonderful sense of humor that she seems to have passed on to her descendants. Her daughter-in-law Patsy Dreher says her stove always "had pots full of the best food you'd ever eat . . . just good old country stuff, like fresh snap beans with new potatoes and pot roast smothered in onions, and all cooked by *ear.*"

Loisie's Cookies

1 stick butter
1 cup light brown sugar
1 egg
¼ tsp. ground ginger
¼ tsp. mace
¼ tsp. cinnamon
¼ tsp. nutmeg
1 tsp. vanilla extract
1 cup self-rising flour
1 cup pecans, lightly toasted

Use blender to mix well all ingredients except pecans, adding flour a little at a time. Then add pecans. The secret to these cookies is making them small—¼ tsp. each. Scoop a large spoonful of batter, then use a knife to dab a little at a time onto cookie sheet lined with foil. Bake at 375 degrees for 6-8 minutes. These were Murphy Jr.'s favorite cookies, and he was said to eat a quart of them a night until his wife, Patsy, hid them and restricted him to only a pint. The recipe came from Lois Simmons, Murphy Jr.'s great-aunt. "Loisie" lived with Hilda Moss, "Mossie," in a small cabin at Star Hill and always had a welcoming hearth and a batch of cookies in the oven. The ladies loved to tell stories of their experiences during World War I working for the Red Cross, especially the time General Pershing came by the kitchen tent one morning asking for a cup of hot tea; after someone refused him because there was no tea strainer, Loisie obligingly used her petticoat as a strainer and served the delighted general.

Loisie's Honey Pecan Balls

1 cup shortening
¼ cup honey
2 tsp. vanilla extract
2 cups sifted flour
½ tsp. salt
2 cups finely chopped pecans
Powdered sugar

Cream shortening; add honey and then vanilla. Mix well. Add flour, salt, and nuts. Mix well. Form into small balls the size of a nickel. Bake on a greased cookie sheet at 300 degrees for 40-45 minutes. Roll in powdered sugar while hot, then again when cool.

Patsy's Crawfish-Broccoli Casserole

1 bunch broccoli
1 pkg. thin noodles
2 cups chopped onions
1 cup chopped bell pepper
½ cup chopped celery
1 stick butter
1 can sliced water chestnuts
1 large can sliced mushrooms
1 lb. peeled crawfish tails
¾ cup chopped green onions
2-3 cups shredded Swiss cheese

Boil broccoli in seasoned water; chop and set aside. Boil noodles until done, then drain and set aside. Sauté onions, bell pepper, and celery in butter in skillet until tender. Add water chestnuts and mushrooms. Add crawfish tails and sauté for about 10 minutes. Add green onions and cheese, reserving some cheese for topping. Fold gently all together. Pour into buttered casserole dish and top with cheese. Bake in 350-degree oven for about 30 minutes, until cheese is bubbly and lightly browned. Cooked rice can be substituted for noodles if desired, and if a creamier dish is desired, fold in a can of cream of mushroom soup.

Patsy's Crawfish Crepes

2 eggs
½ cup flour
¼ cup milk
¼ cup chicken broth
¼ tsp. salt
1 tbsp. butter + more to cook crepes
½ stick butter
1 cup chopped green onions
1 can sliced mushrooms
Hot pepper sauce
Juice from ½ lemon
1 lb. peeled crawfish tails
2 cups half & half
1 cup or more shredded mozzarella cheese

To make crepes, mix eggs, flour, milk, chicken broth (use bouillon cube), salt, and 1 tbsp. butter. Mix well and cook in small Teflon skillet, using about 3-4 tbsp. butter for each crepe. This takes a bit of practice, but it's worth it. For filling, melt ½ stick butter and add green onions, mushrooms, pepper sauce as desired, and lemon juice; sauté crawfish tails in this and cook about 15-20 minutes. Now add half & half and cheese. If too thin, thicken with a little flour or cornstarch. Fill crepes and roll up to serve, topping with a bit of the filling. Patsy Dreher says Murphy Jr. thought this was "'bout the best dish ever."

Little Chase and Big Fat Aunt May

In the life of each child, or each lucky child, is at least one very special older person, sometimes a relative but not always . . . a special friend to whom that child can go in moments of doubt or trouble, someone who always has time to share to explore the deeper meanings of life.

Just such a relationship was preserved forever in the award-winning series of *Little Chase* books, called in one review "lessons in life, learned from a quintessentially southern childhood replete with bourbon pie and frozen mint tea, hounddogs under porches and tomcats in baby clothes, wise old aunties next door and lots of old-fashioned charm."

The small child Chase, in these stories, is forever going to Aunt May's to learn about living and loving, the necessity for manners, the joys of friendship, the consequences of greed, the harmfulness of prejudice, even the inevitability of death.

The lessons are taught with humor in stories peopled with real honest-to-goodness friends and

neighbors and relatives from the St. Francisville area, who vied for the honor of appearing in each subsequent book. There are also lots of animals, from pigs with no manners to scruffy hound dogs indifferent to losing pet beauty contests, from tomcats in baby bonnets hurtling from second-story windows to terriers devoured in one bite by traveling circus tigers.

The lessons are made more palatable by the culinary skills of Aunt May, each of whose 345 pounds in the book is worn proudly as the reminder of some superbly delicious bourbon pie or some other equally delectable rum cake or heavenly batch of divinity fudge. As Little Chase learns, there's no problem so serious that it doesn't look better over a heaping bowl of Paradise Pudding.

Consequently, to accompany the two storybooks, *Little Chase and Big Fat Aunt May* and *Little Chase and Big Fat Aunt May Ride Again*, there was the *Little Chase and Big Fat Aunt May*

Recipe Book—A Cook's Tour of Hog Heaven, from which several of Aunt May's best recipes are reproduced here. The three books, now condensed into two volumes combining stories and recipes, are available by mail from Anne Butler, 8345 U.S. Highway 61, St. Francisville, LA 70775, or online from Xlibris.com/bookstore.

In real life, Aunt May was the late Mary Minor Pipes Butler, nowhere near as fat but almost as wise, and certainly just as good a cook as in the stories.

And if Aunt May's specialties did run to rich and spirited desserts, and if Little Chase as a tiny tot embarrassed her mother, the author of the books, by always responding to interview questions about her very favorite recipe in the books being bourbon pie, it's just like the story said, "Chase's mother didn't exactly approve of her eating bourbon pie, but Aunt May said it would give her character, and Aunt May said character was very important."

Weidmann's Bourbon Pie

1 box chocolate snap or Oreo cookies
½ cup melted oleo
25 marshmallows
1 13-oz. can evaporated milk
½ pt. whipping cream
3 tbsp. bourbon whiskey
½ pt. whipping cream
Chocolate cookie crumbs

To make the crust, crush chocolate cookies (remove and discard filling if using Oreos), mix with oleo, and pat into a 9" pie pan. Bake in 350-degree oven until hardened, 8-10 minutes. Sides of pie pan can be lined with unbroken cookies for scalloped effect. For the filling, melt marshmallows in undiluted milk, being careful not to boil. Chill mixture. Whip ½ pt. cream, then fold cream and bourbon into marshmallow mixture. Pour into cooled crust. Refrigerate 24 hours until set. Whip ½ pt. cream. Top pie with whipped cream and garnish with crumbs.

Betty Rinaudo's Rum Cake

½ cup chopped pecans
½ cup water
1 box yellow butter-cake mix
½ cup light rum
1 small box instant vanilla pudding
4 eggs
½ cup oil
1 stick butter
1 cup sugar
¼ cup rum
¼ cup water

Prepare Bundt pan and sprinkle nuts in bottom. Combine ½ cup water, cake mix, ½ cup rum, pudding mix, eggs, and oil. Mix 2-3 minutes. Pour batter into pan and bake at 350 degrees for 50-60 minutes. For glaze, mix butter, sugar, ¼ cup rum, and ¼ cup water, then boil about 2 minutes. Pour most of glaze over hot cake and let stand in pan for 30 minutes. Remove cake from pan and pour remaining glaze over top of cake.

Grasshopper Pie

14 Oreo cookies
2 tbsp. butter, melted
24 marshmallows
½ cup whole milk
4 tbsp. green crème de menthe
4 tbsp. white crème de cacao
½ pt. whipping cream, whipped

Remove and discard filling from cookies. Crush cookies and mix with butter. Pat into pie pan. Refrigerate. Melt marshmallows in milk over medium heat. Cool. Add liqueurs and whipped cream. Pour into crust and freeze.

Black Bottom Pie

1½ cups gingersnap crumbs
6 tbsp. melted butter
2 env. plain gelatin
6 tbsp. sugar
2 eggs, separated
1½ cups milk
1¼ cups rum
½ cup whipping cream
¾ cup semisweet chocolate chips
1½ cups vanilla ice cream
1 tsp. vanilla extract
8 tbsp. sugar
½ cup whipping cream, whipped
Chocolate curls or grated chocolate

Preheat oven to 350 degrees. Combine crumbs with butter and pat into 9" pie pan. Bake 5 minutes, then cool. In medium saucepan, mix gelatin with 6 tbsp. sugar. Beat egg yolks with 1 cup milk and blend into gelatin. Let stand 1 minute. Stir over low heat until gelatin is completely dissolved. Pour ¾ cup of this mixture into a large bowl, stir in rum, remaining milk and ½ cup cream. Chill, stirring occasionally, until mixture mounds slightly when dropped from spoon. Meanwhile, to remaining mixture in saucepan, add chocolate. Continue cooking over low heat, stirring constantly, until melted. With rotary beater or wire whip, blend in ice cream and vanilla; pour into prepared crust and set aside. In medium bowl, beat egg whites until soft peaks form; gradually add remaining sugar and beat until stiff. Fold into rum mixture. Chill 15 minutes, stirring gently 2-3 times, until mixture thickens and can be mounded onto chocolate layer. Chill until firm. Garnish with whipped cream and chocolate curls or grated chocolate.

Paradise Pudding

½ cup butter
1 cup sugar
4 eggs
1½ cups milk or thin cream
2 tbsp. flour
1 cup chopped pecans
1 large can shredded pineapple, drained
1 box marshmallows, cut fine
1 pt. whipping cream, whipped
Ladyfingers
Whipped cream (optional)

Place butter, sugar, eggs, milk, and flour in a double boiler and cook as for custard, stirring frequently. After thickened, let cool. About 1½ hours before serving, add nuts, pineapple, marshmallows, and whipped whipping cream. Line dishes with ladyfingers, put in pudding, and serve with a garnish of whipped cream if desired.

Gardening by the Moon

As a widow in her 80s living on a small fixed income, Ethel Metcalf of rural Weyanoke didn't plant a vegetable garden for fun; her garden to her meant adequate food, indeed, life. So when she gave gardening advice, it was like E. F. Hutton dispensing investment counsel. Others *listened*.

And her primary piece of advice was this: *Plant by the moon.*

She'd followed her own advice for more than half a century, carefully observing the heavens and consulting the almanacs as she prepared for planting each season.

As the oldest of 14 children, Ethel learned early in life the importance of bountiful harvests; cotton was the cash crop, but the vegetable patch fed the family. She herself had only four children. "I often sits up here and thinks," she mused, "if I hadn't lost three children, I might have had one to take up time with me now. My daughter, she takes up some time with me, but she loves the big city and I don't."

So Ethel took up time with her bountiful garden. Her yard blossomed with camellias, azaleas, jasmine, fruit trees, magnolia and chinaberries, spirea, flowering quince, Japanese tulips, climbing roses, wisteria, Spanish daggers, dahlias, and rooster comb. And just down the hill was a quarter-acre garden plot providing year-round food—collards, cabbage, rutabaga, turnips, beets, mustard, lettuce, carrots, sweet and Irish potatoes, onions, garlic, butter beans, snap beans, tomatoes, cucumbers, and field peas, with another plot for corn and watermelons. So when Ethel went to town for her monthly shopping, she only needed meat, meal, flour, seasonings, shortening, and butter.

Why was her garden always so productive? She used some commercial fertilizer on her potatoes and chicken manure under her greens, but she attributed her success to this: "It's because I plant by the moon. I know it works, 'cause I've done it, I've used it, I've experienced it, and I *always* have a good crop."

The proper time for planting, the almanacs say, is when nature has the earth ready and when man has prepared the soil for crops as indicated by the signs of the heavens and when the moon is in the right phase and zodiacal sign. At just that time, farmers are virtually assured successful harvests.

Ethel Metcalf favored *MacDonald's Farmers Almanac* and the *Ladies Birthday Book* almanac for information on when to plant and harvest by the moon, for it is the moon's influence in the ecliptic of the zodiac that affects vegetation.

Vegetable seeds planted in the wrong signs of the zodiac, the "barren" signs, are doomed to produce plants deficient in the "vital call-salts" needed for good health and strong growth. Seeds planted at the proper time give better yields and higher profits.

From the time of the moon's last quarter until the new moon, the earth's interior cools and the earth slows down; upward growth slows too, so this is the time for planting root crops such as potatoes. Crops with primary growth above ground should be planted during the increasing moon, when the earth's interior is warm; the stalks shoot up quickly and make much top growth, wasting little energy on the root.

But never plant on the day the moon is changing quarters. The moon is considered as increasing in light during the first and second quarters, decreasing the third and fourth quarters.

Ethel Metcalf set out her onions, garlic, turnips, potatoes, cabbage, collards, mustard, rutabaga, and beets on the dark of the moon. "That way," she said, "the onions make big bunches and multiply. If I set them out on the light of the moon, they'd just grow beautiful tops and the roots and bulbs wouldn't do much. But if I planted snap beans, say, on the dark of the moon, I'd get gorgeous vines and blossoms but the flowers would fall off before they made any beans. Same with mustard; if I planted it on the growing moon, it'd shoot up tall and make big flowers, but planted on the dark of the moon it makes big bunches of good leaves and lasts a long time."

Medical surgery performed during the influence of the increasing moon offers fastest healing and fewer complications, so Ethel Metcalf told the dentist when she'd have teeth pulled, not vice versa. She also consulted her almanacs and the moon for the most propitious times to set eggs for hatching, destroy weeds, wean babies, catch fish, predict the weather, shingle a roof, and cut lumber or fence posts, and she said fruits and vegetables gathered just before the full moon would hold up better and be fresher.

Does all this work, or is it just a bunch of bunk? Ask Ethel Metcalf, and she'd tell you she *knew* it worked. Since she always had a garden good enough to provide her with vegetables throughout the year, when Ethel Metcalf talked about gardening by the moon, people listened.

Katharine Butler's Corn Pudding

2 cups corn grated off cob
2 cups milk
2 tbsp. sugar
1 tsp. salt
2 eggs, beaten
2 tbsp. butter

Combine ingredients, adding more milk if corn is particularly dry. Place in oven-proof dish set in pan of water. Bake at 350 degrees for 1 hour.

Mary Butler's Eggplant Casserole

2 large eggplants
1 medium onion
Salted water
¾ cup chopped yellow cheese
10 salty crackers (Ritz or Saltines), crumbled
1 egg
1 small can shrimp
½ cup milk
¼ stick butter or oleo, melted
Salt and black pepper to taste
Swiss cheese, grated, to top

Peel eggplants and cut into chunks. Peel and chop onion. Boil both in small amount of water until just done; drain. Add chopped cheese, crackers, egg, shrimp, milk, butter or oleo, and seasonings. Mix well. Top with cheese. Bake about 30 minutes in oven set at 350-400 degrees.

Quick Spanish Gazpacho

1 can tomato soup
½ can water
2 tbsp. white-wine vinegar
2 tbsp. olive oil
2 large garlic cloves, pressed
Freshly ground black pepper
4-5 ice cubes
¼ cup diced cucumber
¼ cup diced tomatoes
¼ cup diced bell pepper
¼ cup seasoned croutons

Mix soup, water, vinegar, oil, garlic, and pepper. Add ice and shake until thoroughly chilled. Add vegetables and croutons. Serve at once in large soup bowls. Or serve vegetables and croutons in separate dishes and let each diner sprinkle atop his soup as desired.

Chocolate Zucchini Cake

2 cups all-purpose flour, unsifted
¼ cup unsweetened cocoa
½ cup buttermilk
1 tsp. baking powder
1 tsp. baking soda
1 tsp. cinnamon
¼ tsp. salt
3 eggs
1½ cups sugar
½ cup oil
1½ cups shredded zucchini
1 cup chopped walnuts
½ cup raisins
4 oz. cream cheese, softened
2 tsp. butter or oleo
1 cup sugar

Combine flour, cocoa, buttermilk, baking powder, baking soda, cinnamon, and salt. Beat eggs and 1½ cups sugar in large bowl until light and fluffy. Gradually beat in oil. Slowly add flour mixture to egg mixture. Pat zucchini dry with paper towels and add zucchini to mixture. Add nuts and raisins. Bake in greased and floured 9x13x2" baking pan at 350 degrees for 30-35 minutes. For frosting, combine cream cheese and butter until smooth. Beat in 1 cup sugar until fluffy. Refrigerate. Cool cake in pan on wire rack 10 minutes, then remove from pan and cool. Frost top with cream-cheese frosting.

Violet Pate's Pattypan Squash Pie

8-10 small pattypan squash
Water
¾ cup sugar
3 eggs, beaten
1 tsp. vanilla extract
1 tsp. cinnamon
1 tsp. nutmeg
2 tbsp. flour
3 tbsp. butter or oleo
Unbaked pie shell
Butter or whipped cream

Wash squash; remove stem ends but do not peel. Slice thinly and boil in small amount of water until tender. Drain and mash well. To squash add sugar, eggs, flavorings, flour, and 3 tbsp. butter; mix well. Pour into pie shell and bake at 350 degrees until firm and browned. Serve hot topped with butter or whipped cream.

Biscuits

While they certainly didn't bring their axes to the table, the Hungry 'Jacks Leola Metz cooked breakfast for just might have done like Lizzie Borden and given *her* 40 whacks if she had tried to serve them store-bought biscuits from a can!

Leola Metz regularly cooked a hearty and *very* early breakfast for her lumberjack husband Carl (universally called "Dump"), son Julius, Carl's brother Julius (otherwise known as "Moochie"), plus assorted other members of their logging crew. They needed a big meal before sunup to keep up their strength during the demanding day in the woods and swamps, and Leola knew just how to supply that.

After all, as one of seven children in a farming family in the country, she had gotten an early start, helping her mother fix huge meals to sustain her father and brothers in the field. She began baking as a small child under her mother's watchful eye and developed her biscuit recipe through years of cooking experience.

While living with her family in a log home near Big Bayou Sara in the Solitude community of West Feliciana Parish, Leola baked her biscuits in an oven hotter than most people use, but the results were some of the best biscuits around. Leola's recipes were for fairly large quantities, given all those hungry lumberjacks waiting at her breakfast table every morning to devour platefuls then and fill lunch pails with more biscuits for later, but they can easily be reduced.

Sausage Biscuits

Use leftover biscuit mix. Roll very thin on floured board. Top dough with cooked sausage (well drained). Roll in jellyroll fashion and slice. Bake at 450 degrees about 15 minutes until browned.

Angel Biscuits

2 pkg. yeast
3 tbsp. lukewarm water
5 cups self-rising flour
¼ cup sugar
2 tsp. baking soda
1 cup shortening
2 cups buttermilk

Dissolve yeast in water. Sift dry ingredients together, cut in shortening, and add dissolved yeast and buttermilk. Roll dough out onto floured board. Cut it into desired shapes. Let dough rise about 30-45 minutes. Bake at 450 degrees for 10-15 minutes, until browned on top. Makes about 40 medium biscuits.

Leola Metz's Biscuits

4 cups self-rising flour
1 cup oleo
1½-2 cups milk

Sift flour. Cut in oleo until well mixed. Stir in milk. Roll dough out on floured board and cut out into biscuit shapes. Place on greased pan and bake at 450 degrees for about 15 minutes until browned on top. Makes about 40 biscuits, but can easily be cut in half.

Cinnamon-Roll Biscuits

Use leftover biscuit mix. Roll very thin on floured board. Melt some butter or oleo and spread on top of dough, then sprinkle sugar and cinnamon on top. Roll in jellyroll fashion and cut into slices for small rolls. Place on greased pan and bake as biscuits, at 450 degrees for 15 minutes or until lightly browned. Can glaze tops with fruit jelly if desired.

Greenwood Plantation

In a region noted for its elegant plantation mansions, Greenwood near Weyanoke in West Feliciana Parish of Louisiana stood out as one of the finest. Its story began in 1798, when Olivia Ruffin Barrow, a determined widow, embarked by covered wagon on the long journey from North Carolina to the Spanish lands of the Feliciana district, bringing with her 6 children, possessions, slaves, and the wealth with which to build a new life in a new land.

One son, William, supervised construction of the first family homestead in the area, Highland Plantation, and became a leader in the West Florida Rebellion. One of William's sons would elope with vivacious young Eliza Pirrie, Audubon's pupil.

William's second son, William Ruffin Barrow, married a cousin and in 1830 engaged prominent architect James Coulter to build a fine home on 12,000 acres his family had purchased from Revolutionary War financier Oliver Pollock.

The massive result was Greenwood, called the finest example of Greek Revival architecture in the South, nearly 100 feet square and completely surrounded by 28 huge Doric columns of slave-made brick supporting a solid copper roof. A 70-foot central hallway was flanked by spacious rooms with 14-foot ceilings on the first and second floors, while the third-floor attic was topped by a rooftop belvedere from which Barrow could survey his lands and look out as far as the Mississippi River several miles away.

Surrounded by a park of more than 100 live oaks and a reflecting pond, Greenwood was one of the South's most magnificent mansions, toured by thousands, featured in photographic magazines, and in demand as a movie setting. Saved during the Civil War for use as a hospital, the home was restored by Frank and Naomi Fisher Percy in 1910.

A half-century later, on the night of August 1, 1960, the elderly Percys had retired to the rear of the home to enjoy the company of a visiting grandson. The lights went out as a storm front passed through. Thunder crashed and lightning rent the summer sky.

The storm's noise prevented anyone from hearing an ominous crackling until it became a roar, the roar of flames consuming the old, dry house. Lightning had struck the northwest corner. Within 3 hours, nothing was left of Greenwood but 28 Doric columns and some chimneys.

For nearly a decade the stark grandeur of these tragic ruins languished untouched, until they touched the hearts of Ricky Barnes and his family. Instead of seeing the columns and chimneys as an ending, however, they saw them as a beginning, and now, after nearly 2 decades of hard work, Greenwood stands complete again, rebuilt as closely as possible to the original thanks to photos and family memories.

The home once again welcomes visitors and has been the setting of a number of movies, including the television production of *North and South;* a Bed & Breakfast operates just across the reflecting pond. May Percy DeLaureal recalls the joys of growing up in the magnificent home shortly after the turn of the century, happy memories flavored with such Southern specialties as old-fashioned spoon bread for breakfast, plus plenty of mouthwatering pralines made with pecans grown right on the place.

Spoon Bread for Breakfast at Greenwood

½ cup cornmeal
1 tbsp. baking powder
¾ tsp. salt
2 cups milk
1 tbsp. butter
2 eggs, beaten separately

Mix meal, baking powder, and salt. Add milk and cook slowly in a double boiler, over low heat, stirring often. When cooked, pour into a mixing bowl and beat in the butter. Slowly add egg yolks, and then the egg whites. Pour into a buttered pan or casserole and bake at 400 degrees for about 30 minutes, or until golden brown. If too thick, milk can be increased.

Greenwood Pecan Pralines

2 cups sugar
1 cup light brown sugar
1 cup evaporated milk
½ stick butter or oleo
Pinch salt
2 tbsp. corn syrup
⅓ tsp. cream of tartar
2 cups toasted pecans
1 tsp. vanilla extract

Butter sides of pot or skillet. Add all ingredients except pecans and vanilla. All white sugar can be used if desired. Cook until a soft ball forms when a small amount is dropped into a cup of cold water. Add pecans after removing from stove. Let cool slightly, then add vanilla. Beat until ready to drop (the praline mixture, not the cook!). Drop onto wax paper by spoonfuls, and let harden.

Greenwood Fruitcake

½ lb. dried figs
2 lb. currants
3 lb. raisins
2 lb. dates
½ lb. candied pineapple
½ lb. cherries
½ lb. citron, sliced
1 lb. pecans
1 lb. almonds
1 lb. English walnuts
½ lb. black walnuts
Flour for dredging
1 lb. butter
1 lb. sugar
12 eggs, separated
1 lb. flour
2 tsp. baking powder
2 tsp. cinnamon
1 tsp. ground cloves
1 tsp. ground allspice
½ pt. sherry
½ pt. whiskey
1 cup molasses
Grated rind of 1 lemon
Grated rind of 1 orange

Have all fruit and nuts prepared and chopped coarse, except for citron, which is sliced. Dredge raisins and currants in flour. Cream butter and sugar. Beat yolks and add. Sift flour with baking powder. Add spices. Beat whites. Add flour alternately with whites to butter mixture. Add liquids alternately with nuts and fruit, except for citron. Add lemon and orange rinds. Place citron in layers as you pour in pan or pans. Bake 4 hours in slow oven. In place of citron you can use watermelon-rind preserves, and in place of dried figs use fig preserves, and you will find it is much improved. If desired, candied orange and lemon peel chopped fine may be added. Taken from the old *Feliciana Recipes* cookbook published many years ago by Grace Episcopal Church, this recipe is attributed to "the first Mrs. Ruffin Barrow of Greenwood, who, to show her scorn of superstition, had thirteen house servants."

Texas Longhorns

"*P*romote beef, run over a chicken!*" says a sign in one area stockyard, only half-jokingly, for cattlemen have been going through some tough years while beef was getting a bad name in a cholesterol-conscious American society. Now, though, the cattle industry has wised up and is beginning to breed animals with less fat and lower cholesterol levels in the meat, as recommended by dieticians and doctors.

The improvements are being made through the application of genetics. Said Woodville cattleman John Hewes, "We used to have short, thick, pampered British breeds with thick rinds of fat, but now we only want enough fat to insulate the meat from the air to add to its shelf life. Cattle are being bred to be faster growing, with a higher percentage of red meat and less waste fat. It's more expensive to produce fat anyway, and the butcher is just going to cut it off."

Crossbreeding is an important method of making improvements in cattle herds; said Hewes in layman's terms, "You've got half the cake baked with the mama, and you can change the ingredients with the sire to produce whatever kind of cake you want." Improving the recipe makes for more profit for the cattleman and a healthier product for the consumer.

Other cattlemen, like cardiovascular surgeon Dr. B. Eugene Berry of West Feliciana's historic Wakefield Plantation, are turning their eyes backward to the colorful breed of cattle known as the Texas Longhorn, picturesque speckled animals brought to the New World with Columbus on his second voyage in 1493. Cortez took descendants of these Spanish Andalusian cattle into Mexico, then others moved northward with Coronado's expedition and roving Spanish priests.

Scattered by Indian attack, weather, and stampede, many cattle escaped into the wilds, where they multiplied. Only the hardiest survived, growing immensely long horns, some up to 9 feet across, to fight off wolves and hook down high-growing greenery in spare range conditions, able to live on next to nothing with rarely an extra ounce of fat.

Before the Civil War, these cattle were used primarily for tallow and hides, as well as for occasional sport hunting. But after the war, as scarred veterans returned to find their ranches in ruin and the populace of the East clamoring for beef, a new industry developed to lead the Lone Star State out of bankruptcy.

The great cattle drives began, with immense herds of Texas Longhorns driven along the Chisholm Trail to the railhead in Abilene, or north to fatten on Midwestern grasses, or to the Plains

States to restock ranges deserted after the buffalo were slaughtered. It was not uncommon for a tightly packed, moving mass of cattle to snake unbroken along the trail for some 40 miles.

Later, as fatter European breeds of cattle took precedence, the rangy Longhorn breed nearly died out, saved from extinction in the 1920s by a few loyal ranchers and the federal government's establishment of a seed herd of purebreds on an Oklahoma wildlife refuge in 1927.

But now the breed is enjoying a comeback, thanks to its 400 years of genetic honing. Always known for high fertility rates and calving ease, the Longhorn is also disease resistant, hardy and long lived, with cows productive well into their second decade, all factors important to the cattleman in producing less expensive beef.

More importantly to Dr. Berry as a heart specialist, Longhorns have been found to yield lower-fat, lower-cholesterol choice beef that is just as tasty as fatter marbled varieties. The genetics of the Texas Longhorn, Dr. Berry feels, just could revitalize the beef industry and give red meat a newly vindicated role in the American diet, while preserving a little Wild West history and lessening the incidence of heart disease all at the same time.

Oriental Flank Steak

1 tbsp. grated or ¾ tsp. ground ginger
½ cup soy sauce
3 tbsp. oil
3 tbsp. honey
2 cloves garlic, minced
2-4 lb. flank steak

Combine ginger, soy sauce, oil, honey, and garlic and place in a glass, enamel, or stainless-steel dish. Marinate meat in this mixture for several hours at least, turning occasionally. Broil or grill meat. This is also an excellent marinade for venison, round steak, or any cut that needs tenderizing and flavorizing.

Ormond Butler's Barbecue Sauce for Beef

Oil
2 tbsp. sugar
2 tsp. salt
1 tsp. dry mustard
½ tsp. Worcestershire sauce
2½ tsp. hot pepper sauce
¼ cup apple-cider vinegar
Juice of ½ lemon

Fill a 1-pt. container with enough oil (not peanut oil) to reach 1" below top. Add other ingredients. Shake well and use to baste beef while grilling. Believe it or not, this also makes an excellent dressing for a green salad, as well as a good marinade. Makes 1 pt.

SHIPPING CATTLE

Hamburger Casserole

1 lb. ground beef
1 clove garlic, crushed
1 onion, chopped
Salt and black pepper to taste
Chili powder
1 bell pepper, chopped
1 medium can corn
1 medium can tomato sauce
1 medium can peas
1 medium can sliced mushrooms or substitute fresh
1 box cornbread mix

Sauté beef, garlic, onion, and seasonings until tender; drain well. In large casserole dish, put all ingredients except cornbread mix. Mix cornbread according to package directions and spread over top. Cook according to cornbread directions (about ½ hour at 350 degrees usually). This is a good and economical 1-dish meal.

Indian Beef Barbecue

1 lb. top round steak
1 tsp. ground coriander
½ tsp. turmeric
½ cup fresh lime juice
½ tsp. chili powder
Salt and black pepper to taste

Trim away outside fat, cut steak into 1" slices, and place in glass dish. Mix remaining ingredients and pour over beef. Cover and refrigerate, turning steak occasionally, at least 3 hours but no longer than 24. Cook beef on oiled barbecue grill 4" from medium-hot coals for 8-10 minutes, turning occasionally and basting with marinade while cooking. Serves 4, with only 173 calories per serving.

Better Than Sex and Other Sinfully Rich Cakes

Sometimes cooking can be a gamble, and there are times when it pays, just as it does at the racetrack, to take a chance on an unknown just because of its catchy name.

Such is surely the case with this rich and delicious Better Than Sex Cake, the recipe for which was given to Sharon Gauthier by a Baptist minister's wife who shall remain nameless (and who was so embarrassed that she had to write down the name to pass along the recipe rather than verbally repeating it).

And then there's the Cajun Cake recipe, shared with Sharon by a cook who said it was so named because "only a Cajun would mix together all those ingredients!"

Patsy Welch Dreher, who furnished the Sock It to Me Cake recipe, says it was her father's favorite, and, not to tell any tales out of school, she could guarantee he would always double the recipe for the glaze, as her sister Johnnie Welch Bennett would eat a cup of the glaze all by herself!

Better Than Sex Cake

1 box yellow or white pudding cake mix
1 20-oz. can crushed pineapple
1 cup sugar
3 tbsp. cornstarch
1 small box vanilla pudding mix
4 bananas, sliced
1 small carton whipping cream, whipped
½ cup pecans

Bake cake according to mix directions in 9x12" pan. Cook topping of pineapple, sugar, and cornstarch, then let cool. Make vanilla pudding according to package directions, either instant or cooked. Punch holes in warm cake with a fork. Spread with pineapple mixture. Then spread pudding on top of that. Then spread bananas on top of that. Cover with whipped cream, then top with pecans.

Cajun Cake

2 cups flour
1½ cups sugar
2 eggs
1½ tsp. baking soda
Pinch salt
1 1-lb. can crushed pineapple
1 cup sugar
1 stick oleo
1 large can evaporated milk
1 cup pecans
1 cup shredded coconut

Mix flour, 1½ cups sugar, eggs, soda, salt, and pineapple. Beat vigorously for 2 minutes. Bake at 300 degrees for 45 minutes. Remove from oven. Boil 1 cup sugar, oleo, and milk for 5 minutes. Add pecans and coconut. Pour this mixture over cake. Be sure to refrigerate.

Milky Wonder Cake

13 small Milky Way bars
1 cup butter or oleo
2 cups sugar
4 eggs
2½ cups sifted flour
½ tsp. baking soda
1¼ cups buttermilk
1 tsp. vanilla extract
1 cup chopped nuts
Powdered sugar (optional)

Melt candy bars and butter in saucepan over very low heat. Let cool. Add sugar. Add eggs one at a time, beating well. Add flour and soda with buttermilk and stir until smooth. Stir in vanilla and nuts. Bake in tube pan in moderate oven for 1 hour and 20 minutes or until top springs back when touched. Can sprinkle top with powdered sugar if desired.

Sock It to Me Cake

1 box Duncan Hines Golden Cake mix
1 cup sour cream
⅓ cup oil
¼ cup sugar
¼ cup water
4 eggs
2 tsp. cinnamon
2 tbsp. brown sugar
1 cup or more chopped pecans
1 cup powdered sugar
2 tbsp. milk
1 tbsp. butter
½ tsp. vanilla extract

To mix batter, combine cake mix, sour cream, oil, sugar, water, and eggs. Beat on high for 2 minutes to mix well. To mix filling, combine 2 tbsp. cake batter with cinnamon, brown sugar, and pecans. Mix and set aside. Preheat oven to 375 degrees. Pour ⅔ of the batter into a greased and floured 10" tube pan. Over this, spread the filling. Then put the rest of the batter on top. Bake 45-55 minutes. Cool right side up 25-30 minutes, then remove. Glaze this with a mixture of powdered sugar, milk, butter, and vanilla, mixed well.

St. Francisville and the West Feliciana Parish Area of Louisiana

Sick Calls—Fireballs of the Eucharist and Other Infernal Ailments

Surely nowhere but the South is being sick such a ritualized, *social* sort of thing. Such an *occasion!*

We *enjoy* ill health. While we're doing that, we know all our friends and neighbors and well-meaning relatives will show up bearing zucchini bread and armed with stories of their own ill-health experiences.

And with all those people present, the patient absolutely *has* to entertain them, right? No matter how *sick* he might be.

And that's where the Southern penchant for storytelling and embellishment melds with the social aspects of sickness.

We couldn't waste the time and effort of our audiences with just plain *ordinary* illnesses, could we? How *boring!*

So we combine our generalized ignorance and disdain of modern medical and technological jargon with our imaginations, and Lord, look what we come up with . . . or down with.

We've all seen those highfalutin chorus girls do their high kicks from Las Vegas or Gay Paree on television if not in person, ruffled garters holding up sexy black fishnet stockings on shapely legs. Imagine our horror, then, to hear the doctor diagnose the swelling at our neckline as being a *"garter"* in our throats. So what if that doctor does write it down in his records as "goiter"; we feel as if we might just as well have the entire Radio City Music Hall chorus line kicking out our tonsils.

And pity the poor black patient from the country who goes to the big city hospital and comes home to report he is suffering from *"sick-as-hell anemia"* instead of sickle-cell anemia. The former is probably a much more apt description, taking into account the feelings of the low-sick patient.

Then there are the poor older folks with failing vision due to having *"cat tracks"* across their eyeballs. We've all seen what a muddy kitten can do to the shiny surface of a just-washed car or floor; just *think* what one can do to the sensitive eyeball of a sufferer. And if the doctor wants to write it as "cataracts," well, that's just fine with us, but we know what it is. And we know, too, that our senior moments are most aptly blamed on that dreaded "Old-timer's Disease."

One poor soul journeyed to the city hospital during the polio scare of several decades ago to visit a stricken young relative and returned home to report with horror that the patient was *"in an iron casket and they's ironing her lungs!"* Which is probably a fitting description of the horrors of confinement in an iron lung, and thank God for the polio vaccine.

Straining to lift heavy weights can cause such awful conditions as *"high onion,"* otherwise known as "hiatal hernia," and one poor soul who still caught rain water the old-fashioned way without city pipes or reservoirs was horrified to hear the doctor say she had *"pulse in her cistern,"* which turned out to be an infection causing the release of pus into her system.

We *"make water"* or *"hold water"* in place of more graphic descriptions for the urologist, suffer from *"high blood"* or *"low blood"* or *"sugar"* or *"pressures"* instead of the more mundane hypertension or diabetes, and sometimes when we get well the doctor in his wisdom will give us a *"sister, if it itch,"* which might otherwise be known as a certificate.

The descriptions of our ailments flourish in the fertile ground of the sickroom and sprout to amazing heights and breadths when carried out into the community by our visitors. And when those ailments can be used as examples of punishments visited on our moral failings, there's no limit to their expansion.

One poor soul whose character was none too

pristine and whose nighttime activities had long been the despair of the neighborhood preacher found her unfortunate hospital confinement the subject of his weekly sermon, when the fibroids on the uterus diagnosed by the doctor blossomed into the dreaded divine judgment visited upon her under the minister's colorful name of *"fireballs of the Eucharist!"* There could surely be no better cause for immediate repentance and prayers for salvation!

In the old days, though, not everybody could get to a doctor or hospital, and when the creek was up so that the nearest horse-and-buggy country doctor couldn't get to the patients, they just had to do the best doctorin' they could at home But what they missed in not being able to reinterpret the professional diagnosis, they made up for in imaginative cures.

Colic in a baby, for instance, old country folks will tell you could be cured by blowing smoke from a pipe into his diapers and onto the soft spot on his head. A baby's hiccups could be stopped by crossing two broom straws in the crown of his head.

Whooping cough in a baby could best be cured by riding a stud horse until he got real hot, then letting him breathe in the baby's face. Diarrhea was cured by setting a spoonful of whiskey on fire and scorching it before making the poor patient drink it.

A piece of flannel could be browned in the oven to put on the chest to cure colds, which could also be cured by rubbing the throat and chest with coal oil, turpentine, or catfish oil. Rheumatism was eased by patting limbs with a bottle of table salt mixed with a can of cayenne pepper, sure to take the mind off the aches and pains.

Snake bit? Run quick to the hen house, kill a chicken, and remove its gall bladder to apply to the bitten area and draw out the poison. If you haven't got chickens handy, put coal oil or kerosene and soda on the affected area, fast.

Step on a nail? Apply fat meat and turpentine to the puncture to stop the bleeding, or cover with spider webs. To draw out thorns or reduce swelling in boils, wrap with okra blossoms or salt meat.

And if you wake up with a bad crick in your neck, go outside to the hog pen and rub the neck on a fence post where a hog has rubbed. You can make a tea of hog-hoof scrapings and cure colds or pneumonia, too.

To bring out measles, drink tea made of boiled cornhusks. Mumps, on the other hand, could be eased by rubbing sardine oil on the cheeks and tying them up with a scarf. *Pew!*

A tea made of dried ginseng leaves was recommended to settle nervous indigestion, and the plant was also supposed to be effective in treating rheumatism and chronic cough. But finding the ginseng was the tough part, since this shy little plant was thought to hide from man and disappear unless watched. Long considered an aphrodisiac, ginseng was also said to give "the strength of the horse, the mule, the goat and the ram and the bull."

These country cures are based on common sense, often as not, and common sense should be applied before trying them. Before you rush out to put a chicken gall bladder on a snakebite, get to the doctor. On the other hand, a little whiskey and honey never hurt anyone with a cold and has probably helped generations of sufferers, being surely as effective as any modern cure for that common ailment.

And it beats the bourbon enema prescribed by one old-time doc for a fussy little teetotaler hysterical after her husband's death. *Worked,* too. Calmed her right down, then made her drunk as a coot! As another doctor later remarked about the case, "Terrible waste of good whiskey, if you ask me!"

But the point was, it made a good story, besides effecting a cure, and that's what was important.

This zucchini bread, with several variations (yellow squash can be substituted for zucchini, if desired), is a wonderful offering to take on sick calls. It's delicious enough to tempt even the sickest to try a taste and provides lots of nutrition as well, being almost a foolproof method of getting vegetables into small picky eaters. It can be frozen for later delivery and is also handy to keep in a hospital room for snacking and sharing.

Linda Pruitt's Zucchini Bread

3 eggs
2 cups sugar
1 cup oil
2 tsp. vanilla extract
2 cups peeled, grated zucchini
3 cups flour
1 tsp. salt
1 tsp. baking soda
¼ tsp. baking powder
2 tsp. cinnamon
½ cup nuts

Beat eggs until light and fluffy. Add sugar and beat well. Stir in oil, vanilla, and zucchini. Sift together flour, salt, baking soda, baking power, and cinnamon. Mix with zucchini mixture. Add nuts and pour into 2 loaf pans. Bake at 350 degrees for 1 hour or until done.

Virginia Smith's Zucchini Bread

3 eggs
2 cups sugar
1 cup oil
2 tsp. vanilla extract
2 cups peeled, grated zucchini
1 tsp. salt
1 tsp. baking soda
¼ tsp. baking powder
2 tsp. cinnamon
3 cups flour
1 cup chopped nuts
1 cup raisins
1 8½-oz. can crushed pineapple, drained

Beat eggs well, add sugar, and beat. Stir in oil, vanilla, and zucchini. Sift dry ingredients and seasonings. Mix with zucchini mixture. Add nuts, raisins, and pineapple. Pour into 2 loaf pans and bake at 350 degrees for 1 hour.

Berries

All those folks lining the ditches with buckets, all those straw-hatted children wandering through pastures with pans, and those other folks walking the creek beds with pots . . . they're a sure sign that it's berry-pickin' time along the Great River Road. The dewberries and blackberries are especially lush growing along the banks of the Mississippi, and where else could you pick fresh fruit and wave to the venerable *Delta Queen* at the same time! It's also snake time, so besides the pots and pans, you'll be well advised to arm yourself with a stout stick to beat the bushes before beginning to pick.

Once you've located a likely looking briar patch or vine, follow this advice: berries should be picked as early as possible in the mornings, before the outside air gets too warm. Fruit picked later on a hot day will surely spoil faster than that picked in the cool of the morning. Besides, the picker will be a lot more comfortable before the sun gets too high.

Berries should be picked when ripe but still firm and need to be handled with care to prevent bruising or crushing. That treasured purple juice needs to be saved for the jelly pot, not wasted on fingers or the sides of the bucket.

Store berries in a cool place as soon as possible after harvesting. Temperatures over 75 degrees cause rapid deterioration of the fruit. Washing and freezing berries allows for their use months later, if desired.

The dewberries, which come in first in the spring, are sweeter than the later blackberries; still later in the summer come the wild plums, growing on small trees in the woods. Wild plum jelly is tart and more suitable for enjoying with meats and wild game, while dewberry and blackberry jellies are perfect topping for toast or muffins and make wonderful cobblers, pies, and cakes.

The muscadines that grow on vines cascading over creek banks and dangling from the treetops in wooded areas make delicious jelly, and other berries like huckleberries, growing wild on bushes, rival the blueberries, which are just beginning to be cultivated here. Several nice "u-pick" farms in the area feature blueberries and domesticated blackberries, too, and a visit to these farms makes an enjoyable outing for the children while at the same time providing fresh fruit that is usually larger and more perfect than the wild varieties and a whole lot more accessible, too.

Here in Audubon plantation country along the Great River Road, we are blessed to be located so close to Louisiana's famous fertile strawberry

fields. Late each spring our roadsides are dotted with truck farmers and other vendors selling flats of luscious red berries. We put them in shortcakes and in homemade ice cream, preserve them in jam and blend them into delectable daiquiris, serve them fresh with cream and a sprinkling of sugar or freeze them for later use. But there's no better way to enjoy the fresh natural taste of a good Louisiana strawberry than in Mary Powell's Strawberry Pie.

You can use berries for plenty of things besides jellies and jams, pies and cobblers, though. Many of our older residents, who don't mind investing a little time, can make a mean batch of blackberry cordial or elderberry wine or wild cherry bounce.

Mary Powell's Strawberry Pie

1 qt. strawberries
1 cup sugar
2 heaping tbsp. cornstarch
1 pie shell
1 cup whipping cream, whipped and
    sweetened

Wash and hull berries. Mash half of the berries until juice is extracted. Bring mashed pulp and juice to a boil. Mix sugar and cornstarch and add to pulp. Cook, stirring, until clear and very thick. Meanwhile, bake pie shell. Slice the other half of the berries and put into pie shell. Over these, pour the hot cooked mixture. Place in refrigerator until very cold, then top with whipped cream.

Mary Butler's Wild Plum Jelly

Gather and wash firm ripe plums. In large jelly pot, cover with water 1" above fruit and bring to boil over high heat. Turn down to medium heat and boil 30-45 minutes. Drain through muslin or jelly bag into another pot. Put fruit back into jelly pot, cover with ¾" water, bring to boil over high heat, turn down to medium heat and boil 30-45 minutes again, and strain out juice into yet another pot through jelly bag. For 3rd boiling, return fruit to jelly pot and cover with ½" water. Bring to boil over high heat. Turn down to medium heat and boil 30-45 minutes again. Keep each boiling's juice separate as each will have a different capacity to gel. Combine 2 cups from each boiling to make 6 cups juice. Add ¾ cup sugar for each cup of juice. Dissolve sugar and boil at high temperature without reducing heat for 25-26 minutes, or until the liquid sheets off a silver ladle looking "like old ladies' drawers" (slightly coagulating and clumping together like pants' legs instead of in single drops). Pour into preheated clean jelly glasses and skim foam off top. Cool and seal with paraffin.

Dewberry Jam

Usually you use the pulp left over from jelly making to make jam. Gather, wash, and stem ripe berries. Boil once in water about 1" above berries for 30-40 minutes. Mash fruit through coarse sieve after removing juice through jelly bag or muslin strainer and using the juice for jelly. To fruit pulp, add ¾ cup sugar for each cup of pulp. If too thick, add a small amount of the juice. Cook at high heat for 25-26 minutes, boiling, until thick. Pour at once into clean jam jars or jelly glasses that have been preheated. Cool. Can be sealed with paraffin if not using immediately for Jam Cake.

Gertrude Veal's Jam Cake

2 cups sugar
2 sticks butter
5 eggs
3 cups flour
3 scant tsp. baking powder
¼ tsp. salt
1 cup milk
1 tsp. vanilla extract
1 stick butter
1 stick oleo
Dewberry Jam (recipe preceding)
Sugar

Cream 2 cups sugar and 2 sticks butter thoroughly. Add eggs and beat well. Sift flour, baking powder, and salt together. Add half of the mixed flour and half of the milk to the butter mixture. Then add the rest of the flour and milk. Add the vanilla. Put about 4 heaping tbsp. batter in each of 6 cake pans, thinly covering bottom of pans. Cook until done and remove from pans. Melt 1 stick butter with oleo and spread on the layers. Spread on jam thickly and then lightly sprinkle with sugar. Repeat process until you have used about 2 pt. jam. This makes a 6-layer cake with jam filling between each layer and on the very top, but not on the sides except where it drips out from the layers.

Barbara Major's Blackberry Ice Cream

2¼ cups sugar
4 cups milk
1 pt. half & half
½ tsp. salt
2½ pt. light cream
4 eggs
½ pt. whipping cream
1 tsp. vanilla extract
2 cups dewberry juice

Mix all ingredients and freeze in ice-cream freezer according to freezer directions.

Cherry Bounce

¾ gal. fresh wild cherries
Bourbon whiskey
3 lb. sugar

Wash and stem cherries and put into a 1-gal. container. Fill with bourbon whiskey. The better the bourbon, the better the bounce. Leave for 14 days, shaking jar occasionally. Strain off. Make syrup by placing sugar into a ½-gal. measure and adding water to fill; bring syrup to a good boil. Cool syrup and then add to ½ gal. cherry juice. Bottle and seal.

Muscadine Wine

1 gal. muscadines
½ gal. water
Sugar

Set muscadines and water in stone crock; cover with cheesecloth and ferment for 5 days. Strain juice through cloth to get rid of pulp and stems. Sweeten with sugar until desired sweetness. Ferment another 7-10 days. Sample; if not strong enough, add more sugar and ferment 3 more days. Strain through cloth and bottle.

Cinnamon Rolls and Benefit Barbecues

I t was a marriage made in heaven . . . or maybe in the kitchen, this union of "Miss Betsy" Daniel Maryman and Ray Shilling.

Both long widowed, they'd had plenty of time to develop renowned culinary skills individually, and the combination of those skills in one kitchen was enough to make strong men salivate and women turn green with envy.

Big Ray grew up in St. Amant, an outstanding high-school athlete who gained statewide recognition as the barefoot backfield runner who was nearly a one-man team in the days of six-man football. After moving to St. Francisville to clerk in a cousin's grocery, he became an indispensable part of the community, a charter member of the vitally important volunteer fire department and its assistant chief for more than three decades.

Benefit barbecues, livestock shows, church affairs, fire department fundraisers, fairs, parades, donkey baseball games . . . you name it, and over the years Shilling's jovial face was consistently seen reddening as it roasted above the hot coals of the barbecue pit. If he wasn't actually cooking, he was carrying out the garbage or helping to serve lunch to thousands of visitors at the annual spring pilgrimage or selling the concessions at ballgames or pitching in to help in any way he could.

After he went to work for the town as utility superintendent, every elderly widow in town had his home phone number and never hesitated to use it when the gas pilot light went out in the middle of the night or the pipes froze or the water leaked. His small acts of helpfulness to the nighttime meetings of the Episcopal auxiliary called St. Luke's in the 1940s led many of the ladies to call *him* St. Luke, and there wasn't a house in town untouched by his kindnesses over the years.

Meanwhile, practically within spittin' distance across one of St. Francisville's deep hollows, Miss

Betsy was raising children, getting involved with church and 4-H and a myriad of other activities besides holding down a demanding job and stirring up a storm in the kitchen. She'd practically raised her own brothers and sisters, and had plenty of experience with cooking pots and baking pans long before she ever had a kitchen of her very own. The results were soon famous.

A consistent cooking winner at the parish fair, in the fifties she even heard from the famous New York ad agency J. Walter Thompson after taking

first place for yeast rolls; they sent her a copy of Fleischmann's latest baking cookbook, which was her prize, and added her name to the special roster of top cooks in the country receiving complimentary packages of Fleischmann's yeast.

From that vintage cookbook (no longer in print; Miss Betsy tried to get copies for some of her 4-H kids but couldn't), she adapted her famous cinnamon roll recipe. Says she of their road to fame, "I used to make them just for the family, but then I made the mistake of making some for one of Boss's pig roasts, and that started the ball rolling. I took two big pans to the pig roast, and Sonny Nettles for one like to have *popped* from eating them. After I retired, every time I turned around, it was somebody wondering when I was going to make some more."

Miss Betsy's cinnamon rolls were in such demand that a small business began, with clubs and other groups ordering big batches to serve at meetings and get-togethers. Miss Betsy's father was longtime sheriff's deputy and her brother was sheriff,

so that office has always had a special interest in the bounties of Miss Betsy's kitchen, and to this day there are deputies who she swears have no trouble devouring an entire *panful* of her cinnamon rolls. (Her yeast roll recipe, as contributed to the *Woodville Red Recipes* cookbook by daughter Mable Clark, is listed in this book, as in that one, as "Mable Clark's Mamma's Homemade Rolls.")

And as for Ray, before he died Miss Betsy said he was a big help in the kitchen, when he wasn't off helping with benefit barbecues or keeping his hand in at performing small kindnesses for everybody in town.

The recipe for Miss Betsy's famous cinnamon rolls follows, along with a couple of favorite barbecue sauce recipes. The one for chicken was given to Miss Betsy by one of LSU's poultry experts during her 4-H days, and the one for beef or pork came from longtime county agent Leslie Flowers (Miss Betsy says this sauce is best for barbecuing beef or pork but is so good she can eat it plain on bread).

Miss Betsy's Famous Cinnamon Rolls

⅔ cup milk
½ cup sugar
1¼ tsp. salt
6 tbsp. shortening
⅔ cup lukewarm water
2 tbsp. sugar
2 pkg. Fleischmann's yeast, dry or compressed
3 eggs, beaten
3 cups sifted all-purpose flour
3 cups sifted all-purpose flour
Melted shortening
Melted butter
Cinnamon
Sugar
Raisins
½ cup sifted powdered sugar
2 tsp. milk
⅛ tsp. vanilla extract

Scald ⅔ cup milk. Add ½ sugar, salt, and 6 tbsp. shortening, stirring in well. Cool to lukewarm. Combine the water and 2 tbsp. sugar. Sprinkle or crumble in the yeast, then let stand until dissolved. Stir. Add milk mixture. Add and stir in eggs. Add and stir in 3 cups flour; beat until smooth. Add and stir in an additional 3 cups flour (about). Turn dough out on lightly floured board. Knead. Place in greased bowl and brush top lightly with melted shortening. Cover with clean towel and let rise in warm place, free from draft, until doubled in bulk, about 1 hour and 25 minutes. Roll out in rectangle. Spread with melted butter. Mix cinnamon, sugar, and raisins and sprinkle on top. Roll up. Slice about 1" thick. Let rise until double in size. Bake at 425 degrees about 20 minutes or until done. To make the powdered-sugar icing, combine powdered sugar with 2 tsp. milk and vanilla, and beat until smooth. While tops are still hot, ice rolls.

Dr. Hathaway's Chick-n-Cue Sauce

½ cup corn oil
¾ cup lemon juice or cider vinegar
¼ cup water
2 tbsp. salt
2 tbsp. sugar
1½ tsp. Tabasco sauce
1 tbsp. Accent

Mix ingredients well. Bring to boil. After sauce cools, use to baste chicken while grilling. Enough for 3 fryers.

C. L. Flowers' Barbecue Sauce

½ lb. or 1 No. 2 can okra
1 large bell pepper
1 lb. onions
1 large sour pickle
½ clove garlic
1 lb. butter
1 qt. oil
Juice of 1-2 lemons with rind
¼ bottle hot pepper sauce
1 qt. catsup
1-2 pt. beef broth
3 tbsp. mustard
1 bottle Worcestershire sauce
Salt and black pepper to taste
Vinegar and other spices to taste

Mince all vegetables. Mix ingredients well. Bring to boil and cook until tender. Baste meat frequently while grilling. Delicious on beef or pork. Freezes well.

Pilgrimage Workshops

The monumental task of readying an entire parish or county as well as carefully selected featured homes to receive thousands of pilgrimage visitors each season is handled with consummate skill and great tact by hundreds of dedicated and hardworking volunteers.

Committee chairpersons have found, however, that, just as the way to a man's heart has traditionally been through his stomach, so workshops and organizational meetings have far greater attendance when a carrot is dangled . . . or better yet, a chocolate-peppermint square *instead* of a carrot.

This is all the more important in West Feliciana, where the tremendous amount of work required to stage the annual Audubon Pilgrimage is done strictly by *unpaid* volunteers.

Here are a few recipes for delectables dangled by former Audubon Pilgrimage chairwoman Anna Bess Kelley of St. Francisville in assuring good turnouts for her planning workshops, prepared by the hardworking members of her social committee.

Emily Honeycutt's Chocolate-Peppermint Squares

½ cup butter, softened
1 cup sugar
2 eggs
½ cup all-purpose flour
Pinch salt
2 1-oz. squares unsweetened chocolate, melted
½ cup chopped pecans or walnuts
1 cup sifted powdered sugar
2 tbsp. butter, softened
1 tbsp. milk
½-¾ tsp. peppermint extract
2 1-oz. squares semisweet chocolate, melted
1 tbsp. butter, melted

Cream ½ cup butter; gradually add sugar, beating until mixture is light and fluffy. Add eggs one at a time, beating well after each addition. Combine flour and salt; add to mixture and beat well. Add unsweetened chocolate, beating until thoroughly blended. Stir in nuts. Pour batter into greased 9" square pan. Bake at 350 degrees for 20 minutes. Cool thoroughly. Make peppermint filling by combining powdered sugar, 2 tbsp. butter, milk, and peppermint extract, then beating until smooth. Spread peppermint filling over cake and chill. Make chocolate glaze by combining semisweet chocolate with melted butter and stirring well. Spread or drizzle chocolate glaze over filling and chill. Cut into squares and store in refrigerator.

Patsy Hardouin's Cheese and Strawberries

1 lb. grated sharp cheese
1 cup chopped nuts
1 cup mayonnaise
1 small onion, grated
Dash cayenne pepper
Dash Tabasco sauce
Strawberry preserves or jam

Combine all ingredients except preserves or jam. Put in ring mold, or form into a ball. Let stand overnight. When ready to serve, unmold and put preserves or jam in center, perhaps in a small bowl or, if made into ball, in an indentation in the center of the ball. Serve with crackers.

Evelyn Smith's Jacko Applesauce Spice Gems

3 cups flour
1½ cups sugar
1½ cups chopped pecans
1½ cups raisins
Pinch salt
1½ tsp. nutmeg
2 heaping tsp. cinnamon
1 tsp. ground cloves
2¼ cups sweetened applesauce
3 tsp. baking soda
½ cup butter or oleo, melted
3 eggs
2 tsp. vanilla extract
¾ stick oleo
1 1-lb. box powdered sugar
Evaporated milk to thin
1 tsp. brandy or rum flavoring

Grease small cupcake tins and preheat oven to 350 degrees. Mix flour, sugar, pecans, raisins, salt, and spices together. Combine applesauce and soda, then add to dry ingredients. Add melted butter, eggs, and vanilla. Drop about ½ tsp. dough into each tin. Bake about 15 minutes or until done. Cream ¾ stick oleo well, adding powdered sugar and milk to make creamy and of easy spreading consistency. Beat well and add brandy or flavoring, then use to frost gems. These are better made several days in advance and aged in tins; they can be frosted anytime. Makes 5-6 dozen.

Aline Harelson's Spiced Tea

2 cups sugar
4 cups water
2 sticks cinnamon
Whole cloves
12 cups boiling water
½ cup tea
Juice of 4 oranges or 1 can frozen orange juice
Juice of 4 lemons
1 medium can pineapple juice

To sugar and 4 cups water, add cinnamon and cloves to taste. Boil for about 3 minutes. Set aside. In another pot, mix 12 cups boiling water with ½ cup tea (a small box) and let steep for 3 minutes. Mix both mixtures together and add juices. Heat and serve.

Betty Dawson's Lemon Squares

2 cups flour
1½ sticks oleo
½ cup powdered sugar
4 eggs, well beaten
2 cups sugar
3 tbsp. flour
½ tsp. baking powder
6 tbsp. lemon juice
Grated rind of 1 lemon

Mix 2 cups flour with oleo and powdered sugar, blending well. Pack in greased and floured 9x12" cake pan. Bake at 350 degrees for 15-20 minutes. Mix remaining ingredients. Pour over baked crust and bake at 325 degrees for 25-35 minutes.

Sue Powell's Banana Nut Bread

½ cup butter
1 cup sugar
2 eggs
3 tbsp. buttermilk
3 bananas, mashed
1 tsp. vanilla extract
2 cups flour
1 tsp. baking soda
½ tsp. salt
1 cup chopped nuts

Cream butter and sugar. Add eggs and buttermilk. Mix well, then add bananas and vanilla. Sift dry ingredients and add to first mixture. Flour nuts and then add. Pour into large greased and floured loaf pan. Bake at 350 degrees for 1 hour.

Cushaws

Most dictionaries don't even have the word, and most big-time cookbooks don't include any recipes for it. City-born patrons of farmers' markets probably think it's a lopsided watermelon or an overgrown underripe squash. Somebody even purchased one, if accounts can be believed, to use as a doorstop!

But get out in the countryside where the *real* farmers are and you'll find the lowly cushaw held in high esteem. A member of the pumpkin-squash group of vegetables, it's also known as a winter crookneck and is highly prized for its long-lasting nature.

In general, the cushaw can be cooked in nearly every recipe used for pumpkin, winter squash, or even sweet potatoes—casseroles, breads, pies—or simply split and baked with lots of butter and cinnamon.

Finding a cushaw, though, can be a little like finding recipes for it . . . you either have too many, or none at all. Seeds are available by mail order or from country hardware and feed stores, but the best bet is to find someone with a cushaw who will save and dry the seeds for you for replanting the next season.

Even the novice gardener is assured of success with this huge lopsided vegetable, which will grow anywhere and in great profusion. The poorer the soil, the better the hardy cushaw likes it. Seeds can be simply scattered upon a pile of old leaves and will sprout, sending out millions of runners, upon which big blossoms of brilliant yellow precede the green-and-white-striped vegetables.

From just a few plants, the gardener will get enough cushaws to last a year. They can be stored just like pumpkins or sweet potatoes, unrefrigerated, or can be parboiled and cut into manageable slices for freezing until use.

Cushaw Pie

1 cushaw (to yield 3 cups cooked mashed cushaw)
Water
1 cup sugar
3 beaten egg yolks
⅛ cup flour
½ tsp. salt
1½ tsp. cinnamon
½ tsp. nutmeg
¼ cup evaporated milk or cream
¼ cup melted butter or oleo
1 9" unbaked pie shell

Peel cushaw, scrape seeds away, cut into manageable pieces, and cook, covered, in a small amount of water until tender. Drain well and mash well. Mix remaining filling ingredients with cushaw. Pour into pie shell. Bake at 450 degrees for 10 minutes, then reduce temperature to 325 degrees and bake 30-60 minutes longer, until knife inserted in center comes out clean. May be topped with meringue or sweetened whipped cream.

Lucie Butler's Cushaw Bread

3 cups sugar
1 cup oil
4 eggs
3½ cups sifted flour
3 tsp. baking soda
½ tsp. salt
1 tsp. cinnamon
1 tsp. nutmeg
⅔ cup water
2 cups cooked mashed cushaw
1 cup chopped nuts (optional)

Combine sugar and oil; beat well. Add eggs and beat. Combine flour, soda, salt, and spices and add to egg mixture alternately with water. Stir in cushaw and nuts. Pour batter into 3 small greased loaf pans. Bake at 350 degrees for 1 hour.

Gertrude Veal's Baked Cushaw

1 cushaw
1 cup sugar
2 eggs
⅔ cup flour
1 stick butter
1 13-oz. can evaporated milk
Cinnamon and nutmeg to taste
1 tsp. vanilla extract (optional)

Wash and clean cushaw, cut into pieces, and remove seeds. Boil cushaw until tender and remove rind. Mash well, add other ingredients, and mix well. Bake in buttered baking dish at 350 degrees for about 30 minutes.

Pig Tails at the Races

In the old days in this part of plantation country, each isolated early farmstead or plantation had to be a nearly self-sufficient empire, producing as much of what was needed as possible. Much of the food was grown right on the place; the building materials were wrested from the surrounding woodlands, though sometimes sent upriver for finishing, and augmented by bricks baked in kilns right on the spot; the wool was sheared and cleaned and carded and woven into cloth for making clothing.

The plantation master put special emphasis on his livestock, all-important in keeping the plantation running smoothly. He imported new strains of cattle to improve his herd, having Brahmans sent by sailing ship from India to introduce more heat-resistant genes, for example, and breeding sturdy oxen and strong stubborn mules to pull heavy-laden wagons and haul his cotton crop to the riverport for shipment aboard the steamboats to factors in New Orleans.

But his special love was his fine horseflesh. For riding across his immense acreage every day to check his crops and supervise his workers, he bred smooth walking horses with easy-riding gaits.

To pull the family buggies or carriages he bred matched pairs of high-stepping bays or blacks, strong and showy too.

And for those gentlemanly wagers made after dinner, when the menfolk had retired to leather-lined libraries amidst cigar smoke and flowing political talk and fine brandy, he bred stablesful of swift Thoroughbreds to race, sometimes on his own racetrack.

Even after the Civil War when the livin' wasn't so easy, fast horses were prized. An 1888 issue of the *Woodville Republican,* Mississippi's oldest continually published newspaper, includes this feature: "A race came off last Saturday at Fort Adams between Capt. J. D. Cage's bay horse Chain Lightning, and Frank Williams' California Filly Mollie McQuirter.

Distance 400 yards. Williams got the experience and Cage got the cow by about 50 feet."

Most of the old plantations have given up their racetracks now; the Rosedown Plantation racetrack, for example, was laid off into streets and lots for a modern subdivision development. But the thunder of hooves still sounds under a cloud of dust on some Sunday afternoons in the area, on straight 350-yard tracks at Laurel Hill and Centreville, Cheerful Valley or Solitude, and other small communities in East or West Feliciana or southwest Mississippi.

The horses now are locals, for the most part, and

not necessarily Thoroughbreds or even quarter horses, just plain horses, the faster the better. The jockeys may work in banks during the week or go to school, but their small stature and good riding ability place them in great demand on weekends.

The races are two-horse competitions, with 4 or 5 such races taking place each race day. From the starting gate the horses thunder along the dirt track, cheered on by crowds of upwards of 100 or maybe even 200 spectators shading themselves beneath the trees lining the board fence marking off the racecourse.

And under the shade trees may be found cold drinks and, if you're lucky, a big black iron pot for frying pig tails. Scott Simms, who raced a horse or two in his time, said the pig tails were cooked just like fish, seasoned with plenty of salt and pepper and then fried in a big black iron wash pot over a blazing fire.

It's not exactly like the old days; the pig tails, surprisingly fleshy and 6 to 12 inches long, are often purchased by the case, frozen, and sometimes they're cooked just like crawfish with propane burner heating the pot of fat.

A couple of hundred pounds might be sold, at 50 cents a tail, on a good day, when there are well-known horses running with heavy wagers riding on the race, or a longstanding grudge match taking the field.

Once the horses start to run, the time period could be today . . . or it could be 1850, and nothing matters but the sweating straining horses, the pulsing crowd cheering on favorite horses and jockeys, the beating sun and choking dust from the track, after which nothing beats a good cold beer and hot fried pig tail.

Scott's Fried Pig Tails

Pig tails
Water
Plenty of salt and black pepper to taste

Purchase tails frozen; thaw when ready to cook. Build fire under big black iron pot; heat small amount of water thoroughly, so it sputters when a drop of water is splashed in. Season pig tails well with salt and pepper. When water is good and hot, put a few tails in at a time. As they cook, fat will be released and the tails will fry in this just like cracklin's. Cook until browned, just as if frying fish. When the pig tails are done, they'll float to the surface.

St. Francisville and the West Feliciana Parish Area of Louisiana

Rabbits

When Robert Ruiz' granddaughter Catherine, now a young mother, was a tiny tot, her parents gave her a blue-eyed bunny rabbit one Easter.

Catherine named the bunny Hoppity. It turned out that Hoppity was a buck, or male rabbit.

And one fateful day Catherine decided that Hoppity was lonely. A lovely doe rabbit was obtained and introduced to Hoppity.

The rest, as they say, is history.

Grandpa Robert Ruiz inherited the menagerie and found himself in the rabbit business, some years raising as many as 200. He had pink-eyed blacks and blue-eyed whites and everything in between. He had rabbits with big Bugs Bunny teeth. He even had one rabbit he could lead around the yard on a leash.

Mostly, though, Robert Ruiz led his rabbits straight into the gumbo pot. Or the sausage grinder.

Domestic rabbits, he said, lack the wild gamey taste of rabbits hunted in the woods. Pen-raised rabbits taste very much like chicken and can be used in much the same way. Ruiz, who grew up on Bayou Plaquemine as one of six children not long after the turn of the century, ate his share of wild game in his mother's stews and gumbos as a child.

Most of his domestic rabbits were New Zealand ones, which he said were better for eating. He had a regular warren of tin-roofed hutches full of rabbit families and fed them plenty of fresh lettuce, cabbage, carrots, and pellets of dried rabbit chow.

"You don't want a rabbit too big for eating," he advised. "Six months old is big enough. Much bigger and you'll have to grind him up for sausage or make gumbo; the small young rabbits make the best fryers."

Ruiz and his wife mostly made sausage and rabbit salad, but daughter Sharon Gauthier uses rabbit in spaghetti, ragout, and gumbo; she also makes a rabbit jambalaya, her recipe for which, she says, can't be shared because it is simply "pour dis in, pour dat in!"

And did they ever eat Hoppity, whose descendant Hoppity V was the latest head buck? Well, yes. But don't tell Catherine.

Rabbit Gumbo

2 tbsp. oil
3 tbsp. flour
2 rabbits, cut up
1 cup chopped white onions
1 cup chopped green onions
1 clove garlic, minced
Salt to taste; start with 1 tsp.
4 cups water
2 cups long-grain rice

Put oil in pot, add flour, and brown rabbits well. Add onions, garlic, and salt, then add water. Cook slowly for 40 minutes. Add rice and cook until rice is done.

Rabbit Spaghetti

1 clove garlic, minced
1 bell pepper, minced
½ cup chopped celery
1 large onion, chopped
3 sprigs parsley, chopped
2 tbsp. oil
2½ cups chopped canned tomatoes with juice
1 can tomato paste
8 oz. mushrooms, sliced
¼ tsp. thyme
2 tsp. oregano
2 bay leaves
2 rabbits, cut up
2 tsp. olive oil
Cooked spaghetti for 5-6

Gently cook garlic, pepper, celery, onion, and parsley in oil in kettle for about 15 minutes. Add tomatoes, tomato paste, mushrooms, and herbs. Cook slowly. Brown rabbits in olive oil, then add to sauce and simmer for 1 hour. Serve over spaghetti.

Rabbit Sausage

Boil rabbit until meat falls off bone. Grind meat in sausage mill. Add pork-sausage seasoning according to seasoning directions. Make into patties and cook as any sausage.

Rabbit Salad

1 rabbit
2 cups minced celery
1 cup chopped pickles or relish
½ onion, minced
2 tbsp. minced fresh parsley
1 cup rabbit broth
½-1 cup mayonnaise
1 tbsp. mustard

Boil rabbit until meat is so tender you can take all the bones out. Then either grind or chop the meat into small pieces. Add celery, pickles, onion, parsley, and broth. Mix well. Add mayonnaise and mustard. Mix well. After making, keep refrigerated.

Sandwiches

Summertime is sandwich time in most Southern households, with the children out of school, worn out from a busy morning of play, heading off to fish with a cane pole from the pond bank, or rushing between swimming and tennis lessons. The noontime meal usually calls for something quick and cool, but who hasn't tired of long-time favorite standbys like peanut butter and jelly or tuna on white?

Robin Roberts of St. Francisville's Magnolia Café comes from a creative family, with a father who's a woodcarver and siblings who paint. But Robin uses a pita for her palette more often than not, embellishing that plain surface with a richness of textures and colors and tastes to satisfy her own creative urges.

Many of her recipes evolved in that time-honored fashion familiar to all creative cooks. "I look in the refrigerator," she admits, "and use what I've got, combining whatever I think will taste best together."

In a cafe that began life as a filling station and then evolved into a health-food store, Robin continues to approach mealtime with good health in mind, using natural foods and fresh ingredients without preservatives or additives in some of the most scrumptious sandwiches around.

Many of the creative combinations are served on pita bread, preferably whole wheat, which should be stuffed first and then toasted lightly for a moist inside and crunchy outside. Bean sprouts are a flavorful and healthy addition to many of the sandwiches, particularly loved by children who enjoy making the sprouts themselves.

The secret to making delicious and healthy sandwiches, Robin says, is not being afraid of combining ingredients in unexpected ways. Here are some of her specialties, which have turned Magnolia Café into everybody's favorite little local restaurant.

Bean Sprouts

Use alfalfa seeds, readily available in most groceries. Put in a jar and soak overnight covered in room-temperature water, drain, then rinse twice daily, covering top of jar with a tea strainer or mesh. Turn jar on its side for sprouting, and the last day be sure to place the jar in a sunny window to give sprouts a lush green color. Three or 4 days is generally sufficient for a sweeter, nuttier taste; at 5 days, sprouts begin to taste too much like grass.

Famous Turkey Special

1 pita bread
Mayonnaise
Mustard
3 oz. cooked turkey breast
2 oz. Swiss cheese
2 tsp. guacamole
Bean sprouts
Chopped tomatoes

Cut pita in half crosswise. Spread very little mayonnaise and mustard inside pita halves, then stuff with turkey, cheese, guacamole, sprouts, and tomatoes. Toast lightly.

Magnolia Special

Pita bread
Blue cheese dressing
3 oz. sliced cooked roast beef
2 oz. shredded mozzarella cheese
Bean sprouts
Tomatoes

Line pita bread with blue cheese dressing. Add beef and cheese. Top with sprouts and chopped tomatoes. Toast lightly.

Veggie Pita

Sliced mushrooms
Black olives
Chopped celery
Chopped green onions
Chopped bell peppers
Chopped tomatoes
Swiss, cheddar, and mozzarella cheese
Bean sprouts
Oil and vinegar dressing

Like all Robin's sandwiches, the measurements here are flexible. Just put on however much of each ingredient you desire. This veggie pita has only 260 calories, making it a dieter's delight and a whole lot tastier than most diet plates. With no meat or mayonnaise and not too much cheese, it's a low-cal treat. Fill pita with mushrooms, a few black olives, celery, green onions, bell peppers, tomatoes, and cheeses. Top with sprouts and an oil and vinegar dressing. Toast lightly.

Guacamole Sandwich

Toast pita with cheese of choice, either mozzarella, Monterey Jack, or cheddar. Fill with guacamole and top with bean sprouts and chopped tomatoes. Bacon strips may be added.

BLT Pita

Fill pita with small amount of mayonnaise. Add chopped lettuce, tomatoes, bacon, sliced avocado, and bean sprouts. Toast lightly.

Stir-Fry Pita

Heat small amount of olive oil in wok, throw in fresh sliced vegetables such as bell peppers, onions, and mushrooms, and cook just until they begin to sizzle. Add sliced roast beef and stir-fry briefly. Add tamari sauce to taste (better than soy sauce because it's aged longer, Robin says). Serve in a pita with mozzarella cheese. Any vegetable or meat or even seafood can be substituted. The mixture is just as tasty served over rice as in a pita.

Vanilla

Lots of area sportsmen hunt in Mexico, often in the region around Guererra with its lakes, and usually bag their limit of doves. They're just as happy to bag another treasure there, though, proudly bringing back cases of Mexican vanilla.

While Mexican vanilla earned a deserved reputation for its strength and cheapness, it had also earned a just-as-deserved reputation for unsafeness. The toxic substance *coumarin,* an extract of the tonka bean with an odor much like that of vanilla and prohibited for use as a food ingredient in the United States since 1954, was in the past regularly added to cheap Mexican vanilla to enhance the flavor.

The American Food and Drug Administration labeled coumarin a poisonous substance when tests showed it to cause liver damage in test animals. Now, reputable Mexican manufacturers of vanilla leave the substance out, carefully labeling their bottles *"No Contiene Coumarina."* Of course, there are now American manufacturers of vanilla who've never added the substance in the first place.

Vanilla has been a popular flavoring extract in Mexico since the 1500s, when Emperor Montezuma introduced a favorite royal beverage containing vanilla pods, cacao beans, and honey to the Spanish explorer Cortez. Vanilla was considered not only delicious but medicinally valuable as well, described in an Aztec herbal manuscript dated 1552 as capable of reviving energy, fortifying courage, and building strength.

Cortez and his *conquistadores* took home with them tales of this delicious flavoring, and within 50 years Spanish factories were manufacturing vanilla-spiced chocolate. For years the use of vanilla was limited to combinations with chocolate, but in 1602 an apothecary to Queen Elizabeth I of England insisted that vanilla was an exquisite flavoring in its own right.

Mexico was the only producer of vanilla for more than 300 years because transplantation was unsuccessful until the late 1830s, when a means of artificial fertilization was devised. Now, the plant from which vanilla comes flourishes in hot damp climates within about 20 degrees latitude on either side of the equator, being cultivated in four major areas other than the fertile Mexican valleys where it was first discovered: South America, Java, Madagascar and surrounding islands, and Tahiti.

Vanilla comes from one of the world's 20,000 species of orchids, the *Vanilla planifolia* orchid, which produces clusters of delicate white and lemon-yellow unscented flowers. The blossoms open along the cluster a few at a time, lasting less than a single day. If pollinated by midday, the flower forms a long unscented fruit.

It was the Aztecs who first discovered that when wilted, shrunken, and browned by months of heat and humidity, these seemingly inedible beans would acquire a wonderful aroma. They called it *"Tlilxochitl"* or black flower; only later would the Spaniards call the fruit of this orchid *"Vaynilla"* or little pod.

The French took the vanilla orchid to Reunion, an island in the Indian Ocean, in 1822, and there a young slave perfected a quick and simple method of artificial hand-pollination using small bamboo picks. From Reunion, the plant traveled by 1860 to Madagascar, which today produces 75 percent of the world's crop. From a primitive port at the edge of a jungle on this island lying down near the eastern coast of Africa, some 120 million vanilla beans are shipped yearly to the U.S., harvested by 200,000 workers.

There are few large vanilla plantations in Madagascar. Most of the vanilla beans are grown on little plots of only about 500 vines. A year before the plot is set out, one quick-growing jungle tree is planted to furnish shade and support for each vanilla vine. In its wild state, the vanilla orchid vine will ramble 50 to 70 feet straight up the trunk of a tall tree, but on controlled plots, the vines are pruned back or bent into loops to force the sap into the developing pods within reach of workers who must fertilize and pick the beans.

It takes 3 years of good weather and careful attention before the vine bears fruit, with the peak of production reached at 7 or 8 years of age. While a healthy vine might bear up to 1,000 blossoms, only 50 or 60 of these are fertilized to produce beans. The blooming period covers about 2 months, with only a few of the blossoms appearing at any given time, allowing the women workers to go from vine to vine and pollinate only those flowers spaced so as to permit development of fine, straight pods. An experienced worker, called a *"fleuriste,"* can treat 1,500 blossoms a day.

After pollination, long slender beans form, attaining full length in 4 to 6 weeks but not reaching maturity for 6 to 9 months. The beans ripen in the same order in which blossoms appear, so only a few are cut from each vine daily.

Once harvested, the beans undergo a process of curing or fermentation, then are bundled for shipment, acquiring their characteristic flavor during this curing process of 4 months. The entire process of pollination, harvesting, curing, drying, and bundling is still very primitive and for the most part done without mechanization.

Caramel Custard

½ cup sugar
2 cups milk, scalded
⅛ tsp. salt
3 eggs
1½ tsp. vanilla extract

Preheat oven to 300 degrees. Caramelize ¼ cup sugar in a skillet and pour into 8 custard cups before adding custard mixture. Beat milk, ¼ cup sugar, salt, eggs, and vanilla together, then add to custard cups. Put cups into pan and add hot water to pan about halfway up the outside of the cups. Bake at 300 degrees for 30 minutes. Turn upside down onto serving dish.

Conville Lemoine's Homemade Ice Cream

3 cans condensed milk
1 can evaporated milk
1 tbsp. vanilla extract
½ gal. milk
½ pt. whipping cream

Mix ingredients and freeze in ice-cream freezer according to freezer directions.

Bob Butler's English Trifle

4 eggs
2 tbsp. butter
½ cup sugar
⅛ tsp. salt
½ tsp. vanilla extract
2 tbsp. cornstarch
2 cups milk
Pound cake
Melted butter
Grand Marnier
Lemon juice
Raspberry preserves
Fresh fruit

Separate eggs. Beat whites and keep separate. Beat yolks and keep separate. Melt butter. Mix sugar, salt, yolks, butter, vanilla, cornstarch, and milk; stir over medium heat until thickened into very thick custard. Cool. Add egg whites and chill. Cut cake into small pieces. Arrange some cake in clear glass trifle dish or bowl. Splash with melted butter, Grand Marnier, and lemon juice. Top with preserves. Top with some custard. Repeat layers. Refrigerate until chilled. Serve topped with fresh fruit.

W. C. Percy's Turtle Stew

The first thing to remember about making turtle stew is that a good-sized loggerhead can get up to a hundred pounds or so in size and has jaws so powerful that it can snap a 2-by-4 into pieces and can just as easily take off your arm or leg.

And even a smaller snapping turtle of only 8 or 10 pounds can do plenty of damage.

So make sure your turtle is good and dead before you fool with it. Which is easier said than done.

Says retired longtime sheriff W. C. Percy of St. Francisville, a real turtle stew *aficionado,* of the turtle's propensity for continuing muscle movement, "You could cut his head off this morning and he'd still be moving if you skinned him this afternoon. Just like when you cook a bullfrog—he can be frozen solid, and when you put him in that skillet he'll still quiver."

Percy is a dedicated hunter and outdoorsman who cooks deer, turkey, ducks, squirrels, rabbits, and frogs as well as turtles. He knows all the likely farm ponds and old lakes for turtle hunting from his 33½ years in the sheriff's office, 28 of them as sheriff, a job that seems to run in the family. His father-in-law, Fred C. Wilcox, father of Percy's wife, Adele, and 11 other children, was in the sheriff's office from 1904 to 1936, "riding the parish from Angola to St. Francisville on horseback for $2 a day and damn glad to get it!" And before that, Mr. Fred's father-in-law, John H. Clack, had been sheriff for 28 years.

Anyway, riding the range to enforce law and order, W. C. Percy kept his eyes peeled for snappers and loggerheads, and over the years perfected his recipe for turtle stew, trying it out annually on the courthouse gang or the boys at the hunting camp.

The snapping turtle pictured here was caught by Percy's grandson Chaille Daniel in Mississippi using a hook baited with cut-up fish. Snappers, Percy explains, have big heads, long tails, dark shells with 3 vertical ridges, and usually get to be about 10 pounds in weight, while what he calls loggerheads get much bigger, about as big around as you can circle your arms. These bigger turtles, sometimes also known as alligator snapping turtles, are found in rivers and backwater areas, as well as the ponds and well-established lakes favored by the smaller snappers.

The first step in making turtle stew, after catch-

215

ing the turtle, is for the safety of the skinner—cutting off the clawed feet and then cutting off the head and tail; a hatchet comes in handy for this step, but a good sharp skinning knife is the main tool for the rest of the process.

"Turtles are hard to fool with," Percy says. "They'll scratch the devil out of you, and bite you too. And they're damn hard to kill." For the head to be removed, it first must protrude from the shell, and the turtle is not always anxious to assist quite so readily in his own beheading; a hot coal from the wood stove placed on the tail usually accomplished this in the old days—out came the head and down came the ax.

After cutting off the legs and head, hang the turtle to let some of the blood drain out, then cut off the breastplate of the shell to expose the meat. Says Percy, "Some people say turtles have got different kinds of meat in 'em, beef and chicken, because they've got both white and dark meat. They've really got some good meat." He estimates that about a third of the total weight will be in usable meat, which makes a good *sauce piquante* and some fine soup as well.

After discarding the intestines, carefully remove all skin from the meat. Once again, this is easier said than done. "When you skin a deer or squirrel," Percy explains, "once you get the skin started, you can peel it right off, but a turtle is different. With this rascal, you've got to skin him with your knife every step of the way. I guess it's because the skin is so close to the meat, and because of the bones attached to the shell."

Rinse the meat well, being sure to remove all leeches. The legs, neck, and tail are fleshy, and on a loggerhead there are lots of pockets of white meat just like chicken breast alongside the backbone. Percy freezes his turtle meat in cardboard half-gallon milk cartons until he has enough to make a batch of stew, removing most of the bones before freezing and cutting the meat into bite-sized chunks.

W. C. Percy's Turtle Stew

About 24 lb. turtle meat
Oil
14-16 large yellow onions, chopped
10-12 cloves garlic, pressed
5 large bell peppers, minced
1 bunch celery, minced
Water
2 8-oz. cans tomato sauce
2 10-oz. cans hot Ro-tel tomatoes
1 cup flour
8-10 bay leaves
1 pt. sherry
2 lb. fresh mushrooms, chopped
Salt, cayenne pepper, and Worcestershire
    sauce to taste
2 bunches green onions, minced
½ cup chopped fresh parsley
5-6 cups raw rice

Turtle meat should have been deboned and cut into bite-sized pieces before freezing; retain a few bones for flavoring. Cover bottom of skillet with oil and fry turtle meat until browned well. In separate skillet, sauté onions, garlic, bell peppers, and celery in oil. Put turtle in big black iron pot and add water to cover. Add sautéed vegetables, then add tomato sauce and tomatoes. Cook slowly over low heat at a slow boil. Meanwhile, make a dark roux of flour and a little oil in a separate skillet, then add it to the stew. Throw in the bay leaves and cook 3-4 hours or until meat is tender. Add the sherry about 30-40 minutes before done. About 20 minutes before done, add mushrooms, salt, cayenne, and Worcestershire. Cook the rice. Throw the green onions and parsley into the stew right at the last minute. Serve over rice. Should serve 30 at least.

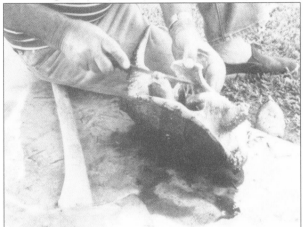

W. C. Percy's Venison Sauce Piquante

20-25 lb. venison stew meat
2-3 lb. beef stew meat
Oil
12-4 onions, chopped
5-6 bell peppers, chopped
1 bunch celery, chopped
2 15-oz. cans beef broth
Water
4 bay leaves
1 10-oz. can Ro-tel tomatoes
4 8-oz. cans tomato sauce
1 cup flour
10-12 cloves garlic, pressed
1-2 lb. fresh mushrooms, chopped
2 bunches green onion tops, chopped
½ cup chopped parsley
Salt, cayenne pepper, and Worcestershire
    sauce to taste
Cooked rice

Use cut-up venison hams and front shoulders, and cut the meat into bite-sized pieces. Adding a few pounds of beef stew meat improves the flavor. Fry meat down in small amount of oil until browned. In separate skillet, sauté onions, peppers, and celery. Put meat in big black iron pot with broth and water to cover well. Add bay leaves, sautéed vegetables, tomatoes, and tomato sauce. Cook over low heat. Make a dark roux of flour and oil; add to stew pot. Add garlic and cook 3-4 hours until the meat is tender. Add mushrooms 20 minutes before done, then add green onions and parsley toward the end of cooking time. Add seasonings. Serve over rice. Serves 40-50.

PHOTO INDEX

Introduction: Levering Lawrason in one photo and three of his sisters, including Annie Mathews Lawrason Butler, in the other; author's collection. Tea party with teddy bears at Butler Greenwood; photos by author.

Grand Village of the Natchez Indians: Chase Poindexter examines thatched roof of typical Indian house. Wild turkeys; photos by author.

Natchez Trace: Stewart Hamilton, age two, at section of the old trace roadbed; photo by author.

Rosalie: Two views of Rosalie; photos by author.

Concord: Stephen Minor's great-granddaughters Margaret Minor (in hat) and Mary Minor. His great-great-granddaughter Katharine Minor Pipes in costume as Tom Thumb's bride; author's collection.

Historic Jefferson College: Little girls in butterfly costumes; West Feliciana Historical Society collection.

Natchez Under-the-Hill: Vintage postcard; author's collection. Saloon and steamboat; photos by author.

Green Leaves Audubon China: China; photo by Ed Prince.

Melrose: Drawing room. Side frontal view of house. View from library through parlor to sitting room. Butler Fred Page. Rear servants' quarters and kitchen now used as visitor center and bookstore; photos by author.

Steamboatin': Steamboat diners at table. Steamboat dining room. The *T. P. Leathers* loaded with cotton; photos printed by photographer Ed Prince, from Norman Collection negatives.

Dunleith: Front of house. Baby carriage; photos by author.

Stanton Hall: Cutting the cake at the Stanton Hall wedding reception of Charlotte Ferguson and George Murrell; photo courtesy Edna Ferguson.

Magnolia Hall: Portrait of Sally Polk Richards; photo by author.

Longwood: House. Oak tree with old farm implements; photos by author. Young folks at their leisure (Jim Kilbourne holding tennis racquet); West Feliciana Historical Society collection.

Antiques Shopping in Natchez: Tea table set at H. Hal Garner Antiques. H. Hal Garner himself; photos by author. Vintage postcards showing downtown Natchez; author's collection.

Eola Hotel: Photos courtesy Natchez Eola Hotel.

Goat Castle Murder: Dick Dana and Octavia Dockery outside and inside Glenwood; photos courtesy Sim C. Callon.

Mammy's Cupboard: Elizabeth Lehmann beside Mammy to show scale; photo by author.

Aunt Freddie: Aunt Freddie Bailey. Stained-glass window. House; photos by author.

Muscadine Winery: Dr. Scott Galbreath examining growing muscadines; photos by author.

Natchez Santa Claus Club: Chase Poindexter with doll in pilgrimage costume; photo by author.

Stone-Ground Cornmeal: Patrick and Jesse Calhoun of Calhoun Bend Mill; photo courtesy Patrick Calhoun.

Natchez Humane Society Barbecues: Humane Society board member Elizabeth Eustis Lehmann with her dog Peanut, salvaged from, naturally, the Humane Society shelter, along with his mate; photo by author.

The Pig Out Inn: Nearby restored Canal Street Depot; photo by author.

Pinckneyville: Old saloon; West Feliciana Historical Society collection.

Rosemont and Jefferson Davis Pie: Early portrait of Jefferson Davis, photo courtesy Rosemont Plantation.

Woodville Red Recipes: Mary Fort Thompson holding C. Stewart Hamilton III at his christening at Grace

Episcopal Church in St. Francisville. Charles S. Hamilton with son and Camilla Bradley Truax; photos by author.

Pond Store: Vintage photo of oxen pulling wagon; West Feliciana Historical Society collection. Store; photo by author.

Crawfish Etienne: Three Craw Daddies partners, left to right Deborah Whetstone, Edine Seal, and Sally Treppendahl; photo by Andy Lewis. Crawfish boiling in pot; photo by author.

Parlange: House; photo by Robert H. Power. Lucy Parlange holding wedge-shaped brick used for columns and mold in which it was made; photo by author.

Open-Fire Cooking from East Feliciana: Bill McClendon in colonial garb preparing to cook over his open fire; photo courtesy Oakland Plantation.

Bear Corners: Horse-drawn advertising. Old grocery store; West Feliciana Historical Society collection.

Jackson's Miss Bea and Miss Dud: Vintage photos of young ladies; West Feliciana Historical Society collection.

Milbank: Victorian family; author's collection. Milbank; photo by author.

Linwood: House; photo by author.

Asphodel: Miles Poindexter II relaxing on front porch at Butler Greenwood in early 1970s; photo by author. Asphodel house. Levy house; photos courtesy Asphodel.

Jackson Assembly Antique Show: Seated on cabin steps at Butler Greenwood are cousins top left to right Eleanor Eustis and Virginia Bruns, bottom Anne Butler and Pat Butler. On garden bench are Annie Mathews Lawrason Butler of Butler Greenwood Plantation in West Feliciana, holding baby Anne Lawrason Butler as cousins Virginia Bruns and Murrell Butler look on; author's collection. Old cars on Royal Street; West Feliciana Historical Society collection. Child in front of vintage car is Charles Mathews Butler at The Cottage Plantation, West Feliciana, around 1913 or so; author's collection.

Glencoe: House view; photo by author.

Feliciana Peach Festival: Mr. and Mrs. David Washington Pipes of Beech Grove, Clinton. Young David W. Pipes, born 1845; author's collection.

Plantation Country Cookbook: Cattle drive through St. Francisville. View from courthouse looking west. Weydert Hardware (now West Feliciana Historical Society building). Burton House hotel in Bayou Sara. Train in flooded area of lower St. Francisville in May of 1912. Boating in Bayou Sara in 1912 after the levee broke. Floodwaters around Jos. Stern Livery in lower St.

Francisville at foot of hill in 1912; photos from West Feliciana Historical Society collection (Burton House from Norman Collection negatives).

Catholic Church: Church; photo by author. View from Catholic Hill; West Feliciana Historical Society collection.

Family Reunions: Stirling family reunion, May 26, 1934, at Wakefield Plantation, West Feliciana Parish; Stirling-Alston collection, courtesy Ann Alston Stirling Weller.

Rosale: House; photo by Ann Stirling Weller.

Audubon Pilgrimage: Oakley house. Longtime costume chairman JoAnn Lawrason in pilgrimage costume. Vintage print of Audubon with gun and dog; photos from West Feliciana Historical Society collection.

Christmas in the Country: Tony Sansoni Store at Foot-of-the-Hill, St. Francisville. Charles Weydert building with buggy (courtesy Miss Gretchen Weydert); photos from West Feliciana Historical Society collection. Current photos of Christmas in the Country celebrations by author.

Barrow House B&B: Dr. A. Feltus Barrow taking his wife, her sister, and his young niece Camilla Bradley for a spin in his early auto; photo courtesy Camilla Bradley Truax. House; photo by author.

The Rural Homestead: Cracklin' cooking. Oliver ("Preacher") McNabb shoeing a horse. Spinning; photos by Grady Smart for West Feliciana Historical Society. Danny Magee minding the gristmill; photo by author.

Butler Greenwood Plantation: House; photo by Jerome Chauvin.

The Cottage: House; photo by Ann Stirling Weller. In Civil War uniform is Capt. Edward G. Butler, son of Judge Thomas Butler, who apparently lost an arm in the war. Col. Edward George Washington Butler was raised by Andrew Jackson upon his father's death, became a hero of the Mexican War, and married Geroge Washington's close relative Frances Parke Lewis, daughter of Nellie Custis and Lawrence Lewis, on April 4, 1826; his daughter Caroline married William Turnbull of Rosedown; author's collection. Butler state carriage and antique baby buggy; photos by author. Charlie Butler at The Cottage with cat around 1913; author's collection.

Catalpa Tea Parties: Mary Thompson at Catalpa pouring tea for Stewart Hamilton, Amanda Floyd, and another young visitor; photo by author. Sam Lawrason, Charlie Mathews, and Charlie Fort; author's collection. Mamie (left) and Sadie Fort as children with dog; photo courtesy Mary Fort Thompson. Butler Greenwood tea party; photos by author.

Grace Church Dinners: Bishop Leonidas Polk; from early Grace Church history. Crowds on the occasion of

Grace's 175th anniversary; photos by Ann Stirling Weller.

Rosedown Housewarming: House; West Feliciana Historical Society collection. Copy of Martha Barrow Turnbull portrait; from *Reflections of Rosedown,* by Ola Mae Word.

Black Church Suppers: Aunt Dicey and Sally Mathews at Butler Greenwood Plantation. 1972 photo showing the late Rev. Lafayette Veal by cross in pond on Rosedown Plantation after baptizing a candidate from Rosedown Baptist Church; author's collection.

St. Francisville Inn: Inn; photo by author.

Ice-Cream Socials: The flood of 1912 at Bayou Sara and floodwaters rising on the Irvine House; West Feliciana Historical Society collection.

Christmas Desserts: Mamie Thompson enjoys eggnog and admires holly; author's collection. Old hunting scene; West Feliciana Historical Society collection.

Sweet Potatoes: Irv Daniel's wife, Betsy, serving as Audubon Pilgrimage chairman, in costume at Butler Greenwood Plantation; photo by Heritage Portraits. Vintage photo may be the late Levering Lawrason; author's collection. Old buggy at Butler Greenwood; photo by author.

Bopotamus Festival: Bayou Sara Fair and carousel; West Feliciana Historical Society collection.

Little Chase and Big Fat Aunt May: Chase Mathews Poindexter and her great-aunt Mary Pipes Butler enjoy a light moment at Butler Greenwood; photo by author.

Gardening by the Moon: Ethel Metcalf at work in her garden in Weyanoke; photos by author.

Biscuits: Unidentified gentlemen and dog; West Feliciana Historical Society collection.

Greenwood Plantation: Vintage photographs of the original home; West Feliciana Historical Society and author's collections.

Texas Longhorns: Longhorn; photo by author. Vintage 1915 shot showing "Shipping Cattle, Bayou Sara"; H. Anne Plettinger collection.

Better Than Sex and Other Sinfully Rich Cakes: Mrs. Lewis of Afton Villa; West Feliciana Historical Society collection.

Sick Calls—Fireballs of the Eucharist and Other Infernal Ailments: Gentleman on barrel with cigar after levee break of May 3, 1912, flooded the Bayou Sara Lumber Company. L. P. Kilbourne's Drug Store, 1886; West Feliciana Historical Society collection.

Berries: Mary Pipes Butler instructs her great-niece Chase Poindexter in the fine art of making wild plum jelly; photos by author.

Cinnamon Rolls and Benefit Barbecues: Ray and Betsy Shilling; photo by author.

Pilgrimage Workshops: Costume chairman JoAnn Lawrason in 1820s costumes for Audubon Pilgrimage; photos by author.

Cushaws: Linda Jean Vessell shares the back steps with two huge cushaws; photo by author.

Pig Tails at the Races: Scott Simms cooks pig tails with Woodlawn barn in background; photos by author.

Rabbits: Robert Ruiz holds one of his many rabbits; photo by author.

Sandwiches: Bayou Sara flooded by the Mississippi. Elisabeth Kilbourne Dart gardening at a tender age; West Feliciana Historical Society collection.

W. C. Percy's Turtle Stew: W. C. Percy prepares snapping turtle for stew; photos by author.

INDEX